W9-CZX-797

מסורה

ArtScroll Series®

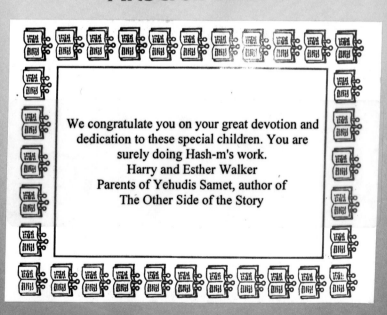

Rabbi Nosson Scherman / Rabbi Meir Zlotowitz

General Editors

The Other Side of the Story

Published by

Mesorah Publications, ltd

„הוי דן את כל האדם לכף זכות"

The Other Side of the Story

Giving people the benefit of the doubt — stories and strategies

by Yehudis Samet
assisted by Aviva Rappaport

FIRST EDITION
First Impression . . . November 1996
Second Impression . . . December 1996

Published and Distributed by
MESORAH PUBLICATIONS, Ltd.
4401 Second Avenue
Brooklyn, New York 11232

Distributed in Europe by
J. LEHMANN HEBREW BOOKSELLERS
20 Cambridge Terrace
Gateshead, Tyne and Wear
England NE8 1RP

Distributed in Israel by
SIFRIATI / A. GITLER — BOOKS
10 Hashomer Street
Bnei Brak 51361

Distributed in Australia & New Zealand by
GOLDS BOOK & GIFT CO.
36 William Street
Balaclava 3183, Vic., Australia

Distributed in South Africa by
KOLLEL BOOKSHOP
22 Muller Street
Yeoville 2198, Johannesburg, South Africa

Please address any comments regarding this book to:

Yehudis Samet	Ita Goldberg
Kiryat Mattesdorf	792 Elvira Avenue
Panim Meirot 10	Far Rockaway, NY
Jerusalem	11691

ISBN:
0-89906-519-8 (hard cover)
0-89906-520-1 (paperback)

Printed in the United States of America by Noble Book Press Corp.
Bound by Sefercraft Quality Bookbinders, Ltd., Brooklyn, N.Y.

Rabbi CHAIM P. SCHEINBERG
Rosh Hayeshiva "TORAH-ORE"
and Morah Hora'ah of Kiryat Mattersdorf

הרב חיים פינחס שיינברג
ראש ישיבת "תורה-אור"
ומורה הוראה דקרית מטרסדורף

בס"ד
ירושלים
ד' חשון תשנ"ז

How fortunate it is for the English-speaking readers of *Klal Yisrael* to be presented with this outstanding contribution to Torah literature.

The subject of this book is one of utmost importance. The mitzvah of *limud zechus* is the prerequisite for proper fulfillment of all mitzvos *bein adam l'chaveiro*. It is essential for peaceful communal living and a wellspring of personal tranquility. This mitzvah teaches us how to develop a positive attitude towards people and life in general.

My dear friends and neighbors, Rabbi and Mrs. Yehuda Samet, have been involved in Torah education for the last twenty-five years. Throughout this time, they have come to me to clarify and discuss at length *halachos* and *hashkafah* relating to matters of *Shemiras HaLashon*. The Samets have a great share in awakening the understanding of the importance of *Shemiras HaLashon* that we see today in *Klal Yisrael*. Their *shiurim* reach out to inspire and educate not only in Yerushalayim but in *kehillos* all over the world.

Those who read this book and absorb its teachings will not only earn for themselves a good judgment, as *Chazal* tell us: "Whoever judges his fellow man favorably will merit a favorable judgment in Heaven." but they will also share in creating the greater peace and unity in *Klal Yisrael* which *Chazal* tell us is necessary to herald the *Geulah Sheleimah,* may it come speedily in our days, as it is stated in *Devarim Rabbah* 5: שאין הקב"ה מבשר את ישראל שיהיו נגאלין אלא בשלום — *HaKadosh Baruch Hu* will not proclaim the *Geulah* to Yisrael until there is peace amongst them.

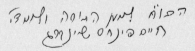

רחוב פנים מאירות 2, ירושלים, ת. ד. 6979, טל. 371513-(02), ישראל.
2, Panim Meirot St., Jerusalem, P. O. B. 6979, Tel (02)-371513, Israel

עטרת זקנים בני בנים ותפארת בנים אבותם

Dedicated by

Mr. and Mrs. Harry Walker

in memory of their beloved parents

Rev. Chaim Ephraim and Leah Speiser ע"ה

ר' חיים אפרים בן אריה לייב ז"ל

ט' טבת תש"ל

לאה בת יעקב ע"ה

ט' ניסן תשכ"ג

R' Shlomo and Tzirrel Walker

ר' שלמה בן אברהם אבא ז"ל

י"ח כסלו תשכ"ד

צירל בת ישעיה אליעזר ע"ה

כ"ה אב תשל"א

ת.נ.צ.ב.ה.

In loving memory of

Mrs. Gittel Samet

גיטל בת יצחק דוד הלוי ע״ה

א׳ טבת תשנ״ב

לזכרון עולם

Rabbi Pinchos Weiner

הרב פנחס ניסן בן מרדכי ווינער ז״ל

י״ט כסלו תשנ״ה

Table of Contents

A Note to the Reader:

Much of the material presented here is based on the works of our great sage Rabbi Yisrael Meir Kagan (1839-1933), the foremost rabbinical leader of his generation. Although he authored numerous works, he is known by the title of his first publication, the *Sefer Chofetz Chaim*, a major treatise on the laws of *lashon hara*, in which he gathered together Talmudic and Rabbinic sources on the subject of proper speech. Presented in a clear, concise manner, it has become the classic and definitive guide for all generations. In that work, together with its complementary second half, *Sefer Shemiras HaLashon*, we find the laws as well as the deep understanding of the value of judging favorably. It is the Chofetz Chaim who inspires and promises us:

> *"The pathways of zechus will never be closed to one who wants to judge favorably."*

The following three expressions, which appear frequently in this book, were retained in their original Hebrew (transliterated) because they have so much more breadth of meaning than can be captured by any one translation:

zechus (zechuyos)— merit(s); also: explanation; excuse; defense; justification

dan l'kaf zechus — lit., judge to the side of merit; also: to give the benefit of the doubt; to judge favorably

limud zechus — looking for extenuating circumstances; searching for mitigating or redeeming factors

Throughout the book you will see these words used in these different ways.

Author's Preface

This book's origin goes back almost thirty years, when my husband and I and our eldest daughter, then four months old, came to settle in Kiryat Mattersdorf, a newly-founded neighborhood in Northern Jerusalem. It was in those early years that several women formed a group to study the classic work on the laws of *lashon hara* by the Chofetz Chaim. At each session a different participant was responsible for presenting the material. This preparation gave each one of us the opportunity to familiarize herself with the Chofetz Chaim's work.

When we completed the *sefer* for the first time, we made a gathering. HaGaon HaRav Chaim Pinchas Scheinberg, *shlita*, *morah d'asrah* of Mattersdorf and Rosh Yeshivah of Torah Ore, spoke about judging others favorably, particularly stressing the happiness we can bring into our lives when we look at people positively. His words inspired us to continue.

Yom Kippur 5733 / 1973

Can we ever forget that Yom Kippur morning when the sirens sounded, and we all rushed to shelters, suddenly finding ourselves in the middle of yet another miraculous and tragic war?

As we emerged from our building's shelter hours later, we knew there was much to be thankful for, many to mourn for, and plenty to think about. While we were busy with the physical, technical side of our safety, some of the neighbors urged that we not forget about protecting ourselves spiritually. The suggestion was made to start a study group in our building. Gathering together and learning the laws of *lashon hara* would benefit all of us and preserve the sense of unity we had felt so strongly that day. Since I had some experience from the original group, I was asked to prepare. And that is how our class in *Shemiras HaLashon* (guarding the tongue) began.

At first we were a small group, but as interest in the subject increased, we grew in size. Our basic texts were *Sefer Chofetz*

Chaim, on the laws of proper speech, and *Sefer Shemiras HaLashon*, teachings of our Sages on topics relating to proper speech. We also studied new books published to explain and supplement these original sources, continuing each week to explore the laws and philosophy of "Jewish Speech" from different angles, on many levels.

My husband worked with me on the weekly presentation, explaining difficult material and clarifying complicated issues with the great Torah authorities, the *talmidei chachamim* of Yerushalayim. Under his direction, the ideas and concepts which formed the basis of the classes — and this book — were developed.

Always on the alert for practical suggestions, our group's interest was kindled when we read these words of the Chofetz Chaim: "The more a person habituates himself in judging favorably, the less he'll be caught in the snare of *lashon hara*."

Speech begins with thoughts. Proper thoughts produce proper speech; negative thoughts are the soil in which *lashon hara* grows. Go to the root of the problem, encourages the Chofetz Chaim, and learn to judge favorably.

We decided to move in that direction, paying attention to daily incidents where we had misjudged an innocent person.

People began submitting personal stories. The stories got us thinking. And as they poured in, they kept us thinking, and rethinking, annoyances, suspicions, and resentments — even those that had been held on to for years. Week after week we read new stories prefaced with statements like, "Wait till you hear this one," or, "You'll never believe this . . ." It was a powerful lesson when we suspected someone and felt sure in our conclusions, and then discovered a surprise ending — that they had done nothing wrong at all.

Reactions were fast in coming.

"I came in to class with a closed fist, and slowly it unclenched."

"I wasn't aware of the mitzvah to judge favorably, but now that it has become such a meaningful part of my life, I wonder how I functioned without it."

Students, young marrieds, grandmothers, visitors — all participated. Many went on to start classes in their own communities nearby. Others, here for only a few years, began classes when they returned home to destinations all over the world. Other women began groups based on tapes of the sessions which were sent to them. These new groups gathered their own stories.

Over the years, we received enthusiastic phone calls, letters, and tapes.

"I started a class in our community and we all share stories. I'm sending along some of the best ones."

"It's added a new dimension to our relationships."

The words varied, but the theme was the same: "It's changed our lives."

From seminary classes, private classes and lectures on both sides of the ocean, people became caught up with the idea and shared their stories.

The stories you will read here are true. They are based on the personal accounts of hundreds of people around the world, individuals from all walks of life, that have been collected over the last two decades.

Since these stories portray people acting in a questionable manner, much thought and effort have been expended to disguise the identity of all characters involved. Not only were all the names changed, but new "scenery" and "props" (time, place, gender, and relationships between people) were substituted to protect the anonymity of all persons mentioned.

At the same time, no effort was made to minimize or disguise the impropriety of behavior, both on the part of the accused *and* the accuser. The nature of our subject demanded a portrayal of non-exemplary behavior. However, the incidents recounted here should certainly not serve to establish norms nor condone conduct contrary to Torah values.

In these pages we find stories of people upset about a wide range of actions and interactions. About some of these situations we might feel, "How trivial!" — unless we realize that each one of us has his own issues which would seem petty to outside parties. The mitzvah of judging favorably helps us deal with minor as well as major obstacles, the small annoyances and the big ones that cramp us and sap our energy. Judging favorably enables us to recoup and reroute this energy into serving Hashem with joy and living together with others in peace.

Acknowledgments

I cannot truly call this volume my own and therefore take this opportunity to thank those who have a great share in making this book a reality.

To my beloved parents, Mr. and Mrs. Harry Walker, without whom this work would never have been undertaken nor brought to completion. It is they who envisioned a project which would enable a wider audience to have access to and benefit from these inspiring teachings of the Chofetz Chaim, and who encouraged and gave generous support throughout.

My father has been the initiator and catalyst of countless Torah projects and was the driving force behind this undertaking. His inspiring optimism and ability to see the bright side of every situation exemplify the teachings presented in this book; his conviction of the importance of Torah learning and of sharing it with others made it happen.

My mother's wisdom and good judgment fill our lives. It is she who implanted in us an appreciation for the values found in these pages by giving them priority in our home, whose discerning guidance enhances all that we do and whose sound advice has been particularly valuable in the preparation of this writing.

Words cannot express my immeasurable gratitude for their deep concern and devotion and their constant interest in all our undertakings. May *HaKadosh Baruch Hu* grant them long and happy years filled with much *nachas*.

I acknowledge with profound gratitude the tireless work of my husband, Rabbi Yehuda Samet. From the time I began teaching, he has unfailingly given me hours of time from his busy schedule to explain the *halachos* of *lashon hara* and the words of the Chofetz Chaim so that I could teach them to others. I am indebted not only for his clarification of the halachic and hashkafic concepts, his research of Talmudic sources and commentaries, and gleanings from numerous *sifrei kodesh*, which represent hours and hours of study and explanation, but for the daily example of how guarding one's speech and judging others favorably can look when put into practice. This book was written under his direction, and certain sections in particular are to be credited to his authorship.

I am deeply grateful to Mrs. Aviva Rappaport, my editor, partner and friend, who shared the work of organizing the material, writing, editing, re-editing, and who helped me make the leap from lectures to printed page. Her literary skills, exceptional creativity and sensitivity to the subject are felt in every page. Her wonderful sense of humor made the long hours of working together a delight.

My husband and I wish to sincerely thank HaGaon HaRav Chaim Pinchas Scheinberg, *shlita,* for his invaluable guidance and for generously giving us many hours of his time.

We would like to thank the *Rabbanim, shlita,* who gave of their time to review the manuscript, each of whom has authored an important *sefer* on the laws of *lashon hara*: Rav Shmuel Dov Eisenblatt, who reviewed the entire manuscript and who offered many suggestions, corrections, and keen insights which were incorporated into the final version; Rav Zelig Pliskin and Rav Yitzchok Berkowitz, who read and commented on parts of the original draft, which improved the clarity and accuracy of the text, and for their continual encouragement.

My sincere and heartfelt appreciation is extended:

To my brother-in-law and sister, Rabbi Mendel and Ita Goldberg, and my brother and sister-in-law, Don and Ellen Walker, for the time they spent reviewing the manuscript and for their excellent advice and practical suggestions since we began writing. With warmhearted readiness, they have offered their assistance at all stages and with all aspects of publication. Their enthusiasm and encouragement have been a great motivation and support.

To our children, who are very much a part of this project and who have continually given their all over the years.

To Mrs. Carol Weinberger and Mrs. Adina Goldman, of Loshon Marpeh Torah Tape Library (with branches in Har Nof and Bayit V'Gan), for taping the classes week after week, year after year, with much dedication, and for creating an index and making the tapes available to the public locally and internationally. They deserve major credit for the enthusiasm and reawakening of interest in *shemiras halashon* we see today in *Klal Yisrael*.

Thanks also to Yehudit Bloch for her share in the taping.

To the Artscroll staff on both sides of the ocean, particularly to Mr. Shmuel Blitz who heads the Jerusalem office, for the care and concern he has given this book, for his availablity and for his energetic and dedicated efforts to guide this book to fruition.

To Miriam Zakon and Reb Yonasan Rosenblum, whose editorial talents and expertise enriched the manuscript.

To Rabbi Avie Gold for reviewing the manuscript.

To Tova Finkelman for her sensitive review of the final draft.

To Devory Bick and Bassie Gutman for their diligent typing, and Eli Kroen for the beautiful cover.

Almost every book has a list of acknowledgments. Our list must be longer than most.

How can I thank all the contributors of stories over the past twenty years?

Those who told me a quick story as we were riding in the elevator

Those who met me in the grocery store and remembered a story they wanted to share

Those who sat down next to me on the bus and told me "the best one yet"

Those who waved from across the street and then crossed to tell me how they had suspected their neighbor / sister-in-law / child / maid of wrongdoing — but in the end, the funniest thing . . .

Those who wrote

Those who called — locally and from across the seas:

"Do you have a minute? I have the greatest story for you."

We offer thanks to *Hashem Yisbarach* for enabling us to complete this book. May it be His will that this book bring benefit to its readers and honor to His Name.

Introduction

What's all the complaining about?

A man blames his staff for shirking responsibility. A worker criticizes the supervisor for inconsiderate demands. A woman accuses her sister-in-law of being aloof, and reproaches a different relative for her stinginess. Cries go up about salesmen, bank clerks, teachers, all kinds of repairmen, any number of friends and neighbors, each one faulted for something else . . .

"How could she refuse after I've done so much for her?"

"We all contributed — why couldn't she?"

"I left two messages . . . but he never called back."

"The rest of the family came, where were they?"

"Why would he give him a raise and not me?"

"How come they invited them and not us?"

"He knew that was my customer."

"Look at that! They left without saying good-bye."

"Why would she say such a thing?

"Where's their thank-you?"

"What's taking them so long?"

"She pushed ahead of me in line . . .

. . . and took my turn . . .

. . . grabbed my parking space . . ."

And on and on . . .

. . . drowning in a sea of criticism and condemnation . . .

When we live in the company of others, we are sometimes insensitive, stepping on toes, guilty of injustices. However, we do live together in an interdependent society, and although the stumbling blocks are ever-present, we derive great benefit from living together with others. The company of our fellows provides material, intellectual, emotional, and social advantages. In addition there is still another important benefit: these interactions provide the stage on which our performance in this world is tested.

As Jews, we have been given guidelines for successfully dealing with people and for overcoming the constant challenges that our interactions present. Our mitzvos were given for the purpose of creating, increasing, and ensuring peace in the world. In fact, we are told[1] that peace is so important that the entire Torah was given for the purpose of making peace in the world, as it says: "Its [the Torah's] ways are pleasant and all its paths are peaceful." Since the Torah was given to ensure a life of peace, and a major part of being a Jew means striving to be a peaceful person, we wonder: Why are many people's lives filled with discord, accusations, fault-finding, and prolonged misunderstandings? And what can we do about it?

If the guidelines for a life of harmony have been provided, should we not take full advantage of them? Should we not avail ourselves of the abundant advice offered to us by our Torah, those mitzvos that sweeten our lives and bring us peace both between one and another, and within each individual?

Our purpose here is to spotlight one of those mitzvos: Judging others favorably.

Voices

Mrs. Beck arrived promptly for her scheduled x-rays — four in all. She sat in the waiting room until her name was announced. After the x-rays were taken, she was told she could wait outside until she was called. When the technician finally called her over, though, it was not to hand her the x-rays, but to apologize. She was sorry, she hadn't put her in the right position and now she would have to repeat two of them.

Mrs. Beck felt her muscles tense. *Because of this technician's incompetence I have to be re-x-rayed!*

The technician took her back into the room, and prepared her once more for the repeats. Already annoyed, Mrs. Beck was fit to be tied when the technician clumsily pushed her up against the screen.

Again, she asked her to wait outside.

The technician finally opened the door and came over to Mrs. Beck. She told her to come back in a week for the results. Mrs. Beck was surprised. "I always get them on the spot," she said.

"No, I'm sorry. You must come back," was the reply.

This is too much: incompetence, such clumsiness in taking the x-rays, changing the rules so arbitrarily and making it so difficult.

She left before she said something she might regret.

A week later Mrs. Beck returned to pick up her x-rays and bring them over to her doctor.

"Here you have the best hospital in the city," she blurted out as soon as she sat down on the chair in his office. "The most modern equipment. How could they hire such an unqualified technician?" and she told him what had happened.

I work as a secretary in a small office. Over the years, I have been given an increasing amount of responsibility and I know my boss, Mr. Green, counts on me. So when he gave me a project with a two-week deadline, I gave it my best. On Tuesday, the day before the deadline, my boss left early. I was sitting at my desk, working feverishly to finish, not even stopping for a cup of coffee, when I realized that I needed to clarify a major point before I could continue. Although I don't like to bother Mr. Green at home, this was one of the occasions when I knew he would want me to pick up the phone.

I dialed and Mr. Green answered.

"I'm trying to finish this up, but I ran into a problem. Do you have a minute?"

"No, I really don't."

"Mr. Green — you know they're coming for this tomorrow. I just need a few minutes of your time."

He hardly responded. As a matter of fact, he didn't even seem to be listening. I tried again.

"Mr. Green," I continued, "without your input, I'm not sure I'll be able to work through some of this information. It'll just take a few minutes."

"Sorry," I heard him say. "I can't."

Hey, I thought, this is for you, remember?

"Try to figure it out," he said. And the next second he was no longer on the line.

I did the best I could . . . and went home fuming.

*M*y uncle was checking in his baggage for an overseas flight. The man in front of him was taking forever. He kept demanding special consideration — and was getting it! The ticket agent told him that there were two very good seats for him. But this man wasn't satisfied. He insisted that two weren't enough — he needed four (!) so that he would be comfortable and well rested. They finally agreed to that and began checking in his luggage.

My uncle watched as the man insisted that one of his large suitcases remain with him on the plane because he had to change during the flight. And they gave in. There were a few more points he wanted clarified and he insisted on speaking to a supervisor, who was called over and listened patiently and agreeably to all he had to say.

Now it was my uncle's turn. He stepped up to the counter and all he asked for was an aisle seat. The ticket agent said he was sorry, but there were no aisle seats available. After having witnessed the service given to the man in front of him, my uncle muttered under his breath, I'll never use this airline again!

We hired a painter, who came highly recommended, to give our deck a new coat of paint. He came a few days later and I was quite impressed with his promptness and efficiency. I had to leave for work, so I left him to work on his own. By the time I got home he had finished and gone. Looks nice, I thought. But as I got closer to the house, I couldn't believe my eyes. The whole front window was speckled with paint, as were our brand-new storm door and dining room windows.

Maybe he'll still be back to clean it, but better not take any chances. I quickly called him and left a message on his machine. The next day when I got home from work I found that he had come by and had left a bill in my mail box — but he hadn't touched the windows. If he left a bill, he must think he's finished! Maybe his other customers accept this — but I certainly won't!

These are the voices of people who are annoyed. And it would seem that their grievances are justified. However, these stories are only told from one point of view. In the coming chapters you will read . . .

THE OTHER SIDE OF THE STORY

1
Challenging Our Perceptions and Assumptions

As we go through life, our eyes see, our ears hear, our brains register and we draw conclusions. These conclusions seem to explain events logically and accurately, and we feel comfortable with them. And yet sometimes we are fooled.

While attending an all-day conference out of town, I saw a woman whom I had met six months earlier when we were both guests at the home of mutual friends, the Shulmans. Then, I had spent considerable time referring her to some resource people for a project in which she was involved. In the following weeks we were in touch by phone and I gave her as much help as I could.

Now, after the session, I spotted her and was very happy to have a chance to renew the friendship. I walked over to her with a warm smile and greeting. She returned a barely discernible nod and turned to talk to someone else.

I was puzzled by her lukewarm response. She had been very nice and friendly and we had really hit it off at the Shulmans. And I was hurt at the lack of gratitude for all the time I had spent helping her.

Could it be that she was annoyed at me because she wasn't satisfied with the people I sent her to?

A few months later, I saw her again at a dinner, but got the same cool response as the last time. I guess she was only friendly when she needed me, I thought, and left it at that. At the end of the evening, it turned out that we got a ride home in the same car.

I found myself sitting next to her in the back seat. For an opener, I brought up the subject of our old connection, the Shulmans. She didn't seem to recognize the name. "Don't you remember?" I asked, a bit surprised at her poor recall. "I met you there about half a year ago. Remember — they had just moved into their new home?" She claimed she didn't know the family and had never been there.

It only took another blink to get it. A striking resemblance, a close second, but . . . she was not that same girl.

Almost . . . but not quite the same.

"Look-alikes" are a frequent challenge to our perceptions. Most all of us have at one time or another mistaken someone for somebody else, or have ourselves been mistaken for someone else. At times, these incidents might be embarrassing, but usually they are innocuous or even humorous. On some occasions, though, such mistakes can lead to misjudgments and recriminations.

This morning I was at a staff meeting of all the nurses on the ward. As we sat around the table, I saw to my dismay that one of the nurses was wearing a pair of earrings I had been missing for two months. I must have taken them off during work and left them somewhere on the ward. The earrings, a gift from my mother-in-law, were not only expensive but very unusual in design and stone.

How could she just wear them? Why hadn't she posted signs and tried to find the owner — ME! Maybe she assumed she'd never find the owner. Maybe she didn't know she was supposed to look.

How could I handle this? I tried to imagine how I might be able to get my earrings back. What could I say to her? No matter what I would say, it would surely be embarrassing for both of us. On the other hand, I was not prepared to give up on getting my jewelry back.

The meeting ended, and I was no closer to a solution. In a quandary, I glanced back longingly at my earrings. Wait a minute. Something looked strange and unfamiliar. I took a closer look — and my eyes opened in surprise. I turned away before she noticed me staring. At the tip of each earring was a tiny gold ball. My earrings never had that.

Funny I missed that, I reflected, as I walked out of the room, happy that thoughts are invisible.

It's not only people who have "look-alikes." We see here that we can mistake objects as well.

Such misperceptions can cause unpleasantness or worse. They may be caught and clarified — or they may not.

One morning, my friend and I were riding along on our way to work. As we neared a prestigious educational institution, my eyes were drawn to the roof of the six-story building where I saw a group of boys playing. Although a safety wall had been built, there were four large openings in it with absolutely no barrier to keep anyone from falling. "Look at that!" I called out in shock to my friend. "Where are those teachers? How can they allow the children on such a dangerous roof?"

My friend looked, and she was just as astonished as I.

The light turned green, and as we drove closer, my eyes remained on the boys. My fear increased as I saw one of them run towards one of the openings. My hand flew to my mouth and I gasped. Then, I saw them. At first blurred, then clearer, and soon distinct. Across those openings were securely welded white wrought iron bars.

Not only can our eyes deceive us, but our ears can as well.

*T*he setting was a boys' dormitory. Benjy had a room on the first floor; directly above him, on the second floor, dormed Rafi. Benjy was not feeling well and wanted to turn in early. As he was about to shut off the light, he heard thuds on the ceiling. This was not surprising, because his upstairs neighbor, Rafi, nicknamed "Mr. Jump Rope," loved the activity and actually taught people who needed to exercise how to jump rope for their health. So when Benjy heard the noise right above him, he realized that Mr. Jump Rope was practicing.

It was about ten o'clock at night, too early to be careful about making noise in a dormitory. But since Benjy didn't feel well, he decided to ask Rafi to do him a favor and practice elsewhere. He went upstairs and knocked at his door, but there was no answer. Benjy really felt ill and was anxious to go to sleep, so he felt annoyed that Rafi was ignoring him. Impatiently, Benjy flung open the door. "I hope you don't mind, Rafi. I'm not feeling well . . ." He stopped in mid-sentence. The room was pitch black.

Benjy was taken aback. He realized he must have walked into the wrong room.

Benjy's entrance had been loud enough to wake up the occupants of the room. Two sleeping forms turned over.

"What's going on, Benjy?" It was Rafi's groggy voice. "I finally get a chance to go to sleep early — what's the problem?"

"Sorry, Rafi," Benjy stammered in confusion, "but I heard you jumping."

This set off Rafi's roommate. "Why burst into a room like that? Why don't you look first to see if there's a light on? Or listen to hear if we're awake?"

Benjy stood there, not sure what had happened. In the silence a noise became apparent. It was the thud of a rope banging rhythmically on the floor of the room next door.

Benjy heard jumping from above. His upstairs neighbor is Mr. Jump Rope. Could there be any doubt where the noise was coming from? An acoustical deception not only caused him to reach an incorrect conclusion, but to act hastily, in a way that he surely wouldn't have if there had been even the slightest doubt in his mind as to its source.

*R*ivky and I are old school friends now busy raising our families. Every so often (in between coping with the essentials like folding laundry and wiping runny noses) we indulge in a long phone conversation.

Yesterday morning we had been shmoozing, when Rivky suddenly interrupted. "Hang on a sec — Eli just woke up from his nap, okay?"

"Sure," I said. This was one of the normal interruptions that was a part of our conversation.

As I waited on the phone, I heard a voice in the background. Somebody must have just dropped in to see Rivky, I thought. I hope it won't take too long. But it did.

Suddenly, I recognized the voice. Hey, I know who that is. It's the woman who gives the Wednesday-night lecture. The minutes ticked by . . . but the visitor didn't stop talking for one minute!

This is really taking a long time, I thought to myself. Why doesn't Rivky just excuse herself for a minute and tell her visitor that someone is waiting on the phone?"

Finally, Rivky picked up the phone. "Sorry it took so long — I just settled Eli with some blocks."

"Uh-huh." Don't tell me it was just Eli, I thought to myself, and couldn't help adding, "Did you finish with your visitor?"

"Visitor? There's no one in the house."

"Then who's that I hear talking?"

"That's a tape of the class I missed last week."

Our senses trick us time and again, yet we continue to believe them, taking them at face value without remembering that they can mislead us. In many cases, we slip up and fall into negative judgments because we accept our first perception of reality, believing our first quick superficial glance or grasping tightly at what we think we heard.

Human beings were created, though, to be dependent on their senses for information about the world. In fact, it is through our senses that we are meant to acquire knowledge. At the same time, our Creator has enjoined us to doubt their infallibility. The mitzvah of judging favorably teaches us that when our perceptions lead us to a negative judgment, we must contest the validity of their testimony.

Not only must we challenge our perceptions, but we must rethink our assumptions. In order to respect people, we have to re (again) spect (look): We have to "look again." We have to be willing to take up "the case" for renewed consideration: Did we jump to erroneous conclusions? Did we add up facts and get the wrong answer?

The baby was drifting off to sleep. It was 3:30 in the afternoon. Maybe I would be able to close my eyes and rest a little. The house was filled with children, friends, and friends of friends, happy sounds. Everything was okay. A good time to nap.

The doorbell rang. I decided to answer it. I'll never go back to sleep anyway.

I pulled on the door handle, more asleep than awake. My face brightened. "Oh, Lea, come on in. How nice to see you."

Lea Newman is one of my good friends, very respected by all. "I didn't come to visit, although I'd like to," she began. "Something important came up and I feel you should know."

There was a sinking feeling in my stomach. What would be coming? Was it about one of my children? My mind flipped through the smiling faces and drew a blank. It was one of those peaceful seasons where everyone was happy with teachers, friends, sisters and brothers, and parents.

She seemed to be waiting for me to say something. I didn't. She leaned forward. "Didn't he tell you?"

Oh, so it was my son. That narrowed it down. What could he have done and why did I have to miss a nap to hear about it?

"You know my daughter Chavie is running the summer day camp. That's where it happened. She felt she had to consult with me before she spoke with you. We decided it would be better if I were the one to come and tell you." My friend's voice was uncharacteristically solemn.

My son was eight and this day camp was for five-year-olds. It must have been pretty bad if Chavie had to tell her mother. Chavie is eighteen and knows how to handle children. What could he have done?

"What's the problem?" I asked her in as casual a tone as possible. Her answer exceeded anything that I would have imagined:

"Yesterday, Chavie was inside giving out pails and shovels for the sand pile when she heard a child crying outside. She looked out of the window and saw your son holding a piece of rubber hose and hitting little Shimmy. He was lying on his back and crying and holding up his hands to protect himself."

I was in shock. Such a picture! Rubber hoses, bullies, helpless victims, defenseless children — it was like a splash of ice water in my face.

I heard the baby crying. But everything seemed far away as I looked into my mind and saw my son's face, from birth until now. I lined up his misdeeds and pulled out from all the files his worst behavior. This horrible picture simply did not fit him.

"Did Chavie actually see him hitting Shimmy?" I asked.

"Absolutely."

"Are you sure it was a rubber hose?"

"Yes. She went right out and took it away."

"Didn't Chavie ask them what it was all about?"

"Yes. Shimmy said the big boys wouldn't let him play with them."

"What was my son doing there anyway?" I asked.

"That's what Chavie wanted to know!" her mother exclaimed.

Remember, I told myself, don't make knots. Don't let her tie up the package and label it forever. There is always at least one other side to a story, if not more.

"Lea, I appreciate your coming over to tell me this yourself. I'll discuss it with my son when he comes home."

"I don't envy the punishment he'll get," she said as she left.

When my son came home, I gave him something to eat and calmly ask him if he had had a good day. "Yes," he said. "Did anything unusual happen today?" "Nope." "Anything you'd like to tell me about?" "No, nothing special." I sighed.

"Today I heard about something that happened and I'd like to hear what you have to say." When I finished repeating what I had heard, this is the story he told me:

"Me and my friends finished learning and went out to play ball. We were playing in the grass next to the fence, outside the camp. A little kid from the camp came out and threw sand in our faces. We yelled at him to go away and he ran inside. He came out after a few minutes with a stick and hit us. We chased him and the teacher saw us and shouted at us not to come in the yard again.

"We were playing again when he came after us. This time he had a piece of rubber hose. We all ran after him but I'm faster. I chased him into the camp playground, near the slide, next to the fence and he turned around and raised the hose to hit me. I grabbed the hose in the air and he stepped backwards to pull it away and he tripped over something and fell on his back.

"Just then the teacher came out and shouted at me. After that we all went to play somewhere else."

Still the detective, I asked him a few more questions. "Why did you chase him? If he was bothering you so much, why didn't you go look for the teacher?"

"We didn't want to get him in trouble."

"So why did you hit him?"

"I never hit him! How could I hit him? He's just a little kid."

Later in the day, we went over to Lea's house. She and her daughter Chavie were both home. My son repeated his story in full. Mrs. Newman turned to her daughter and said: "Didn't you say that you saw him hitting Shimmy?"

"Well," Chavie replied hesitantly, "I'm not sure. I thought I did . . . but I guess I never actually saw him hit Shimmy. I just assumed from the way he was standing and holding the rubber hose that he had hit him."

She added up two plus two — a raised hose in a hand and a child lying on his back on the ground. It seemed like easy addition. Nonetheless, she came up with the wrong answer.

*A*s *an architect I deal with all types of professional people involved in the building trade.*

Recently, one of my renovations was completed and, as usual, a clean-up was in order. The clients asked me to recommend someone, which I did. In fact, I highly recommended a certain company since they had done outstanding work for me in the past and had shown themselves to be completely reliable.

The cleaners were supposed to finish that afternoon. I went over to the apartment to give it my final approval. I was unprepared for what I saw.

As I entered the building, the downstairs neighbor met me in the lobby. "Have you been up yet? Did you hear what happened?"

Slightly alarmed, I listened as the neighbor filled me in on details.

Apparently the cleaner and his helper had arrived at 7:00 a.m. that morning. Because the owner lived too far away to open up for them, he had left the keys with his brother. The brother was there when the workers came, opened the door for them and then left. The owner, my client, arrived at 9:00 a.m. He looked around the apartment only to discover that the fancy imported bathroom fittings were missing. A thorough search did not uncover the missing faucets. Only two people had been there: the cleaner and his helper. My client marched over to them and accused them to their face. At that, the cleaner blew up.

Now they were all there in the apartment as I walked in the door.

Both sides gave me their stories. The professional cleaner begged me to side with him. We had worked together on many occasions and he knew he had proven himself to be honest.

The owner of the apartment, however, had no doubt in his mind who was guilty. He took me aside and asked me if I agreed with his assessment of the situation. I said, "One thing I was never good at was solving 'whodunits.' But I do know that when you think you've discovered the culprit, and you're sure beyond the shadow of a doubt, it's usually someone else!"

I finished checking the apartment and we all left.

Later that evening, I received an agitated phone call from the owner's wife. She explained that her brother-in-law had come in to see the finished apartment after I left. After hearing what happened, he then went over to a cupboard in an adjoining room and returned with the "stolen" bathroom fittings.

The brother explained that because of the house being left open all day he was afraid something might be stolen. He knew how much the fittings meant to his brother and sister-in-law, so he hid them where no one would find them.

Now the wife asked me, "What should we do? We're so embarrassed. Certainly we will pay the cleaners something extra for all the trouble we put them through — but whatever we do, it won't wipe out the embarrassment we caused them.

"But we were so sure," she defended herself. "All fingers pointed to the guilty party. Right?"

Right — but wrong.

Remember this story in "Voices"? Now you'll hear the painter's side.

We hired a painter, who came highly recommended, to give our deck a new coat of paint. He came a few days later and all in all I was quite impressed with his promptness and efficiency. I had to leave for work, so I left him on his own. By the time I got home he had finished and gone. Looks nice,

I thought. But as I got closer to the house, I couldn't believe my eyes. The whole front window was speckled with paint, as were our brand-new storm door and dining room windows.

Maybe he'll still be back to clean it, but better not take any chances. I quickly called him and left a message on his machine. The next day when I got home from work I found that he had come by and had left a bill in my mail box — but he hadn't touched the windows. If he left a bill, it must mean he thinks he's finished! Maybe his other customers accept this — but I certainly won't!!

I called again, and again I got the machine. This time my tone was tense and my message more to the point. I certainly didn't intend to let him get away with it.

When I got home from work the next day there was a message on my answering machine from the painter. He was most apologetic and assured me that he knew he wasn't finished. He had been swamped with work the past few days and was planning to come back and finish up as soon as he could.

Sure enough, he was back the next evening after a full day's work and did a beautiful job.

When our assumptions seem to make so much sense, it is a challenge to question their credibility. Is it not reasonable to assume that if a worker leaves a bill he's finished? The painter, on the other hand, assumed it was obvious that he would not leave a porch in such condition. The bill didn't preclude a return visit, especially since it was an outdoor job and the owner didn't even have to be home.

O ur friends Shoshanna and Eliezer Hermann were making a wedding and my husband and I flew out to be with them for the festivities. My husband made sure to take along his brand new camera for the occasion, happy that he had bought it in time to take a lot of pictures to remember the event.

We had a wonderful time. We were their house guests for two days and it was particularly enjoyable being in the middle of all the preparations and excitement.

It was joyful — and quite lively. Shoshanna's children sure were a peppy crew! It seemed there wasn't a thing they weren't interested in exploring. They were into everything.

A week later I was looking at the newly developed pictures, when I stopped short. Three views of the ceiling and the Hermann's chandelier!

That's what happens when you're lax with children! I thought to myself. If their mother would discipline them properly such a thing would never have happened. Respect for other people's property is a must in education.

I was still incensed when my husband entered the room. "Look at this," I said, waving the pictures.

He came over to see the photos I was holding up. "Guess I missed a few," he said with a little smile. "I'm still not comfortable with this camera. When I was trying to advance the film, it took three shots of the ceiling."

From stories such as those above we see that if we are not trained in judging favorably, instead of seeing the good and the redeeming in seemingly dubious behavior, which is what we should be doing, we may attribute negative behavior to a person who didn't do anything at all, faulting others by the process of elimination or through incorrect assumptions.

When we add up facts and reach a negative conclusion about people, we must be willing to work it through again. Before we bang down the gavel, we must challenge the evidence.

2

Judging Favorably: What Is It? What Is It Not?

Judging favorably — *dan l'kaf zechus* — means finding acceptable excuses for questionable behavior, excuses which make sense to us and leave us with a positive feeling towards the other person. It is based on a desire to see the best in others, to recognize their good qualities despite their shortcomings and to attribute worthy intentions to their actions. It involves using various techniques to understand human nature and the human condition to help us clear our friend of guilt.

When we find ourselves suspecting others, we must ask ourselves: Are there any redeeming factors? Did I miss something? Did I jump to the wrong conclusion?

There are many situations where the evidence seems clearly condemning, and yet the subject is guiltless. Sometimes we lack information without which we cannot draw a clear, fair conclusion. Sometimes our senses fool us, and we must challenge our perceptions.

Judging favorably is an aspect of humility. It is an admission that our perception is limited, and a decision not to allow this limited understanding to trick us into hasty conclusions. Judging favorably means realizing that the other person has his reasons, even if we may disagree with them. It is knowing that it is just as important to go into the depths of the other person's claim as our own.

Judging favorably means imagining untold stories.

Finding merit, discovering a *zechus*, is like finding the missing piece of the puzzle. Suddenly the picture becomes clear.

Giving the benefit of the doubt means recognizing that there might be another side to the story. Then we begin our search, as we attempt to acquit the "suspect" or at least reduce his sentence, so that he becomes, again, a person of good standing in our eyes.

What is it not?

Some people are afraid they will lose out if they judge favorably — "I'll be stepped on!" "I'll be taken advantage of!" "I'll never get my money back!" — but that is not so.

- Judging favorably does not mean looking positively at a negative situation that can or should be changed.
- Judging favorably does not mean whitewashing wrong actions.

If someone is throwing stones at you, you need not say, as you find yourself being pelted, "Maybe he's doing it for some good reason and I should judge him favorably." If you can change the situation or protect yourself, of course you should. If someone is hurling insults, try to get him to stop. If there is a situation — whether intolerable or just plain annoying — which might be improved, go ahead and try to improve it. A person need not stay in that same situation and just "judge favorably." That would be not only foolish, but incorrect, because judging favorably does not mean living with apathy and resignation, and it should not dampen our efforts to help ourselves or others.

In short, judging favorably does not preclude action — it precedes it.

For instance, some parents might think that if their child complains about his teacher, and they judge the teacher favorably, the child will lose out. Judging favorably does not inhibit our efforts at clarification — it's one step before. It reminds us: Maybe the teacher also has something to say; maybe not. Find out.

Some people are worried about monetary disputes: "I'll never get my money back if I sit around 'judging favorably.' " They're worried that judging favorably will paralyze them. Wrong again. Judging favorably does not preclude demanding payment, lodging a complaint, even going to *beis din* — all are acceptable when necessary.

It cannot be emphasized often enough: Protecting yourself, your position, or your property, is not a contradiction to judging favorably. Judging favorably should not hinder you from safeguarding yourself and your rights and the rights of others. However, you will stand your ground, demand your rights, and ease your pain more successfully if you have a desire to understand others. You can try to understand another's position without agreeing with it. Your willingness to consider a second point of view will transform your interactions into more peaceful and, therefore, more successful ones.

3

Judge Your Fellow Man Justly

קְדֹשִׁים תִּהְיוּ כִּי קָדוֹשׁ אֲנִי ה׳ אֱלֹקֵיכֶם
"Be holy because I [Hashem] am Holy."
(Vayikra 19:2)

The Torah commands us to "be holy," and then tells us how. We are given mitzvos that both elevate us as individuals and improve our relationships with others, and through these mitzvos we reach holiness.

Be a holy person, and then together, become a holy nation. The Torah continues, and the next verse places our foot on the first rung in our ascent: "Revere your mother and father." This mitzvah precedes all the other mitzvos in this *parashah* and sets the tone for what follows. We must first submit to our parents' authority, bow to their wishes, learn to accept a "no," and real-ize we can't always have things our way. We must practice yielding to another person as a preparation for the flexibility required to deal successfully with other people.[1]

This essential beginning is followed by far-reaching Torah directives:

Would you like to keep all the money you earn? You can keep most of it . . . but you must share some of it with people less fortunate.

Has your worker finished a day's work? Pay up! Don't withhold wages unnecessarily.

Are you annoyed with someone? Don't curse him! We can do better than that.

Be sure not to give bad advice; don't give advice that benefits you, but harms the one asking.

Do not pervert justice.

If you see someone in trouble, or someone whose life is in danger, help him, guide him . . . or better still, warn him (if you can) before it happens.

Don't steal, cheat, or cause damage. And don't cause damage with your tongue.

Care about the property, as well as the reputation, of others. Want other people to succeed.

Be careful not to embarrass people, especially in public.

Honor the elderly; honor learned and wise people.

If people can't come through for you when you need a favor, try to be understanding. Don't hold a grudge.

Beware of taking revenge, or holding on to concealed hatred.

Fulfilling these and other such mitzvos sets us on the road towards an elevated and successful life. These precepts form the building blocks of the ideal society for which man has been searching from the beginning of time.

From among these many commandments — each of which warrants a lengthy examination — we will focus on one, the admonition not to pervert justice:

לֹא תַעֲשׂוּ עָוֶל בַּמִּשְׁפָּט לֹא תִשָּׂא פְנֵי דָל וְלֹא תֶהְדַּר פְּנֵי
גָדוֹל בְּצֶדֶק תִּשְׁפֹּט עֲמִיתֶךָ

"Do not do injustice in judgment, do not favor the poor, do not honor the great — judge your fellow man justly" (Vayikra 19:15).

Let us look at each segment separately:

◦ Do not do injustice in judgment

What is considered injustice? Rambam explains:[2] acquitting the guilty and convicting the innocent.

◦ Do not favor the poor

How might a judge favor a poor man unjustly? Imagine two litigants, one rich and one poor. The judge might think: The rich man has a duty to support the poor, so I'll decide in favor of the poor man — even if he is wrong — and in this way the poor man will get his support in a respectable manner.[3]

It is true that the rich should help the poor. But we cannot pervert justice in order to attain this otherwise righteous goal.

◦ Do not honor the great

We are not allowed to say: This man is rich or of noble descent — how can I put him to shame by ruling against him?[4] Also, a judge should not address the "important" litigant first or smile to him first, because the other one will feel intimidated and become flustered and won't be able to present his case properly. The result will be injustice.[5]

◦ Judge your fellow man justly

The verse began by admonishing us not to corrupt justice and ends by warning us to judge justly. What does just judgment entail? Rambam[6] tells us it means giving both litigants equal treatment.

What is considered unequal? 1) Speaking congenially to one litigant and harshly to the other; 2) allowing one his full say and telling the other to "keep it short"; 3) positioning one in a preferred seat or allowing one to stand and the other to sit.

Included in the concept of just judgment is the "order of fairness." For example, Jewish law dictates that if the case of an orphan or widow is scheduled, that case takes precedence.

What else is included in the concept of making sure judgment is just? According to *Sefer HaChinuch*, any individual capable, according to Torah law, of judging between parties to a controversy has a mitzvah to do so — because he will judge fairly. Whereas if he defers, less learned and less capable people will judge and pass a corrupt judgment.[7]

Until now, we have been in court: the mitzvah has been dealing with a judge's obligation. What does this have to do with us? We're not sitting on the judge's bench!

But in a certain sense we are.

Sefer HaChinuch explains that the mitzvah of "judging" also includes our obligation "to judge our fellow man favorably and to interpret his actions and words only to the good." Thus, this mitzvah refers not only to courtroom situations, but to our everyday observations and judgments.[8]

We are all, in that sense, sitting on the judge's bench. We pass judgment — all the time. And like judges in a courtroom who are required to judge justly, we too are obligated to judge our fellow man justly.

Wouldn't it be better if nobody ever judged anybody else? Isn't it preferable to strive to become non-judgmental? Wouldn't life be less complicated and more peaceful if we could just shut off our minds and stop making value judgments about all the things going on around us?

"Judge . . .

We might think so if we didn't know that we were created with the ability to perceive, discern, differentiate, and evaluate, for a purpose. We were given active, curious minds in order to fulfill our primary task: to make choices as beings with free will. We start our day by thanking Hashem, "Who gave us the understanding to differentiate between day and night"[9] — between light and darkness, between good and bad. The Torah doesn't say, turn off your mind, don't see, think, or evaluate. We are supposed to differentiate between right and wrong — and choose right.

Along with giving us the ability to make judgments, Hashem tells us how to use that ability. He tells us to judge in a certain way: justly.

. . . Your Fellow Man . . .

What is meant by the words "fellow man?" Who is included? Everyone — except for a small category of people who have willfully and with full knowledge of their responsibilities chosen not to identify themselves with the obligations of the Jewish way of life. However, only a person well versed in Torah law can determine who falls into this category, since many people reject the Torah life through ignorance of what it entails.

Justly . . ."

Rashi explains the Torah's admonition to "judge your fellow man justly" to mean: "Judge your friend to the side of merit, i.e. favorably."[10] But if, as Rashi tells us, the mitzvah means judging people favorably, why does the Torah use the word "just"?

The answer lies in understanding Rashi's use of the word "friend." A friend is a person we know, someone whose behavior is familiar to us because we deal with him all the time, such as a family member, a neighbor, or a fellow worker. We are required to give our friends the justice due them by evaluating any questionable action or statement in light of their usual behavior.

Within this group of people known to us, there are three categories:

1. If the person is known to us to be a virtuous, G-d-fearing person, because we have witnessed his consistently exemplary behavior, and we now see him doing or saying

something objectionable or even committing an explicit transgression, we are required to find a redeeming factor.[11]

Mr. Davis, for example, is known to you from years of experience to be beyond reproach in his business dealings. And now you see him doing something which looks dishonest. For such a consistently upright person, judging justly means assuming there is something in his questionable situation we can't see or don't understand. Even if the situation looks very bad, we must put this one seemingly negative action on one side of the scale, and all the person's history of good behavior on the other. "Favorable" in this case is "just."

If a situation arises where it can be proven that the person did transgress, we would have to say it was unintentional, accidental, or a mistake which he surely regretted and will not repeat.[12] Because of his consistent proper behavior, logic and justice give him this "right" to be so judged.

2. What of the person whose behavior is inconsistent, someone who tries to do the right thing but occasionally stumbles? How can we justly evaluate his behavior when we see him doing or saying something which could be given either a negative or a positive interpretation? Since he generally makes the effort to do the right thing, until we know otherwise, his behavior is entitled to a positive interpretation.

For example, if his check bounced, it could be there were no funds and he knew it, but it also might be an error on the bank's part.[13] In this case, because there is a good chance he was blameless, a "just" judgment is a favorable one.

What happens when we see this same person doing or saying something for which it would be very difficult to find a positive interpretation?[14] He occasionally slips, and this surely looks like one of those times.

Giving him the benefit of the doubt is considered, in this case, beyond what the law requires — beyond a just judgment. Judging him favorably in this case would be considered praiseworthy or exemplary behavior, a *midas chassidus*, as we explain in later chapters.

3. There is a third category: Someone who has an ongoing record of improper behavior. We are not obligated to judge such a person favorably. There is no point in giving him the benefit of the doubt: he has disqualified himself because of his continual discreditable behavior. He is not deserving of favorable judgment in *that* area. (Although we do not use *limud zechus* to whitewash improper behavior, finding merit can be applicable even in such a case. For further clarification see Chapter 11, page 164 "Judging the Whole Person," and the section in Chapter 13, "He's Really Wrong.")

It is worth noting that a person can fall into more than one category with regard to different aspects of his behavior. For example, the same person may be unswerving in his devotion to his parents, inconsistent in his observance of *kashrus*, and totally unreliable when it comes to repaying loans.

The categories mentioned above apply only to people we know — judge your "friend" favorably. We are obligated to give people we know whatever their record has earned them. That's only fair — that's just.

The case of a person we don't know, or don't know well, is different. Because his behavior is unknown to us, we have nothing to put on the scale in his favor. We can't be "just," because his background is unknown to us, and can not shed light on his present behavior.

Then how should we view him? R' Yehoshua ben Perachyah gives us the answer in *Pirkei Avos*: Judge **all** people favorably.[15] Rambam explains: "**All** people — even if you don't know them, and have no basis upon which to evaluate their actions. It is still meritorious and desirable, a *midas chassidus*, to judge all our fellow men favorably."

4
A Multi-Faceted Role

The skill of judging favorably is many-faceted. Taking note of its diverse dimensions helps us appreciate the value of acquiring this essential skill.

It's a mitzvah

Some people think that judging favorably is an elevated behavior expected only of the extremely pious, one which only a *"tzaddik"* is capable of achieving. But the fact that the injunction to judge favorably is included amongst the 613 mitzvos given to all Jews for all generations proves it is not the purview only of the elite. This is confirmation that not only a select few, but all of us, are obligated in its fulfillment. In addition, since we know that any mitzvah given to all of us must also be within the capacity of each one of us to fulfill, we know, therefore, that every person is capable of judging others favorably.

The Torah requires every Jew, from the most intellectual to the least intellectual, from the most sensitive to the least sensitive, to work towards spiritual improvement. Bettering our relationships with others is a great part of attaining this spiritual self-enhancement. Judging favorably contributes crucially to our ability to get along with others.

This is an obligation commanded and demanded by Hashem. It is what distinguishes us and contributes to our uniqueness as a nation.

It's pivotal

"This positive commandment," says the *Mitzvos HaLevavos*, "leads to the fulfillment of all the commandments between man and his friend. It is the pillar on which all other mitzvos affecting man's interpersonal relationships stand."[1]

When we find some redeeming factor which explains another person's disturbing behavior, we surely have a better feeling towards him. Suspicion is a roadblock forcing us to detour into resentment, grudge-bearing, anger, gossip and slander, and sometimes even hatred and disputes. Remove the roadblock and you can go straight through to caring, kindness and peace — all the productive and constructive ways of interacting with others.

It creates peace

Sefer HaChinuch tells us that the main purpose of the mitzvah of judging favorably is to help create a peaceful society. Fulfillment of this mitzvah — removal of one man's false suspicions of another through fair and deliberate judgment — is essential for harmonious living.[2]

Our Sages give us a list of mitzvos whose reward is especially great. One of them is the mitzvah of judging favorably. The Gemara says this list corresponds to another list mentioned in

Mishnah Peah. When we look at this second list, though, we see that the mitzvah of judging favorably does not appear; instead, the mitzvah of promoting peace between man and his fellow man does.[3] Rashi explains: Judging favorably **is** bringing peace between man and man.

Usually when we think of making peace between two people we see it as helping two "other" people solve their problems. No less important, however, is making peace between ourselves and others. If I am willing to give the other person the benefit of the doubt and say, "Maybe what he did to me really wasn't wrong," or, "Maybe it was beyond his control," or, "He did it for my benefit," I can restore the peace between us.[4]

From the Vilna Gaon we learn more about the role that judging favorably plays in creating peace. If you have an enemy, there is a proven and tested method of reversing his animosity. If you judge him favorably — if you understand him sufficiently to consider him completely virtuous — your attitude will affect his, and his enmity will dissipate.[5] We are told in *Mishlei* (27:19): As water reflects the face shown it, so too the heart of one man [is reflected] to another. The Gaon explains: Just as water reflects the face of a man peering into it, so one man's heart reflects another's feelings. We sense what others feel towards us, even if those sentiments remain unexpressed.[6] Feelings are felt . … and returned. If we develop positive feelings towards someone who is angry with us, by judging him favorably, our adversary will pick up those positive feelings and his heart will be swayed.

It's a midah

Judging favorably is both a mitzvah and a *midah*, a character trait, one which we have inherited from our forefathers. Our Sages teach us that when the people of Sodom sinned, Hashem revealed this to Avraham because He knew that Avraham would come to their defense.*[7] In *Tehillim* (45:8) we

---

* Avraham Avinu did not come to the defense of Sodom by condoning their evil. Rather, he pleaded that perhaps there was enough good to be found that would warrant deliverance and salvation despite the evil.

read: "You love righteousness and hate wickedness, therefore Hashem, your G-d, anointed you with oil of rejoicing above your friends." The *midrash* tells us that these words were said by Hashem to Avraham, and explain the words to mean: *You love righteousness* — You love to find righteousness in My creations; *and hate wickedness* — you refrain from faulting them. Therefore I chose you and I raised you above your friends — the ten generations from Noach to Avraham. I rejected all of the ten generations and chose you, Avraham, because of this *midah*.[8]

When R' Chaim Volozhin tells us about the greatness of Avraham he notes: When a *tzaddik* struggles to perfect himself, his children are blessed. They will be drawn towards those same character traits and can acquire them with less effort. Because Avraham excelled in the trait of looking for good in his fellow man, this path has been made easier for us to tread, if we will but make the effort.[9]

Rabbeinu Yonah describes this *midah* based on a verse in *Mishlei* (14:9): "Fools heap condemnation, but for the upright there is satisfaction."[10] Fools, he explains, always want to find people's weaknesses. They are happy to make them look guilty. But the upright take pleasure in noticing people's strengths, and come to their defense when their weaknesses show.[11]

From the above, we learn that we have two levels to strive towards:

- *not wanting to make people look bad, and*
- *taking pleasure in making people look good.*

1. Not wanting to make people look bad

When Noach was lying inebriated, he became uncovered. His son Cham saw him lying in disgrace and ran to tell his two brothers. When Shem and Yefes heard, they took a garment and, turning their heads aside so as not to see their father's shame, covered Noach. What is the *midah* we see exemplified by Shem and Yefes here? The desire to cover over peoples' faults and embarrassing deeds when there is no benefit in revealing them.[12]

2. *Taking pleasure in making people look good*

A virtuous man was walking with his students and they chanced upon the dead carcass of an animal. The students said, "What a foul odor is coming from this carcass!" The virtuous man said, "How white are its teeth!"[13]

Which was true? Which was more obvious?

Both observations were true. Even though the white teeth were much less obvious and easy to overlook in the face of the offensive, overpowering odor of a dead carcass, the virtuous man found something nice to see and to say. He chose to concentrate on the positive. If this can be said concerning a dead animal, how much more so should we try to find the good in a human being.

The Chofetz Chaim reiterates this idea: "A person should try to perfect his character so that he can be counted amongst the worthy, and not the unworthy. What are the traits of the worthy? They help others whenever they are able; they conceal other peoples' weaknesses, as they would their own. And if they see a person angry at another, they try to calm him, by giving him an understanding of the other person's position....

"The unworthy do the opposite. They harm others and are happy when others fail. They reveal their faults, and if a person makes a mistake, they interpret it as intentional wickedness. They cause fights and incite one person against his friend and think they are clever for all this!"

The Chofetz Chaim goes on to ask: What is considered true wisdom and strength? A person who sees his friend at the edge of a roof and gives him a push, or one who sees his friend falling and tries to catch him? One who finds his friend down and kicks him, or one who finds his friend already in the pit and tries to pull him out?

This is the essence of judging favorably. It means that if we find our friend in a situation where it seems he has already "fallen," when suspicions of guilt surround him, we use our mental resources to lift him out of that mess, both in our own mind and in the minds of others. This is what finding *zechus* is about. This is the *midah* to which we are asked to aspire.[14]

אוֹר זָרֻעַ לַצַּדִּיק וּלְיִשְׁרֵי לֵב שִׂמְחָה

Light is sown for the righteous and for the upright of heart, gladness (*Tehillim 97:11*).

Most people in this world seek happiness in some form or other — but where exactly does one turn in order to find this elusive state? King David tells us that if one seeks *simchah*, gladness, he should join the ranks of the *yishrei lev*, the upright of heart. Who are these happy and fortunate people?

R' Yitzchok Hutner, late rosh yeshivah of Yeshivas R' Chaim Berlin, observed that the Targum translates יִשְׁרֵי לֵב as תְּרִיצֵי לִבָּא, which literally means "those whose hearts are full of תֵּרוּצִים, explanations."

The heart of an unhappy person is filled with strong questions on everyone and everything. Such a person is critical and nit-picking, finding fault everywhere and voicing his bitter complaints about everything. "Why did he say that to me? How could she do such a thing? Where was G-d when I needed Him?" Naturally this negative attitude fills him with discontent; joy and gladness are banished from his heart.

The secret of perpetual gladness, says R' Hutner, is to develop a positive attitude whereby you find תֵּרוּצִים, explanations, which justify the actions of the people you encounter. In other words, it is better to explain than to complain.

This message is implied in the first half of the verse as well: אוֹר זָרֻעַ לַצַּדִּיק, light is sown for the righteous, i.e. the righteous know that the justification for an action or event is often not readily apparent. One must dig beneath the surface to discover the "light" which is "sown" and concealed within. The righteous ones are those contented and happy people who have learned the art of unearthing the "light" in everything.[15]

It's the antidote to lashon hara

Fulfillment of this mitzvah offers us another benefit: It counteracts the evil of *lashon hara.*

Lashon hara, literally "evil talk," refers to a statement which belittles others or causes them damage or embarrassment and serves no constructive purpose even though it may be true. The mitzvah of judging favorably is directly followed in the Torah by a warning concerning *lashon hara,* to teach us that judging favorably and refraining from speaking *lashon hara* are closely connected.[16]

The Chofetz Chaim tells us: The more we judge favorably, the less *lashon hara* we will speak.[17]

If we don't think negatively about others in the first place, then we are not in danger of such thoughts ever being expressed. When we are constantly battling with negative thoughts, there is always the possibility that they will prevail and be articulated. If we can obliterate or at least neutralize suspicions as they arise, by judging favorably, then there remain no negative thoughts lurking in our mind waiting for a chance to escape in the form of *lashon hara.*

R' Chaim Shmuelevitz, the late Mirrer Rosh Yeshivah, illustrated the connection between judging favorably and *lashon hara* with the story of the *meraglim* (spies):

The *meraglim* were sent to tour the Land of Israel before the whole nation entered for the first time. When they returned, they gave a negative report about what they had seen. The people believed them, and because of this the entire nation was penalized by having to spend 40 more years in the desert, corresponding to the 40 days of travel by the *meraglim.*

We know that punishment is given measure for measure.[18] Why then did the nation have to spend 40 years in the desert when *lashon hara* was spoken only once? Where's the justice? Where's the "measure for measure"?

R' Shmuelevitz explains that they were punished for the root of the sin — 40 days of *seeing* the negative aspects of the land. If they hadn't seen the negative, they wouldn't have come to speak negatively. Thus the punishment was measure for measure.

The Chofetz Chaim says that almost all the cases of *lashon hara* in the Torah occurred because people did not judge favorably.[19] For example, Miriam spoke against her brother Moshe to her other brother Aharon: "We are also prophets, yet we didn't separate ourselves from our spouses — why did Moshe?" We are told that she misjudged the situation because she lacked information: She did not know that Moshe's level of prophecy had no equal, and therefore his actions were justified.[20]

We think we know, it seems clear, and yet sometimes . . .

*T*ova Rothman needed a babysitter. She had been calling girls all evening, but everyone was either busy or not home, and it was getting too late to make any more calls. By now she was desperate. One of her daughters said eagerly, "Hey, Ma! What about my friend's sister, Dassy Engel?"

"That's worth a try. We haven't used her in a long time. Do we still have her number?

A minute later she was dialing the Engels.

"Oh, Dassy, I'm so glad you're home. I hope you can do me this favor. I need a babysitter for two o'clock tomorrow afternoon. It's very important and I must leave at exactly two o'clock. Are you available?" Tova was thrilled when Dassy agreed and she hung up with a sigh of relief.

The next day at two o'clock Tova was standing with her coat on, ready to walk out as soon as Dassy arrived. The minutes ticked away and no bell was ringing. No one was knocking or calling to say she'd be right over. It was 2:05 and still no Dassy. Tova called the Engels, but their line was busy.

Dassy seemed like such a nice girl. How could she be so irresponsible? Tova let her family know how she felt about a girl who gives her word and then lets you down. She gave them an earful! — and they were only spared the rest by the ringing of the telephone. Tova dashed over. It was her husband. Whatever she hadn't managed to say till now to Dassy's discredit she let out on Mr. Rothman. And for good *measure, she threw in a few choice observations about the Engels. Tova might have said more, but she cut herself short so she could try the Engel's phone again. This time it rang.*

Imagine Tova's astonishment when Mrs. Engel answered and in reply to her question, "Is Dassy home?" said, "Oh, are you the one who called her about babysitting? You hung up and I guess you didn't realize that you never gave her your name!"

Judging favorably is not only the leading remedy for our inclination to speak *lashon hara*, it also offers the primary relief for another related "illness," one that is undiagnosed, unacknowledged, and particularly insidious because of its anonymity: accepting and believing *lashon hara* without clarifying its validity.

Chapters have been written by the Chofetz Chaim on this topic bringing to us the ageless wisdom of the Torah: Be wise, be discerning, don't believe everything you hear. Be willing to challenge your perceptions and be willing to reconsider.

It was late Tuesday night when the phone rang. A good friend of mine by the name of J.P. was calling. "Perhaps you can help me," he said. "I'm making a wedding soon, and I'd like you to recommend a good photographer."

After giving it some thought, I gave him the name of a man who is both an excellent photographer and is also very reasonably priced. "I've heard about him," came my friend's reply, "but I was also told that he was unreliable."

"Oh, really," I said, quite surprised. "What makes you say so?"

"Well, I'm told that he was recently hired for a bar mitzvah and he first arrived after it was half over. He missed half the affair. There's no way I'd hire a person who is so irresponsible," J.P. said.*

It's certainly a severe charge, I thought to myself. "Are you sure about it?" I asked. "That's a very strong accusation!"

---

*J.P. is not required to hire this photographer even though this decision is based on an unproven suspicion. However, he was wrong in accepting this rumor as absolute truth.

"I'm quite positive," was his reply. "Yisroel was the head of the band that night, and he told it to me himself. In fact, I met someone else who attended that same affair, and he verified the facts. I'm not making it up. It's 100% true! Go check it out yourself."

"I sure will," I said. I've learned to be very skeptical as to the authenticity of any story, and I also knew that even if perfectly true, there might be a good explanation.

"Maybe due to unforeseen circumstances he was delayed?" I said to the caller, trying my best to judge favorably. "Perhaps there was some sort of emergency. What makes you so sure that it was a case of negligence or pure laziness?"

"Perhaps you're right," replied J.P., "but I just can't risk it. Besides, there is no reason in the world for coming late. He should have started out early enough so that even if his car broke down he could have taken a car service and made it on time. There is absolutely no good excuse for a photographer to walk in after half the affair is over!"

It was hard to argue with him. He had a strong point, and my defense wasn't too convincing. When I hung up the phone I found myself in a real quandary. Could I really recommend someone who is unreliable? Was it truly negligence on his part? Was my argument in his defense just a cover-up for his lack of responsibility? Truthfully, I wasn't really convinced myself of his innocence, so how could I convince someone else?

Firstly, I decided to check out the story on my own to see if it was really true. I called the musician, who was a close friend of mine, and he verified the entire story. There was no question as to its authenticity.

The very next day, I bumped into my good friend, the photographer. I brought up the subject of the bar mitzvah in question.

"Is it true that you arrived halfway through the bar mitzvah?" I asked.

"Yes, it certainly is," he said. "But why are you asking?" he wanted to know.

"I just recommended you for a job, and the people refused

to take you. They claimed you were unreliable because you didn't come on time."

He looked at me in disbelief and shock, and then began telling me his story. I listened very carefully.

"The job was not mine at all," he began. "The photographer who had been hired for the job failed to show up. I received an emergency call in the middle of the affair to come down immediately. Despite being very busy at that moment, I dropped everything I was doing and raced down to the hall as quickly as possible."

With a hurt look written on his face, he added, "I only did it as a personal favor to them." [21]

The more we practice judging people favorably, the less likely we are to speak against them, because . . .

- the more insight and comprehension, the less disapproval.
- the more we consider possibilities, the less we will censure and blame.
- the more we make an effort to reconsider, the less chance there will be to pass hasty, superficial judgments . . .

because understanding and condemnation are mutually exclusive.

When you hear a report of *lashon hara*, act like a judge in court who isn't allowed to pass judgment until he hears both sides. You can't believe what was told to you until you consider the other side of the story.

It Dispels Anger

Giving the benefit of the doubt is also an effective method for dealing with anger.[22] So many fiery outbursts could be avoided, so many prolonged resentments and grievances could be re-

---

* Sometimes class participants would bring in a story they had clipped from some publication. Four such stories were included because they so perfectly illustrated the point under discussion.

dressed and even prevented from developing in the first place, if we were willing to use this tool.

When we feel ourselves churning and burning, cooking and steaming, we are harming ourselves physically and emotionally. Much has been written and documented about the negative effects of anger and grudge-bearing: High blood pressure, ulcers, lower back pain, tension headaches — the list is long. Trying to understand the other side of the story frees us from our imprisonment in the gloomy darkness of condemnation and resentment. It's the key that unlocks the door to a room full of light. When understanding comes in, anger almost automatically leaves through the back door.

I'm enrolled in a program in a hospital in Jerusalem, and I'm receiving credit from a school in America that sponsors this program. I have a supervisor here who gets paid from the institution in America.

One day in January, I came into the office as usual at about 9:00 a.m. My supervisor, Ofra, was fuming. She was stomping around the rooms and muttering under her breath. I asked her what was the matter, and she said she didn't want to tell me because it wasn't professional. I was sure it wouldn't take Ofra too long to become unprofessional, and, sure enough, fifteen minutes later she couldn't contain herself anymore.

She told me that she had just gotten her paycheck for supervising me. Now mind you, I had been part of this program since October 1993, and it goes until June 1994. Ofra told me that the reason she was so angry was that the people in charge had the chutzpah to send her a check dated November 1, 1994. She could not understand how they could have the nerve to give her a check postdated for almost a year later. I said I personally couldn't believe it because I go to this school and I'd never heard of such a thing. But she really let go, and she was screaming and yelling and telling everyone the whole story.

Now it was already ten o'clock, and she said she was going to go to the National Association to consult with one of the counselors there to ask them what she should do. She wanted to put in a complaint about this program and how they *send students here to be supervised and how their supervisors are paid, or, rather, not paid.*

Ofra kept calling the number of the National Association. I was a little embarrassed, because I felt that maybe I should call somebody in America to let them know before she put in a complaint about them. If they got a big complaint about the school, who knew what could happen.

So she was calling and calling, and the phone stayed busy. Finally she got through and they said no counselor was available. Ofra was willing to leave work and go to this organization to show them the check and file a complaint about the whole situation, but they told her not to bother to come because no one was there to help her. By now it was already eleven or twelve o'clock. Ofra was furious. She didn't even want to talk to me.

Well, finally it was one o'clock and time for me to leave. Ofra still hadn't calmed down. Finally, I said to her, "Are you sure that's what the check says — November 1, 1994? Can you just show me?" She just got more annoyed. "You think I can't read?" And then she said, "You know, I don't think you believe me! I'm going to take out that check and show you."

She took out the check, and the check read: 1.11.94. "This check is for January 11, 1994," I told her.

"What?" She looked at me, obviously confused. Then Ofra remembered that Israeli and American dates are reversed. Locally, 1.11.94 means November 1, 1994.

She was very embarrassed. For five hours she had done nothing but rant and rave. Now she was left muttering, "For this I raised my blood pressure? For this I got so angry and missed a day's work?"

Someone once said: "I had never known anything about judging favorably — I had never heard of such a thing or thought of such a concept. But it's changed my life! And you know what — it's so much better than getting angry!"

*M*rs. S. always took care to leave half a cup of milk in the refrigerator for her toddler's first bottle of cereal in the morning. One morning, Mrs. S. woke up and saw her husband's empty cup of coffee next to the now-empty milk container. Her eyes bulged. How inconsiderate — favoring yourself over a baby! She had the whole day to mull over his selfishness.

When he came home, she let him have it.

At the end of her tirade, her husband asked if he could say a few words. He picked up the baby from the playpen, gave him a kiss, and turned to his wife: "The baby woke up in the middle of the night. I couldn't find his bottle, so I gave him the milk in the cup."

It Promotes Educational and Social Success

יְהוֹשֻׁעַ בֶּן פְּרַחְיָה אוֹמֵר: עֲשֵׂה לְךָ רַב וּקְנֵה לְךָ חָבֵר וֶהֱוֵי דָן אֶת כָּל הָאָדָם לְכַף זְכוּת.

Yehoshua ben Perachyah says: Appoint a teacher for yourself, acquire [buy yourself] a friend, and judge everybody favorably (Pirkei Avos 1:6).

The fact that these seemingly unconnected statements are grouped together indicates that there is a special relationship between them. And so we learn that the acquisition and retention of an educational mentor and guide, as well as harmonious companionship, depend to a great extent on our ability and willingness to judge favorably.

"Appoint a teacher for yourself"
— and judge him favorably.

If we want to grow in our understanding of Torah, we search for a teacher to guide and inspire us. When we feel we have found the right person, we "appoint" him to do this job. We must then be careful to judge him favorably. If we suspect him of wrongdoing, his stature becomes diminished in our eyes and our faith in him as an authority figure is shaken. As a result, we might distance ourselves from him. In doing so, we also move away from our original purpose: to find guidance and inspiration. This rule applies to rebbes, rabbanim, the rabbi of the shul, and all educators.

My Rosh Yeshivah's morning Gemara shiur begins promptly at nine o'clock. Yesterday I had to weave my way through heavy traffic to get there. In a rush, I parked the car and dashed up the stairs. I reached the door only to find it locked. I looked at my watch. It was 9:05. None of us have the nerve to knock on the door once it's locked. We know it's his rule that when the clock hits 9:00, he locks the door and then sits down to teach. Why does he do this? I thought. Doesn't he realize what effort we make to be here on time?

Later in the day, I was rebuked by my Rosh Yeshivah for not being there. I thought to myself, Why doesn't he just leave that door open for a few more minutes? He'd save so many troubles and problems for all of us!

I guess I was particularly annoyed because this was not the first time it's happened to me. The Rosh Yeshivah gives a shiur on the other side of town every Friday night. I usually don't have the opportunity to go, but a few weeks ago we rushed the meal so that I would be able to attend. I'd been waiting for a chance to get to this shiur for some time, so I walked briskly, but when I got there it was only to hear the door being locked in front of me. I blew my top. How does he lock doors when we're dealing with Torah and yiras shamayim? Where's the right? That's how you deal with talmidim?

When I calmed down I thought of the words of the Mishnah telling us to get ourselves a rav and judge him favorably. Maybe my Rosh Yeshivah is trying to teach us something for life, for our own good, a lesson that we'd better learn while we're young: the importance of being on time, if we want to be successful in life, in Torah, in business, with family and friends. He might even be going out of his way just to teach *us this! He was picked by all of us as our rav. We chose him to guide us in all aspects of life. We gave him the job and he's doing it.*

This principle can be applied not only to a rav, but to all people involved in our education.

During my first year teaching in a prestigious girls school, I stood in awe of the principal. She was a well known and highly respected figure, with years of experience in education, and was looked up to by teachers, parents, and students alike. The staff tried to learn as much as possible from her both professionally and personally. We watched her every move and cherished those moments of personal contact we had with her.

One day, after a long, difficult morning teaching, I went up to her office to discuss some of the day's problems. She welcomed me in, and soon I was deeply involved in describing several of the disturbances which had made my day so problematic. She listened with her usual unwavering concentration.

You can imagine my surprise, then, when I saw her suddenly pull out a breath freshening spray from her desk drawer! I was still talking, and it took all of my restraint to continue as if nothing was happening while across the desk from me she opened up her mouth wide and sprayed the freshener into her mouth.

I was flabbergasted, to say the least. How ill-mannered can you be? There are certain things a lady does only in private. She certainly isn't who I thought she was, I decided inwardly. Although I never mentioned this incident to anyone, my respect for her lessened. As time went on, the incident receded from memory — but now that I look back, I realize that my visits to her office to ask her advice tapered off.

Months later, news spread that our dear principal was in the hospital. She had suffered an asthma attack. Suddenly, I realized: Her "breath freshening spray" must have been a ventilator to ward off an asthma attack! How could I have so misjudged her!

Our young children have two main authority figures in their lives: their parents and their teachers. In many countries, the majority of children's waking hours are spent with their teachers. It is to our benefit as parents to strengthen our children's respect for those educating them. Judging teachers favorably is a vital ingredient in enhancing that respect.

As we mentioned before, judging favorably does not prevent us from seeking clarification. We owe that to our children. However, our children should see that we speak respectfully to and about their teachers.

My daughter came home from her first day in 2nd grade practically crying. "I won't go back to that teacher. A girl needed to go and she wouldn't let her leave the room. Then a girl got a bump and she told her she doesn't need to cry."

My first reaction was to sympathize. But then I tried to gather up all my dan l'kaf zechus strength and present it to my daughter. "This is the first day and the teacher has to be strict, otherwise the girls will be taking advantage of her." But my daughter was adamant. Even I started to think, Well, maybe we are in for a difficult year with this teacher. But I didn't say it. Instead, I said, "In your school they only take good teachers. Perhaps she had something else that was bothering her or maybe something happened in the office."

"No, Mommy. Call her! Call the principal!"

I kept calm and told her, "We'll wait a few days. I'm sure this teacher is very nice. It's just the first day and you can't know. You have to give the teacher a chance!" My daughter was still unconvinced, but went on with other things. (I also wasn't 100% convinced and hoped that all I said was really true!)

The next day, after my daughter had come home from school and eaten lunch, she turned to me and said, "Mommy, you know what?"

"What?"

"The teacher is very nice. She called on me a lot, and you know what, I think that something else really must have been bothering her yesterday."

Student dissatisfaction is not sure proof of teacher incompetence. While we should listen empathetically to our children's concerns, we are wise not to accept these reports as facts, thereby being tricked into faulting, embarrassing and sometimes causing damage to a teacher, without first clarifying the issues. One clever teacher warns parents at the first PTA meeting of the year: "Let's make a deal: If you promise not to believe everything your children tell you about me, I'll promise not to believe everything they tell me about you!"

Or, as one experienced mother commented: "It was such an eye-opener for my children when their older sister became a teacher. Then we all saw the other side of the story!"

✍ "Acquire a friend" — and judge him favorably.

Can friendship survive on a long-term basis if we're not willing to judge our friends favorably? Even between friends, and especially between close friends, there are many opportunities for misunderstanding. The closer we are, the more shortcomings we see and the more tests we face.

Sara had been coming to the Lakeview bungalow colony for many years. For Rochel, this was the first time. This is Sara's story:

Rochel went out of her way to become friends with me. I had my group of friends from previous summers, but Rochel, being new, seemed very much to want my friendship. She was always dropping in for a cup of coffee, or to offer to do me a favor or suggest somewhere to go. We did many things together and our friendship grew.

I became very fond of Rochel and a strong emotional attachment developed. As the weeks passed we became inseparable. As I look back, I realize I had become dependent upon — even possessive of — this new friend.

Picture our bungalow colony on an unusually hot, humid Shabbos afternoon, the type of day when you prefer to stay inside with the air-conditioning. You almost didn't see anybody on the winding roads. It was 4:30, time for the weekly

Shabbos afternoon shiur. I went out onto the porch to see if anyone was coming, although I couldn't imagine anyone going out in this weather.

I stood there for a few more minutes, and all of a sudden I saw my friend Rochel coming in the distance, going towards the *shiur.* We exchanged a 'good Shabbos,' and then Rochel continued on her way. I turned to go into my cabin, but a minute later I changed my mind. Why miss a good class? So I hurried back out to the porch and called to Rochel, "Are you going to the *shiur?"* No answer.

I called out again, "Wait for me and I'll go with you." Again there was no reply. She didn't even turn her head. I started to think to myself, *What's going on here?*

I quickly got dressed and rushed over to the hall where Rochel would usually be sitting and waiting for me. Instead, when I walked in I saw my "good friend" busy shmoozing with the other women.

I felt the tears well up in my eyes. I thought to myself, *If I stay another minute, I'm going to completely lose control.* I ran out back to my bungalow, burst through the door and let out my hurt and anguish in a torrent of tears.

Even after I stopped crying, it was hard for me to calm down. *What did I ever do to her? Is that a friend?* I felt overwhelmed and very, very hurt. I couldn't look her in the face.

I acted very distant . . . and Rochel got the message. Something had changed, and the friendship was no longer there. What a bitter summer it turned out to be. All the laughs, the good times, the closeness — gone.

Living in a small bungalow colony, there was no way to really avoid her. Passing by without exchanging a word was just too painful. Should I just pack up and go home? How can I ruin it for the children? Finally, after a lot of agonizing, I decided I had to pull myself together. I just couldn't go on like this. I decided to approach Rochel.

One day, when the children were out, I knocked at her door. She looked surprised, and hesitatingly let me in.

I didn't know how to start, so I just blurted out, with hurt in my voice: "I would just like to know why you ignored me *and refused to answer me that Shabbos afternoon when I asked you where you were going and if you would wait."*

Rochel looked at me, in astonishment, "I don't know whether to laugh or cry. I must have been daydreaming or maybe I was just too far away because — Sara — I never heard you ask!"

We should be proud to be part of a people that for thousands of years has been practicing this mitzvah and cultivating a *midah* which enhances our physical and emotional health, is the antidote to *lashon hara,* stills anger, and quiets grudges. This mitzvah legislates for us what the whole world is trying to achieve: It is the road to social success, it is essential for success in education, and it promotes peace.

Even for this one mitzvah alone, it is a privilege to be part of our great people.

5
The Power
of Zechus

We are in the army. We are all soldiers fighting a constant battle against our baser instincts, winning some, losing some, picking ourselves up, trying again, hoping we are forging ahead.

And we are not unarmed. Our Commander-in-Chief provided us with 613 weapons, the most advanced civilization has known. If we use them correctly, we are guaranteed victory.

In all armies, soldiers express their dedication on many levels. Some do their duty, fulfilling their obligations. Others perform beyond the call of duty. This same distinction exists in mitzvah observance. There is that which binds us all — the letter of the law — and those aspects which go beyond it.

The same holds true in the fulfillment of the mitzvah of judging favorably. Sometimes a person has earned the right to be judged favorably, and we are obligated to do so. At other times, our willingness to justify behavior goes beyond the call of duty and is called a *midas chassidus.*

In most areas of Torah observance, a person has the option to follow the letter of the law and is not required to go beyond its requirements. (While it is preferable and something to strive for, it is not an obligation.) The mitzvah of judging favorably is different. Our Sages have presented to us powerfully convincing arguments as to why we must all master this skill and carry it even beyond the letter of the law. They tell us that here we don't have a choice — **the stakes are simply too high!**[1]

The Torah reveals to us certain rules by which Hashem runs His world. One of the most basic is: The way we measure others is the way we will be measured in Heaven.[2] The way we deal with others, is the way Hashem will deal with us.

The Chofetz Chaim tells us: Whatever we do in this world has a direct effect in the Upper World and evokes a reciprocal reaction.[3] If a person chooses to be merciful, he arouses in the Upper World this quality of mercy and he merits, in return, Hashem's mercy. If he chooses to be uncompromising, dealing strictly with others, he arouses the attribute of strict justice in the Upper World. What he sends up is what is sent back — measure for measure.

We may consider it analogous to pipes linking us to the Upper World. We can open any pipe we choose. We can turn on the pipe of compassion, *rachamim,* and *rachamim* goes up, awakening its parallel in Heaven, to be sent back to us on this earth. Or we may send uncompromising and compassionless behavior through that pipe. Then we strengthen the force of strict justice in Heaven, and strict justice is sent back.

We are told: "One who judges his friend favorably, *he* is judged favorably[4] — measure for measure." The word "he" refers to the person who is doing the judging. If I try to make you look good, I increase your merit and cause you to receive a more favorable judgment; therefore, measure for measure, I also receive a more favorable judgment.[5]

When we act towards people with compassion, we earn

Hashem's compassion. If, when we pass judgment on others, we search for any possible merit they may possess, Hashem does the same for us. When our own actions leave much to be desired, Hashem says, as it were, I am willing to find something face-saving for you, because you were willing to do that for your fellow man.

By being "generous" with others, we are being generous with ourselves.

Another interpretation of "one who judges his friend favorably, *he* is judged favorably," adds a further dimension to the power we wield when we judge favorably. The word "he" refers to the person whom we are judging.[6] By finding merit for our friend, through our good words, we arouse merit and compassion for him in Heaven. Look at the power we have! When I speak kindly about you I cause kindness and compassion to be extended to you. I create defense attorneys on your behalf. Then, in the Heavenly Court, it is said: Oh, that's the way you see it? We'll see it that way, too.

This being so, we can understand why judging favorably is included in the mitzvah of *gemilas chessed*, doing kindness for others.[7] Sometimes we might want to provide a kindness but we can't, because we don't have the time or the money, or distance prevents us. Our Sages tell us there are other ways to reach out. Just as we can always pray for a person, so too, can we help others by judging them favorably. Even if I can't be near you and I can't help you out in other ways, I can bring blessing into your life by speaking positively about you.

We all need the merit that words of favorable judgment add to our lives; we all need Heavenly mercy every second. Yet there are times when speaking up on a person's behalf is especially crucial. *Pele Yoetz* tells us: "When we see a person suffering misfortune, when he is sick, or in need of Hashem's compassion for whatever other reason(s), this is not the time to speak about his shortcomings . . . or to say, 'It must be because of this or that, because he was careless in this or did that sin, that this trouble has come upon him.' "[8]

In the same vein, it is especially crucial not to speak against a person who has just departed from this world. We are taught that at such a time he surely needs mercy. When we speak well of him and defend him, it is as if we are giving him *meilitzim* (defense advocates) in Heaven who will help assure that he comes through with a good judgment.

By acting with compassion, we not only have the ability to arouse Heavenly compassion for ourselves and others, but in addition, the Chofetz Chaim tells us, these individual acts have global consequences.[9] When we act compassionately, that day is "crowned" with the quality of kindliness and mercy in our merit, bringing a benefit to all mankind.[10]

How would any of us like to be judged — with compassion or with strict justice? With the strict hand of justice, or with special consideration — *lifnim meshuras hadin* — more than is coming to us? (Doesn't that sound good!) Our Sages tell us that it is in our hands: If I judge you favorably, when it comes my turn for needing a "favor," I'll get it. If I give another more than he deserves, I'll get more than I deserve.

We are always looking for *segulos*, for special ways to bring blessing into our lives. Isn't this the best way to help ourselves and isn't this a wonderful way to help other people? What greater blessing can a person procure for himself and for others than Hashem's mercy?

When we realize how crucial is the mitzvah of *dan l'kaf zechus,* the far-reaching consequences of judging others favorably, we will understand why we must all master this skill and carry it even beyond the letter of the law. We don't have a choice. We can't afford to say, "I'll forgo this *midas chassidus.*" The stakes are simply too high.

✍ After One Hundred and Twenty Years

The Chofetz Chaim presents us with a forceful and compelling argument for perfecting the trait of *limud zechus.* He tells us that the way we judge others will be the determining factor in the Heavenly evaluation of our whole life![11]

We have been taught that if we leave this world with a majority of good deeds to our credit, we are considered righteous (*tzaddik*). If we have more to our discredit, we will be considered iniquitous (*rasha*).

All of us have some behaviors of which we are not proud, yet we feel we are basically good people. And therefore we are counting on the fact that when the time comes to give a Heavenly accounting — after 120 years — we will emerge on the positive side of the ledger. But we may be fooling ourselves. It is possible to come to the Heavenly Court heavily laden with mitzvos and still find that we are credited with almost nothing!

How could that be? How could a person work a lifetime accumulating mitzvos and yet not get full credit?

The Chofetz Chaim explains: In order for a mitzvah to be considered complete and earn full credit, it must conform to a certain standard. Let's take one example — the proper way to make a *berachah* (blessing) on food:

First, we have prerequisites:

- we must have clean hands;
- the place where the *berachah* is being made must be free of foul odors;
- our mouths must be empty;
- we are not allowed to make a *berachah* until we have attended to our bodily needs;
- before beginning the *berachah*, we must determine which *berachah* the food requires.

When we make the *berachah* —

- the food should be held in one's hand (a right-handed person holds it in his right hand, and a left-handed person in his left — except for bread, which must be held with ten fingers);
- the *berachah* must be said slowly, with attention to the meaning of the words, especially the meaning of Hashem's Names;
- the *berachah* must be recited loudly enough so that one hears himself say the entire *berachah* enunciated clearly;
- one may not recite a *berachah* while engaged in any other activity, like clearing the table, or cutting the food; nor is one allowed to gesture or motion or be involved in any similar form of non-verbal communication.

- we may not make an interruption which invalidates the *berachah*. For example, one may not speak even a single word in the middle of reciting a *berachah*, nor between the saying of the *berachah* and the swallowing of the first bite.

Even if a person did fulfill all the halachic prerequisites, there is still more to making a perfect *berachah*. A *berachah* should be an outpouring of gratitude for Hashem's kindliness, an expression of *ahavas Hashem,* and not a mechanically repeated formula. A *berachah* should be an expression of our awareness of all the wonders and benefits bestowed upon us through the complex miracle of eating. It should give us a feeling of awe (*yiras Hashem*) for the One responsible for all these wonders, and joy (*simchah*) for the privilege of serving Him. To fulfill a mitzvah this way is so difficult that we can begin to comprehend why the Chofetz Chaim himself made the humble claim that he did not merit even one perfect mitzvah![12]

What can *we* say?

Now we can understand why the Chofetz Chaim tells us that even if our mitzvos are as numerous as the sands, if Hashem scrutinizes our actions critically, we will be left with practically nothing to our credit. This mitzvah was done either incorrectly or inexactly, that one was done without proper motivation, and another was done begrudgingly. If any of our mitzvos would be held up for inspection against the ideal, it would be found sorely lacking. If our mitzvos were to be paraded before Hashem and evaluated strictly, they would be a shabby crew, carrying little weight when compared with our transgressions, whose severity remains undiminished. Our mitzvos won't be powerful enough to outweigh our transgressions, and the Heavenly Court will cry: "*Rasha!*" ("Wicked one!")[13] And that title will remain forever.

However, if Hashem chooses to judge us leniently and look for merit in all our actions, even though they leave much to be desired, then we won't lose out: The mitzvos that we spent a lifetime accumulating will remain to our credit.

What happens, though, if we come before the Heavenly Tribunal with more transgressions than mitzvos? Is there any hope for us?

Our only hope is if Hashem Himself will serve as our defense attorney. If He will want to find *zechus* for us — with a claim that some of our transgressions were done because we weren't fully aware of their severity; or that we found the *halachos* numerous and complicated; or that there were other circumstances beyond our control — then the severity of our transgressions will be lessened, the mitzvos will be fully credited, and the scales will tip in our favor!

How can we "hire" the Alm-ghty as our defense attorney? What is His fee? Says the Chofetz Chaim: It all depends on how we treat our fellow man. The way we dealt with others is the way Hashem will deal with us: **measure for measure**. If we judged our fellow man favorably, we too will be judged favorably. But if we were fault-finders, it won't be difficult to find fault with us.

How essential it is for us to know this rule: At the moment we are passing judgment on someone else, we are in fact determining our own judgment for eternity.[14]

Could there be a more powerful incentive to look for redeeming factors in other people's disturbing behavior?

6

How Far Do We Have To Take This?

לֵךְ נָא רְאֵה בְּמַעֲשֵׂה דְשַׁבָּת (קכז): מִמֶּנָּה יִלְמַד הָאָדָם הַיָּשָׁר שֶׁצָּרִיךְ לָדוּן אֶת חֲבֵרוֹ לְכַף זְכוּת אֲפִילוּ אִם אֹפֶן הַזְכוּת הוּא הַיּוֹתֵר רָחוֹק.

Study the incident found in Gemara Shabbos (127b): From there an upright person will learn that he is required to judge his friend favorably, even if the only way to clear him of suspicion is with a far-fetched excuse (Chofetz Chaim, *Shemiras HaLashon, Shaar HaTevunah* 4).

How far do we have to go in judging favorably? The Chofetz Chaim tells us the answer is to be found in a well-known incident related in Gemara Shabbos. From the events described there, we can learn the heights a person can reach in the development and perfection of the trait of judging favorably. A close look at the story, understanding the classic questions and answers asked about the events described, can bring us insight into various aspects of giving the benefit of the doubt:

A story is told of a man from Upper Galilee who hired himself out to an employer in the South for three years. On Erev Yom Kippur, the worker said to his employer, "Give me my wages so that I can go home to provide for my wife and children."

The employer answered, "I have no money."

"Then give me fruit," requested the worker.

"I have none," replied the employer.

"Give me property," suggested the worker.

"I don't have any."

"So give me livestock," asked the worker.

"I don't have any."

"Give me pillows and blankets."

"I don't have any."

Disheartened, the man slung his belongings over his shoulder and went home.

What are some of the questions that can be raised about this first half of the story?

1. **Why didn't the employer have the wages available?** Torah law requires that when an employer knows that the time is approaching to pay a worker, he should have the wages ready.

2. For the three years the worker had been employed, he had been surrounded by his employer's wealth. Luscious fruits dangled invitingly from the trees, cows and sheep grazed on the rambling landscape, and the luxurious furnished home of his employer confronted him daily. This is why the worker asked for them as payment. **Why did the boss refuse to give his employee any of them as payment?** Wasn't a man of such wealth ashamed to say he had nothing to give?

3. **Why didn't the worker press for payment?**

4. **Why didn't the worker at least demand an explanation** instead of slinging his bag over his shoulder and going home?

5. **Wasn't it wrong to let the boss "get away" with this?** Even if the worker was willing to forgo his salary, shouldn't he have considered his wife and family? Also, by allowing his boss to "get away with it" wasn't he encouraging dishonest behavior?

Let's continue the story:

*A*fter Succos, the employer traveled to the home of the worker with the wages he owed him, along with three donkeys laden with food, drinks, and an assortment of delicacies. They ate and drank, and the employer gave the worker his wages. Then the employer asked: "When you asked for your wages and I told you that I didn't have money, of what did you suspect me?"

"I thought that perhaps a very good business deal had come your way, a chance to buy merchandise cheaply, and that you had invested all your cash in this unusual opportunity."

"And when I told you I had no livestock, what went through your mind?"

"I thought that perhaps they were hired out."

"And when you asked for land, and I said I didn't have any land, what did you think?"

"I thought that maybe it was leased."

"And when I told you I didn't have any fruit, what could you have thought?"

"I thought that perhaps you had not yet separated tithes."

"And when you asked for pillows and blankets, and I claimed that I had none, what did you suspect?"

"I thought that maybe you had dedicated all your possessions to Heaven."

The employer exclaimed, "That's exactly what happened! I pledged all my possessions for the sake of my son Hyrcanus,[1] so that he should learn Torah. When I came to my colleagues *in the South, they released me from my vow. And now, just as you judged me favorably, may Hashem judge you favorably."*

If we concluded our discussion here, most of us would agree that this is a story of a boss who took advantage of a naive worker. True, in the end, it turned out that the worker was right in judging his employer favorably. He was paid his wages eventually and his explanations turned out to be correct. But we are still left with questions. Why did he have to wait for his salary? What would have happened if his assumptions about his employer had not been correct? What if he had never been paid? And why did he let his boss get away with it?

Now let us look at this story through the eyes of our classic commentators.

1. Although it appears from the wording of the story that the worker had a three-year contract that ended Erev Yom Kippur, it is also possible that the worker had not set any terms of employment and suddenly decided on *Erev* Yom Kippur that he wanted to go home. Therefore, when he approached his employer on *Erev* Yom Kippur, it was without prior notice. Now we have an answer to our first question: **Why weren't the wages available?** Since the employer was not given time to prepare wages, he was not to blame. (Notice how one fact alone can change our whole understanding of a situation!)

   This leads us to wonder about the worker's behavior: How could he have expected on-the-spot payment if he had not given notice?

   He must have simply assumed that he would not need to give advance warning. He had no qualms about approaching his boss for an on-the-spot payment because it was clear that his employer was a wealthy man with varied assets, vast resources, and a lavish estate, any of which could be used as payment. In such a case, where a person has assets and owes money, he is obligated to pay immediately even though he was not previously notified.

2. We have clarified why the payment wasn't available on the day the worker left, yet we can still wonder: **How could the employer have pledged his possessions if he knew he would eventually have to pay?**[2] What kind of an excuse is that? Would any of us accept this excuse from a boss who owed us money? Wouldn't we feel that our boss had no business putting himself in a position where he wouldn't be able to pay?

   The commentators[3] explain that the employer did *not* actually pledge all his possessions, only his pillows and blankets. He was planning to pay his worker with the land and animals, which were now temporarily hired out. But since the worker's departure was unexpected, the rented and leased property was not available at the moment.

   What about the other assets? Why didn't he just sell the merchandise he had purchased so cheaply and use the money to pay his worker? We read in the original story: "On *Erev* Yom Kippur the worker said . . ." The significance of telling us that it was *Erev* Yom Kippur is to stress that it is a time when commerce is at a standstill; there are no buyers.[4]

   And why didn't the boss tithe the fruits? Again, it was *Erev* Yom Kippur and there was no time.[5]

3. **Why didn't the worker press for his salary?** From the description of the worker *as slinging his belongings over his shoulder and going home,* it is possible to get the impression that he did not make a strong effort to claim his salary. But, in fact, he did *not* readily forgo his due. He did *not* just give in. In fact, he was quite persistent, suggesting alternative possibilities. He asked for cash, fruit, land, animals, and finally, household belongings. In essence he was saying, "If you can't pay me this way, then pay me that way." He made every effort to get his salary — while still judging his boss favorably.

Here we see illustrated the answer to the question that is invariably raised in a discussion of judging favorably: Won't I lose out if I judge people favorably? Not if we understand that we are supposed to make efforts to protect ourselves and doing so is no contradiction to judging favorably.

A favorable judgment is something we can render even as we guard ourselves or others from a loss. As long as we take precautions, and in addition, we are careful not to whitewash improper actions, judging favorably can only be an asset.

4. **Why didn't the worker demand an explanation?** The worker had no need to demand an explanation because he thought of the answers himself:

   a. He knew that he had not warned his boss that he was going to leave and therefore could have no complaints that money was not ready for him.

   b. As for the other possible sources of payment, which did seem to be available, he judged his boss favorably. Though money, land, animals, fruit and bedding all seemed readily available, the worker put his mind to figuring out why the appearances were deceiving.

If all the excuses were correct, we wonder why the employer only acknowledged the last *zechus,* saying: "That's exactly what happened. I pledged all my possessions . . ."[6] The answer is that this was the *zechus* that was consequential, and it was the real exercise in *limud zechus*. At the outset, the worker questioned his boss on alternate methods of payment. If one wasn't available, he still had hope of payment in another way. But when the boss claimed he didn't even have pillows and blankets, the worker lost his last hope. His willingness to explain this non-availability — to find *zechus* — meant that he accepted the fact that there would be no payment, at least for the moment.

To judge favorably when we have nothing to lose, or when it's someone else's problem, may be a challenge. But we face a much greater challenge when we are personally affected, especially when we feel we were deeply wronged. It is a big step to be willing to see it from the other person's point of view.

5. **Why did he let him get away with it?**

   Why does the worker accept the boss's claim of not having assets? The validity of the worker's behavior is based on the assumption that his boss was honest. Three years of working for his employer enabled the employee to understand the nature of his boss from up close. From his experience of three years, he knew that if his boss could pay, he would. Now the worker's job was to figure out why his boss couldn't come up with the salary.

If the employer *had* thought that the employer was evading payment, just asking would not have been enough. He would have made a greater effort, a further *hishtadlus* — even going to *beis din* if necessary — and not just gone home.

Once we've established that the boss had an excuse, we can raise still another question.

6. Why didn't the boss offer an explanation?

Sometimes offering an explanation puts us at a disadvantage. In our story, the boss might have been concerned that people would discover his precarious financial state, i.e., no liquid assets, and cease extending credit. So he gave only a general answer: "I don't have any." This was non-specific enough not to endanger his credibility.

Sometimes offering an explanation is embarrassing. In this case, the boss might not have wanted to discuss the problem he had with his son.

Sometimes we would rather not explain, because we feel others won't understand or accept our excuses, even though for *us,* it's right and acceptable.*

We've looked at what originally seemed to be a one-sided story from other perspectives and discovered new meaning. The guilty party was not as guilty as he originally appeared!

There was another side to the story.

What principles of judging favorably does this story teach us?

• **The explanations given by the worker were specific.**
The best way to fulfill the mitzvah of *dan l'kaf zechus* is to

---

*See "Why Don't People Speak Up"

be as specific as possible. Instead of saying, "There must have been a reason for such behavior," it is much better to consider what that reason might be, as did the worker in the story. The more specific it is, the more believable it will be. Coming up with something specific is usually better than a general assumption, which should only be used for lack of something better.

- **The explanations were also reasonable.**

  Explanations should be logical and reasonable to us — otherwise they won't work. This worker knew that wealthy people do not always have liquid assets, so that excuse made sense to him. He knew property owners lease their land, so this was a reasonable thing for him to think of.

- **Start with the likely, but consider even the unlikely.**

  The worker had a reasonable solution for everything — until he came to the pillows and blankets. Then he was stumped. Nothing seemed likely, and therefore, in order to judge favorably, he had to consider the "unlikely." Pledging one's possessions is not a usual occurrence.[7] The worker only resorted to this excuse when nothing more probable suggested itself.

  We learn from this that when we can't think of a likely excuse, we should be willing to move on to consider excuses that are unlikely.[8]

  It is important to understand that "far-fetched" and "unlikely" are not the same as unreasonable, illogical, absurd, irrational, or preposterous. If we make up nonsensical possibilities we won't believe them — and then we won't accomplish our purpose.

  - Unlikely, far-fetched, or unusual, can still be reasonable;
  - Improbable is also possible;
  - Rare is also credible;
  - Uncommon or infrequent may be worthy of consideration;
    because it just might be so!

Far-fetched need only mean the unconsidered.*

I had just given birth to a baby girl. When I looked at the empty bed in my room, I thought to myself, I sure hope they bring in someone friendly. I'm in the mood to talk.

A few hours later the door opened and I saw a roommate being wheeled in. Even better, I recognized her: Esther Wilman. We used to live on the same street. I hadn't seen her for at least a year, since we moved away. Great! Now we can share the joy and also catch up on old news.

The nurses drew the curtain and got her settled, while I waited impatiently. Eventually, the curtains opened and the nurses left. Esther looked around and our eyes met. She returned my enthusiastic "Hi!" with a weak smile.

Okay. Take it easy, I thought. She just had a baby. Give her a chance. But as the hours passed, her interest in talking didn't increase.

They brought in the babies. She cooed and purred with her little one. They took the babies. She never once turned in my direction.

Maybe something's wrong. Any number of things could be bothering her at such a time. Or maybe, could I have done something wrong?

Visitors came. Esther was in great spirits, even more lively than I remembered her.

[Now try to imagine this happening to you — without knowing that there's going to be a great punch line. Imagine the confusion, the hurt.]

I had been so perfectly happy. Who needed this to dampen my mood?

My husband came to take me home the next morning. I was glad to be going home, leaving this aggravation behind.

---

*This point especially applies to a person who is known to have consistently proper behavior and whose behavior now seems out-of-character. If the only way to clear him is with a far-fetched *zechus*, that becomes the likely. In fact, for a person like this, the worse the behavior seems, the more unlikely it is that he did anything wrong.

Months passed. It was a beautiful day. I had dozens of accumulated errands, so I dressed the baby in an adorable outfit and went to town. As I was leaving the bank, I saw in the distance . . . Esther, wheeling a carriage. She waved to me and greeted me with a big smile. Whatever was bothering her in the hospital sure wasn't bothering her now!

Of course, right away we both looked into each other's carriages. Did I have a shock. "Esther, what in the world have you been feeding him! He looks enormous! He can't be 3 months old!"

Esther says, "You're right. He's 8 months old."

"But we were in the hospital together three months ago!"

Esther smiles. "That must have been my twin sister — she has a 3-month-old baby. We really do look quite a bit alike, don't you think so?"

I certainly do, Esther, I certainly do.

Identical twins are commonly mistaken for each other. And yet we rarely consider that this option is the solution to our dilemma.

My young son was housebound after an operation and I asked my sister-in-law to send me her Fisher Price gas station to keep him occupied. She couldn't find someone to bring it from her home on the other side of town. I was a bit desperate, so, against my better judgment, in the meantime I decided to borrow the toy from a neighbor who lives across from us. This neighbor is much more successful than I am in keeping toys looking like new, and the garage was in excellent condition. We guarded it very carefully. A few days later, this neighbor came in, barely able to contain her anger. She accused me not only of making a shmattah out of her gas station in a few short days, but of being so cowardly as to just leave it next to her front door without a word of apology.

I was stunned! I went into the other room and brought out her gas station intact and exactly as I'd received it.

Now we were both mystified.

She returned home and came back carrying a bruised and

battered gas station, which I immediately recognized as my sister-in-law's!

Later we found out what had happened: My sister-in-law had finally found someone to bring the toy. The messenger found our door locked and left the toy near the door. The man who cleaned the building that day had pushed the toy the short distance to my neighbor's apartment across the hall!

Somebody borrowed something from you, and then you got it back in poor condition. Would you ever think that the item had been changed for another one just like it? Maybe you would, but it never crossed the neighbor's mind.

Nechama and Heshy Shapiro had hired a worker to clean their home and he seemed to be working out well.

Nechama was in the kitchen speaking with a relative who had dropped in. Heshy had gone to the pool, leaving his wallet on a shelf in the closet.

The worker finished his job, but he didn't leave right away. The heel had fallen off his shoe, and he asked for some glue to put it back on. He went into the bathroom to apply the glue and then lingered for some time until it dried.

That was Friday. On Sunday morning, as Heshy reached for his wallet to pay for some groceries, he found to his dismay that the $200.00 in bills that had been in his wallet on Friday was missing.

Heshy went home and quickly asked Nechama if she had taken the money. She assured him that she had not. Who could the guilty party be? Their eyes met: It had to be the cleaner, a new worker. Nechama remembered how he had lingered in the bathroom, which was right near the bedroom, on the pretext of waiting for his shoe to dry. She had been busy in the kitchen. Why hadn't he left his wallet in a safe place, Heshy chided himself.

But that was in the past. What should they do now? Should they confront the worker, or just tell him not to come anymore? Would it help to accuse him? He could just deny it.

Sunday, Monday, and Tuesday passed, and they were still debating what to do.

Wednesday, Nechama needed a flashlight. She went to the closet where it was usually kept. She reached up, but didn't see it. Maybe it was further in. She pushed her hand deeper and deeper into the shelf...her hand touched soft leather. She pulled it into view — her husband's black wallet! And inside — $200.

Oh, no! she laughed. What an extraordinary coincidence!

Nechama realized what must have happened. Heshy had needed a new wallet. She happened to pass by a store having a sale on wallets, and had bought him one. She didn't know that the week before he had already bought one for himself. Now he had two nearly identical black leather wallets. Both had been on the same shelf. Last Sunday, he had grabbed the wrong one.

Improbable? Yes. True? Absolutely!

*M*rs. Abrams' daughter Shira had finished high school and was studying at a seminary abroad. As she traveled around the country she would take pictures of the sights, and then send the film home for her mother to develop.

One day, Mrs. Abrams went to pick up the most recent set of pictures from the photo shop. This is how she tells the story:

"I looked through them and my jaw dropped lower and lower. The blood rushed to my face as I flipped through picture after picture. I thought to myself, I sent my daughter for an uplifting experience. What kind of friends does she have? Where do they go? What are they doing? And look how they're dressed! I was horrified. One picture was worse than the next.

"I walked around in a daze from the fridge to the sink to the stove without even knowing what I was doing. Somewhere, from that fog, I heard my youngest daughter say, 'Mommy, where did these pictures come from?'

"I didn't answer. I was sorry I had left them so carelessly on the table.

" 'They were taken right here,' she continued. 'See our mall in the background? But I don't recognize any of the people.'

"I went over to take a second look, and sure enough, some of those pictures were local. I went through the whole pile and found eight pictures that didn't belong to us at all. Suddenly it occurred to me that the developer must have mixed in somebody else's pictures!

"I have been doing business with this studio for over twenty years and never once did such a thing happen. And not only that, I never even heard of a studio switching pictures before."

Mrs. Abrams had never heard of such a thing, so this possibility simply did not enter her mind.

Aliza Gordon received a letter from her sister Hadassah in America, filled with all the usual family chit-chat, including news of a big family reunion planned by Uncle Meyer.

A short time later, Aliza was on her way to the airport to pick up her parents, the Spiegels, who had come for a visit from the States and would be staying with her for a few weeks.

Before she knew it, she was hugging them and they were in a taxi on the way back home. There was so much to talk about and so much to catch up on. During the conversation Aliza mentioned her sister's letter and the forthcoming reunion. Her parents were surprised. This was the first they had heard of such a reunion. They had enjoyed the previous year's family gathering and wondered why they had not been included this year.

They arrived home, and after they settled down, Aliza took out Hadassah's letter, since her parents were really curious to know about the forthcoming party.

Mr. Spiegel read and reread the letter. Something wasn't right. Then his eye caught it. At first he thought that it was a mistake.

Aliza turned around when she heard her father laughing. She saw him with the letter in his hand and a big smile on his *face. Maybe he was enjoying one of the cute stories about Hadassah's children. But the look in his eye seemed to imply something more.*

"Come here a minute," he called. "Did you notice the date on Hadassah's letter?"

Aliza had. The letter was dated the end of April. She couldn't figure out what he was finding so interesting.

"What an extraordinary coincidence," said Mr. Spiegel, shaking his head. "Off by exactly a year."

Aliza took the letter, and this time she read it more carefully: "April 29, 1994." The date was May 5th, 1995. Slowly, she understood. It really was amazing. It had taken this letter one year to arrive.

A letter written April 29th might arrive May 5th — but not May 5th a year later. That's far-fetched. But that mix-up was nothing compared to one clipped from a New England newspaper.

For almost two decades, Harry and Martha Levine have endured teasing from their friends Larry and Judith Gluck, who never received an invitation to the Levine wedding.

"At least once or twice a year we'd rib them about it," Mrs. Gluck said. "We wouldn't let them forget the fact that they never invited us to their wedding."

So, when an invitation to the Levines' 1969 nuptials arrived in the mail last week, complete with a 10-cent postage stamp, the Glucks immediately assumed it was an elaborate practical joke.

But the invitation was no joke, it was just 19 years late, courtesy of the US Postal Service.

The ivory-colored envelope bearing the wedding invitation arrived at the Glucks' Sun Valley Road home with a yellow postage sticker affixed over the address. "Found Under Machine. Please Excuse," the sticker said.

The letter was addressed to Brindisi, Italy, where Gluck was stationed in the Air Force in 1969, and had been forwarded from the Worcester post office, where it apparently had sat since 1969, to Sun Valley Drive.

"My first reaction was that he's getting even for all the jokes I've pulled on him," Gluck said of Levine. "So I did a little research."

Gluck said he showed the letter to a friend who works at the post office, and he confirmed the postal stamp as almost 20 years old, as well as the legitimacy of the yellow sticker.

Gluck admitted he was a bit taken aback by the news, especially since the Levines had always insisted that the invitation was sent.

The Glucks were gracious in defeat, appearing at the Levines' home with a strawberry cheese-cake and a big apology.

"He still owes us a wedding present," Levine joked. "And I hope it won't take another 19 years to arrive."

Since both my husband and I work, the domestic has keys to our home and cleans in our absence. One afternoon I returned home to find that one of the pieces of glass in the sideboard, where all our lovely dishes were, was broken. We questioned the maid and she said she didn't know anything about it. We couldn't believe that she thought we would believe that. It was obviously her fault, since no one else had been home.

What could we do now? Force her to pay? Fire her? Or "just" hold a grudge?

Three years later, we were all sitting in the dining room when — crash! — the glass in the breakfront shattered . . . with no one anywhere near it!

Once when we were discussing the subject of judging favorably in class I said, "We're not supposed to make up tall tales; it has to be real and reasonable. If we make up some wild idea, we won't believe it and then we won't accomplish our purpose." And I gave an example: "Don't say, 'Oh, maybe the cat dragged it away, or the bracelet must have flown to the other side of the moon . . .' "

I was going back to Yerushalayim after spending a few months in Tzfas. I left my bags with the Golds, a wonderful family I had met while studying there. They happened to be away just then, but they gave me the keys to their house, so that I could come in the morning to get my luggage.

I was late and ran into the house, knowing that the taxi I had ordered would be there soon. As I dropped my pocketbook down in the kitchen, a girl who had just come to Tzfas a few days earlier walked in. I had been introduced to her — she was a traveler, out to see the world. She had a lot of energy, but few resources. She had just come by to say hello to the Golds and was sorry they weren't home. She asked me for a glass of water and I quickly gave her one, and then ran to the back of the house to gather my things.

I came back and she was gone — and so was my pocketbook! The front door was wide open. A few seconds later, my taxi arrived.

I had to postpone going back to Yerushalayim and report the theft to the police. I also had to cancel my checks, and report the missing passport and ID card.

Imagine the audacity of that girl, walking off with my purse right from under my nose!

The next morning I looked around the area with the hope of at least salvaging my bag with whatever the thief had chosen to leave in it.

I did find the pocketbook — across the street, by the garbage bin, barely recognizable since it was covered with mud. I looked inside, and to my astonishment everything was still there — my money, passport, checks; not a thing was missing.

Now I was perplexed. I tried to imagine the scene: She must have made a dash with my bag and as she was rummaging through it, she saw someone watching her. She probably got scared, dropped it and ran. Such an ending to all crooks, I thought. And a happy ending for me.

But that really wasn't the ending. When the Golds returned, I told Mrs. Gold how someone had made off with my bag. But before I could give her any details, I saw her chuckling. Now what's so funny about a theft? I wondered.

Seeing my confusion, she told me that she should have warned me to keep the front door closed because she has constant problems with cats coming in and running off with things. My pocketbook has a long, thin shoulder strap, and obviously it was a fun toy for that cat, who dragged it through the mud and played with it until he found something more interesting to do.

I hadn't really wanted to accuse that girl, but how could I have thought otherwise? The thief — a cat? Come on!

What's the point of telling a story like this? Was the girl at fault for not thinking that the thief might have been a cat? Would you have thought of that possibility? How does *dan l'kaf zechus* fit in here? We are not faulted for not considering an excuse we could never have thought of! We are not faulted for lacking information about cats or other things.

What we can learn from this story and others like it is that there is a lot about life we don't know. That's what these stories are all about: to persuade and encourage us that when we catch ourselves being judgmental and unequivocally condemning, we should keep in mind that it might just be . . . another cat story.

My friend Mrs. G. told me recently about her sister's mother-in-law, who had become a very negative, unpleasant person. The older she got, the more negative and unpleasant she became. Even her grandchildren didn't like her. She made life miserable for her daughter-in-law and difficult for her son. Incredibly, even when one of her sons died, she didn't cry or even look the least bit sad! Nothing seemed to affect her.

Despite the difficult relationship, her son made sure to call daily. One Sunday, when he didn't get an answer, he was concerned. After all, she was eighty-one, lived alone and rarely went out. He called an ambulance and rushed over. They broke open the door and found her unconscious. At the hospital, the doctors discovered a tumor the size of a grapefruit on her brain. It was wrapped around the portion of the brain that controls personality. The doctors said it had probably been growing there for the last 25 years!

Other than her awful personality, she had had no other obvious symptoms. And whatever minor symptoms there had been had been attributed to old age. One doctor said that at her age it didn't pay to operate, but others felt they could do so successfully, so the decision was made to go ahead with surgery.

After the operation, Grandma was a changed person. Now you could hear her saying things like: "My children are so good to me," or, "I have such a wonderful daughter-in-law." Remembering the past, she felt terrible about how she had treated her family. "How did you put up with me?" she asked tearfully. For the first time, she was able to grieve for her lost son. During her stay in the hospital, everyone loved her. She was such a cheerful, lovely person.

As amazing as it sounds, says Mrs. G., the story is true.

Does that mean that every time a person is grumpy or rude, we have to consider the possibility that they might have a serious medical condition? Of course not. This story is at the very extreme end of a continuum. On that continuum of medical problems, from bunions and headaches to life-threatening illnesses, are thousands of conditions that can make a person grumpy and not allow him to be what he would like to be or what he really is.

Each one of us, at some point in life, has experienced physical limitations. Sometimes we are painfully aware of them; other times, we have no idea why we are such unpleasant people to be around. When physical limitation or a medical problem is so often our excuse, why doesn't it leap to the forefront of our mind that the same variety of physical ailments may be behind other people's disturbing behavior?

How far do we have to go in trying to understand the other side of the story? R' Chaim Ozer Grodzinsky was once asked by his students: Everything Hashem created has a purpose. What is the purpose of creating "crooked reasoning" (*krumer seichel*)? His answer: "To be *dan l'kaf zechus.*"

From the mitzvah of judging favorably we understand that the Alm-ghty wants us to be creative thinkers. He wants us to consider alternate routes, to let our minds roam and discover paths we don't usually take.

That's why we tell stories with "unexpected" endings: to make the unexpected more expected, the unbelievable more believable. If we pay sufficient attention to the many occasions in our *own* lives where what seems far-fetched is what actually happened, then we will be more likely and willing to find a *zechus* for others — no matter how "unlikely" that likelihood may appear.

7
Questions
And
Answers

H ere are some commonly asked questions and their answers.

Does every situation require our finding a zechus?

We are only required to give the benefit of the doubt when there is a suspicion of guilt. If you didn't perceive a person's speech or behavior negatively, you need not find a *zechus*. This is, of course, subjective. The very same situation, statement, or action might irritate or provoke one person, while someone else wouldn't be bothered at all.

For instance, some people are bothered about the amounts people pledge to charity. Others say, "Why is it anybody's business how much people give?" One person is offended by being left out. But someone else says, "They can include whomever they like."

If there is something that bothers *you*, the mitzvah of judging favorably is there to help. Although some people are very judgmental and others less so, *all of us* have times when we question people's behavior. When such a situation presents itself, *limud zechus* is there to help us reconsider.

◄ What is the first step?

The first step is becoming aware that it is **wrong** to suspect an innocent person.

There are certain categories of transgressions for which a person is unlikely to repent because they consider them so inconsequential; they don't think they are doing anything wrong. Suspecting the innocent (חשד בכשרים) is one such transgression. A person defends himself with the thought: "I didn't **do** anything to him. I only suspected that he might have done something wrong," without realizing that suspecting an innocent person is itself a transgression (*Rambam, Hilchos Teshuvah*, 4:4).

Suspicions often enter our minds and linger. We are not aware that there is anything wrong with this or that we have an obligation to rid ourselves of these suspicions.

Becoming aware has two components:

1. We must first know there is an obligation to judge favorably, and that if we fail to do so, we are guilty of the transgression of suspecting an innocent person.
2. Then, we have to learn to apply this knowledge **at the time** suspicions arise. This is tricky because we are not always aware of that happening. Thoughts like, "What a nerve!" "How come he isn't . . ." "Shouldn't she . . ." and "Why aren't they . . ." should be a red light signaling us: STOP! Danger! Negative thoughts at work. Before proceeding, judge favorably.

To help us focus on this, R' Alexander Ziskind, in his classic work, *Yesod V'Shoresh HaAvodah*, gives us this advice:

If we see our friend doing something or saying something which appears at first glance improper, we should arouse **awareness** of what is required of us by formulating this thought: *I am prepared and ready to fulfill the mitzvah of judging favorably.*[1]

Generally, we recite these words prior to performing mitzvos between man and Hashem: *tallis, tzitzis, bentching, Sefiras HaOmer, lulav,* and *succah.* Here we see them in a new context, serving as a reminder that if we are troubled by someone's behavior or speech, we must focus on the fact that there may be another side to the story to consider.

R' Ziskind continues: . . . [a person should then] exert intense and enthusiastic mental effort to find some kind of merit on behalf of the one suspected.[2]

How energetic and how enthusiastic an effort should we make?

When a person loses something, he first looks in: 1) places where it's most likely to be; 2) other places he's been; and 3) unlikely places. If we really want the missing item, we even recheck places we checked before, like an empty drawer we've already opened three times. When we want something, we are willing to try everything — even the farfetched — to find what's missing. That should be our attitude to judging favorably.

❧ Where and When?

The mitzvos of judging favorably and loving and caring about others (ואהבת לרעך כמוך) are unique. Unlike other mitzvos which are bound to a place or a time or an object, these two mitzvos can be done anyplace.[3] Even if we find ourselves in a place which, due to lack of cleanliness, is unsuitable for *davening* or reciting *brachos*, we can still be involved in the mitzvah of judging favorably.

The mitzvah of judging favorably can be practiced not only anywhere, but also anytime — day or night, weekday, Shabbos or Yom Tov. There is also a timeless aspect to judging favorably. Even past events can be recalled and reviewed and rewritten.

Even if days, months, or even years have passed, you can always reconsider your negative evaluations.

✍ If my first thoughts are unfavorable, are they counted against me?

A person is not held accountable for the first thoughts that enter his mind. Only when we allow the thought to linger are we held accountable.[4]

✍ What if I can only think of a partial zechus?

There are times when finding a partial *zechus* — making a person look a little bit better — has value, and through it we fulfill the mitzvah completely. Such a case is described by the Chofetz Chaim: If I think someone has cheated me, I am allowed to make an effort to retrieve my loss by speaking to someone else who might be able to help me. There are, however, certain conditions that must be met. One of them is, if there is anything I can say in his favor which will make him look even slightly better, I must be sure to include it, even if this information does not make him look completely righteous but just puts him in a slightly better light. To omit such information is considered a grave offense![5]

*B*enny borrowed $1000.00 from Reuven and it's more than two months past the time he promised to pay. Reuven called him five times and each time Benny says he hopes to have the money by the end of the week. Reuven feels he's getting nowhere. Now he wants to talk to Benny's uncle, Mr. Kramer, who he feels will be able to help him.

When Reuven tells Mr. Kramer what happened, he must include the fact that Benny had been expecting money owed him, but each time people disappointed him. That does not absolve Benny of his financial commitments — he still should have found a way to pay on time — but mentioning it surely makes him look better.

What about the case where a person deserves total exoneration, but we only come up with an explanation that partially clears him? At such times, we are, in fact, not giving him what he truly deserves.

Let's say you were just walloped with a giant insult. Assuming that the hurtful statement was made without much forethought and was surely regretted is preferable to assuming a malicious intent. But considering the possibility that you completely misunderstood the statement is even better. If it was a misunderstanding — the speaker never said it, or didn't mean it the way you thought — then you owe him more than you gave him.

If the best explanation one can come up with at the moment is only a partial *zechus*, then he has fulfilled the mitzvah to the best of his ability. Changing black to gray is also good. At such times, however, it would be worthwhile to keep in mind that the person *might* deserve even more.

ᕽ What if I thought of a zechus but it's the wrong one?

It doesn't say anywhere that we are obligated to discover the *real* reason or the *right* reason for a person's actions. We need only think of a justification that is meaningful to us and clears the person as much as possible.

If it was a logical *zechus*, even if it wasn't the right one, then we are still fulfilling the mitzvah and perfecting the *midah*.[6]

At the same time, however, we must be extremely careful:

- not to whitewash wrong actions — calling bad good;
- not to allow ourselves or others to be harmed.

ᕽ What if I judge unfavorably and I find out I was right?

When one has an obligation to judge favorably and he doesn't, he has transgressed a positive commandment — even if he finds out later that his negative interpretation was correct. At the time he was passing judgment, he did not know the person was guilty, and at *that* point, the person deserved to be favorably judged. Until he discovers otherwise, he must judge the person favorably.

≈ When other people are struggling with disturbing things that are happening to them, is it helpful to suggest "far-fetched" excuses to them?

When we are annoyed and someone tries to pacify us with unlikely explanations, the usual consequence is that we will be annoyed with two people instead of one. If we want to help someone find a *zechus*, we have to come up with something logical and reasonable.

We want to be careful about demanding that others consider the unlikely. But if they are open to suggestions in this direction, then we can help them expand their horizons.

Here is a story that illustrates some of the points we just discussed:

I recently attended a lecture given by an important guest speaker. The hall was packed with hundreds of women, and I was sitting with a friend in the middle of the hall. As the speaker walked in and took his place at the podium, I noticed a lady sitting in the front row — knitting! {[The need to judge favorably can happen anytime and any place.]} *I thought to myself, just look at that woman sitting in the front row facing the speaker with her knitting.* {[Not everyone would care, but since this woman was bothered, she needs limud zechus]}.

What nerve to sit at such an important lecture and knit like that in the front row! At least let her move to the back row, where the speaker can't see her. It's so disrespectful. Doesn't she realize that it's not nice to sit smack in front of the speaker and do something else other than only listen to what he has to say? {[These were her first thoughts.]}

I caught myself. {[Awareness.]} *Well, maybe it's relaxing for her after a hard day's work — she can concentrate more easily this way if her hands are moving.* {[I gave her a partial zechus.]} *Or, maybe she asked the speaker permission before-*

hand, so it's a hundred percent okay to knit now, and there's no problem.

I was busy giving myself imaginary pats on the back for a job well done. As the speaker began to speak, I glanced at my knitter friend in the front row. She was still sitting in her seat, but now her hands were quietly resting in her lap and her knitting was put away in a bag near her chair. {{I thought of a zechus, but it was the wrong one.}}

That possibility hadn't even entered my mind.

8 Caring About Others

Judging others favorably is closely connected with the mitzvah to "Love others as you love yourself."[1] Due to this unique relationship we can broaden our understanding of *dan l'kaf zechus* if we examine the meaning of *ahavas rayim*, loving others.

The Torah tells us it is an obligation to love our fellow Jews as we love ourselves. More, it is a fundamental principle of the Torah and the foundation upon which the whole Torah stands.

Can we say that to love others like ourselves means we must take care of their needs the way we take care of our own? In practical terms, we know that it's not possible. And in fact, our Sages confirm that this is not what is meant.

Our obligation to love others requires us to want their success just as we want our own. To give another everything he needs is impossible for a person; to *want* him to have what he needs *is* within everyone's reach.[2]

Every one of us wants all the happiness, pleasure, and blessing that this world has to offer. *Ahavas rayim* means wanting that for others, too.

I want good health for myself and my family, and I wish the same for you and yours too.

I don't want anyone to damage my property, and I am equally concerned that no harm comes to yours.

I want to make a decent living (if not more), and I want you to be successful also.

I want children who are respected and accomplished, and I desire that *nachas* for you.

I want a good night's sleep, and I hope you get one as well.

And oh, how much I want a peaceful life!

Just as it pains me where any of these blessings are missing in my life, *ahavas rayim* means that I share your pain when this happiness is missing from your life.

Above all, *ahavas rayim* means I should want you to be respected and well thought of, just as I want a good name for myself and the people I love.

Above all? Who says this is what we want above all?

We are taught that jealousy, lust, and pursuit of honor take a person out of this world.[3] The *Mesillas Yesharim* gives us this key insight into human nature by telling us that of the three, the desire for honor wields the greatest influence.[4] A person goes to great lengths so that people will have something nice to say about him. "What will they think, what will they say?" is the thought behind many of our actions and decisions. It is not surprising, then, that seeking honor is called "one of the greatest stumbling blocks facing us."[5]

This raises a question: Why did Hashem implant in us such an overwhelming need for honor if it is such a great obstacle? There must be some very positive and beneficial aspect to this powerful yearning for honor, proportional to the harm it causes if misused. And in fact our Sages tell us that as a motivating factor the desire for honor *does* have great value. The concern with opinions of others drives us to do good and helps prevent us from doing the wrong thing.[6]

But most fundamental, we have a need to feel important because we ARE important.[7] Each one of us has a unique and exclusive assignment in this world that no one else who ever lived, is living presently, or will live, can accomplish. Our individual mission is so important that each one of us should feel that it was worthwhile for Hashem to create the universe and all its galaxies, this whole world and everything in it, as a backdrop for us to pass through this world and complete our task.[8]

The desire for recognition and dignity is implanted in our hearts by Hashem so that we will be drawn to achieve distinction. Not only the distinction that we achieve competitively, but true distinction by discovering the special talents and particular strengths that lie within us and utilizing them maximally.

Because the desire for honor plays such a central role in our lives, we can better understand the definition of *ahavas rayim* as explained by Rambam:

> "It is a mitzvah incumbent upon each of us to love our fellow Jews as we love ourselves, as it says, 'Love your fellow man as you love yourself.' Therefore, we are obligated to speak well of others and be concerned about their material well-being . . . as much as we are concerned about our own material well-being and want people to respect us."[9]

Rambam tells us that our obligation to love others is primarily fulfilled by:

- speaking well of them; i.e. guarding their reputation;
- showing respect and concern for their property and possessions.

Is "speaking well of others" mentioned first because it takes precedence? While both are integral to *ahavas rayim*, our Sages tells us that hurting a person with words **is** considered worse than wronging him financially.[10] For many people, damaging their reputation and causing others to look down at them is worse than causing them financial loss. This is why speaking well of a person is a genuine expression of love and concern for our fellow man. If I am willing to make the effort to notice your virtues and praise you, I am giving you what you want — a good reputation in the eyes of others.

This is the basic connection between judging favorably and *ahavas rayim*. Judging favorably guards a person's reputation. Removing suspicion, making the other person look good or better, returning his good name to him, in our own mind and the minds of others, is caring at its finest.

9
The Double Standard

S ometimes we feel we lack the tools and skills to judge favorably. As a matter of fact, more often than not we feel there could not possibly be any excuse or justification for certain behavior.

We can challenge these thoughts and prove how talented and ingenious we can be in inventing excuses for others by seeing how well we do it for ourselves:

I am, in my own humble estimation, a reasonably considerate, courteous and judicious driver. I obey signs and traffic signals. I have never willfully cut another driver off, signaled right when I meant to turn left, or honked my horn in an officially designated quiet zone. Yes, I believe I can say without fear of reproof that I am a paragon of virtue and rectitude *when I drive a car. It's when I park a car that I exhibit signs of, well, not **thoughtlessness** so much as chronic **unawareness.***

Allow me to explain.

You know how sometimes you're desperately searching for a space in a busy shopping area and you note, with no small degree of annoyance, that someone ruined a perfectly good spot by parking smack in the center of a space that would otherwise easily have accommodated two cars? Well, that was probably me.

And you know how sometimes (usually when you're in a real hurry) you want to pull into (or out of) your driveway but you can't because someone left either the front or back end of their car jutting way into the driveway entrance?

Me again.

Believe me, I have never been proud of these, shall we say, unfortunate tendencies. (Vividly, I recall returning to my car one afternoon, surprised to find a rather nasty note taped to my back window. Much as I'd have liked to, I really couldn't disagree with anything in the note, unless maybe it was the spelling of the word "malicious.") On the other hand, I can't really say I was terribly troubled by them. My attitude, it now shames me to admit, hovered somewhere between "I probably should try to be more careful" and "what's the big deal, really?"

But that was before my miraculous and total rehabilitation. But I'll get to that in a moment; first, one final bit of information.

Since a recent change in my husband's work location necessitated his driving in to the office each day, he and I decided to purchase a small second car for my personal use. Because the driveway we share with our neighbor, Mr. S., is not large enough to accommodate this vehicle, I generally park it in the street in front of our house.

Hence, a typical scenario: I park the car at the end of the day, blocking a good part of the entrance to the driveway. My husband, who always comes home later than I, barely manages to squeeze his car in.

"It took me ten minutes to pull into the driveway," he

informs me. "There's no way Mr. S. is going to get his van in. You'd better re-park the car." Out I go, feeling — dare I admit it? — mildly put out. Okay, maybe there isn't a lot of room, but surely with a little bit of effort . . .

Now to the episode that I fervently believe has cured me forever.

I'd gotten off to a later start than usual that morning. Despite my frantic efforts to get everyone ready for school on time, my sons missed the bus.

"Great, just great," I fumed as I hustled the boys into the car. I had an extremely busy morning ahead of me and then an important early afternoon appointment. Driving the kids to school would take twenty minutes I could ill afford to spare. To top it off, I noticed the needle on the gas gauge was hovering close to empty. Oh well, there was enough gas to get me to school and back — I'd fill up later on the way to my appointment.

Twenty minutes later I was back, smoothly pulling the car up in front of the house as I usually do, leaving the car partially blocking the driveway. I gave the situation some quick consideration — my husband had taken public transportation to a meeting with a client that day and Mr. S. never got home until late in the evening — and then put the matter out of my mind.

The morning flew by. Before I knew it, it was time to leave for my appointment. In fact, if I stopped to fill the gas tank as I'd planned, I'd definitely be late. I'd just have to take my husband's car.

Really racing the clock now, I ran to the driveway, yanked the car door open, jumped in and started backing out. I'd only gone a couple of feet before I hit the brake. What was that I saw in my rear view mirror?

A car?

Was that the back end of a car blocking my driveway?

Had someone actually had the chutzpah, the unmitigated gall, to block my driveway?

How could anyone do such a thing? How could they not stop to think that someone might have to get out? That someone might be in a big hurry to get out?

Forcing myself to keep calm, I tried to determine whether there was any way at all I could maneuver past the vehicle. If I turned the wheel just a couple of degrees to the right and then carefully . . . no, forget it . . . there was absolutely no way out.

Now I was really angry. Would I give this person a piece of my mind when he showed up! Where was he anyway? Tentatively, I hit the horn, a few short beeps. Then a few not-so-short ones. Finally, I leaned on the horn, filling the air with one long, ear-piercing blast. Still no sign of the guy. I realized I had no choice but to start ringing doorbells. Fighting back tears of frustration, I slid out of the car and turned towards the street. One step, two . . . and the awful truth dawned on me at last.

If I'd had the time, I might have written myself a note and taped it to the car window. And believe me, I would have been careful to spell every word right.[1]

Cheating, causing damage, pain, or embarrassment to another person, are all "atrocities" when someone else is the perpetrator. We raise our voices in protest, clench our fists, stomp our feet and scream, "Shocking!" "Irresponsible!" "Deceitful!" "Outrageous!" Yet the behavior we might consider outrageous in another person, we find somehow acceptable when done by us.[2]

‿ When Done By Us

*E*very *morning on his way to work, Suri's husband took their three-year-old son across the street and sent him off to kindergarten. One day, with her husband running late, Suri told him she would take their son across the street.*

Once they were on the other side of the street, little Ari started to fuss, refusing to go by himself. "He's taking advantage of me," thought Suri. "He never does this to his father." She tried a few tactics — "I'll give you a candy," "There's your friend" — but nothing helped. Finally, Suri took him by the hand and walked down the block to the building. At the entrance she turned to leave, but Ari was still reluctant, so Suri brought him into the classroom. When they entered the room, she was not happy with what she saw: a room full of youngsters and no teacher in sight. She was annoyed at the teacher for being so irresponsible as to leave the children alone like that.

As soon as she came home she called the school office and complained to the secretary, who said she would tell the principal.

A few days later, Suri had second thoughts about having made the call in haste. She berated herself for not speaking to the teacher first. She called back the school to try to undo the damage, but before she could say more than her name, the secretary interrupted her by saying she had informed the principal and he had agreed with Suri that children that age should never be left alone. Not only that, but he had spoken to the teacher about it.

The next morning, as little Ari was getting ready to leave with his father, he said, "You know, Mommy came to my school."

"Oh!" said his father in surprise. "When?"

"The other day when you couldn't take me, Mommy took me all the way."

"I'm so sorry that you had to take him all the way there," Suri's husband turned to her. "What did you do with the kids?"

"Well, I left them alone. It was just for a little while. I really didn't have a choice, Ari wouldn't go by himself. You know I would usually never do that, but there was no other way . . ."

As Suri heard herself going on and on she almost choked on her words, thinking about the teacher she'd been so quick to condemn.

Shuli was in town picking up a repaired window. She hailed a taxi and got in with it.

"How much did you pay for that?" the driver asked her.

"Ten dollars," she answered.

She heard a gasp from the driver. "Ten dollars?! That's robbery! I had the very same size window fixed recently for four dollars. That guy is a ganev."

"Are you sure it was the same size?" Shuli asked. "Maybe it was a different kind of glass."

"No. You were cheated. What a nerve."

"Well," said Shuli, "everyone wants to make a living."

"He's a crook!"

When they reached Shuli's home, the driver asked for ten dollars.

"I always pay seven to come home from that part of town," Shuli appealed.

"Nope. It's ten dollars."

As she handed him the ten dollars, Shuli thought to herself, "Right, everyone wants to make a living."

It's the other fellow who's the crook. We? We just want to make a living.

✍ . . . Or Those We Love . . .

We were speaking about the impropriety of bringing small children who can't sit quietly to shul, and all of us were in full agreement that it is wrong to bring them.

But one woman in the group hesitated. "Of course I agree too. I'm surely on the side of those who feel it is inappropriate to bring small children to shul. But I know of an exception. One of my grandchildren is a very exceptional child. My daughter-in-law brought him to shul from the time he was born!* He never missed a Shabbos or Yom Tov. She brought him in every kind of weather. Everyone in shul knows him and loves him! I wish you could talk to the people where she lives to hear how much they all love him.

"Although some children may disturb by crying (I'm sure my daughter-in-law always took him out if he cried) or create halachic problems because of dirty diapers, the experience of

---

*In an area where it is permissible to carry.

being in shul in these early impressionable years imparts something to that child for a lifetime. To this day, my grandson loves shul.

"Surely it would have been a mistake not to take such a child to shul — don't you all agree? Such a child belongs in shul!

"You see, even if he cries a little in the early years, eventually he'll learn about the decorum of a shul and then he'll be the pride and joy of the congregants who would surely be happy to put up with the noise, considering the nachas they'll have from him in later years!"

When we care about someone, it is surprising how easy it is to find a *zechus*, or at least to reserve judgment. Suddenly we become very creative and imaginative. We tap intellectual and emotional strengths we didn't know were there to justify our loved ones.

I joined a group of people who were standing and talking, and as I listened, I heard some very derogatory information about someone whose name was never mentioned. They were painting a black picture about this person, which made a lot of sense based on the information presented.*

Suddenly, as I was listening, the story started to sound familiar. As I continued to hear more and more details, I said to myself, Oh no! They're talking about my daughter! It was my own daughter that they were accusing of doing all of those horrible things! All of a sudden, in one split second, I had twenty good excuses for her.

At first, as this mother listened to the conversation, it sounded like the girl they were talking about was clearly to blame; there was nothing to say in her defense, no excuse. All of a sudden, in an instant, the picture changed. Why? Because they were talking about someone she loved.

---

*See *Sefer Chofetz Chaim* 6:8 for *halachos* of stopping a person from speaking *lashon hara.*

When we see someone we like doing something questionable, we instinctively say to ourselves, "Something good must be going on here," even if we don't know exactly what it is. Very often a defense naturally comes to our mind. No one forced us, no one pointed out: "Here's a case where you have to judge favorably!"

This is the magic in *ahavah* (love): It causes us to overlook the worst sins.[3] We naturally and instinctively want to cover for ourselves and the people we love. Loving others prompts me to stick up for them, to make allowances and smooth over rough spots. *Ahavah* is like a "bribe," bending my judgment to incline my reasoning in your favor.

If we notice how resourceful and ingenious we can be at justifying behavior, how clever and capable we are at excusing ourselves and those we love, then we must acknowledge that if it's difficult to judge **others** favorably, it is not because we are lacking the talent or skill. We are only lacking the will.

> *One of my nieces, of whom I am especially fond, had finally found the time in her busy social schedule to accept my Shabbos invitation.*
>
> *She came Friday afternoon and decided she wanted to bake me a cake. I was busy around the house, and when I came into the kitchen I found it a complete mess.*
>
> *What surprised me the most was my own reaction. I didn't mind. I just picked up everything, cleaned up, and that was it. If anybody else would have done it, I probably would have hit the roof.*
>
> *Shabbos afternoon, when I went to the freezer to give myself the treat I had saved — the last of the chocolate ice cream — it wasn't there! All I could think was, I'm glad she enjoyed it and felt at home.*

It is an important insight for us: **We tend to judge people, not actions.** It really depends on *who* says it and *who* did it and not *what* was done.

> *Goldie wanted to get her daughter Miri into camp but she was told there was no room. She kept calling the*

director, even though he insisted there were no more places. Since most of Miri's friends were going and it was very important to her daughter, Goldie persevered.

Later that week, Goldie got a call from an acquaintance, Mrs. K. Goldie's husband was in charge of a boy's choir and Mrs. K. very much wanted to get her son in. Even though Goldie's husband had told Mrs. K. that there was no room, she wanted Goldie to "push" a little bit. Mrs. K. called several times to see if Goldie had made any headway. By the fourth time, Goldie thought to herself: "What a nudge! There's a limit to how pushy a person can be."

When I do it, I call it "perseverance"; when you do it, you're a nudge. How does the verb "to persevere" become "to nudge"?

My husband and I were celebrating our anniversary and our children came over to spend the evening with us.

Our two daughters walked in with a pre-arranged gift. Debby had brought the flowers, and Mimi, the vase. Each handed me her gift with joy and kisses. As I was admiring the presents, I heard Debby say to Mimi: "What a puny vase!" Mimi's smile disappeared, and was replaced by a look of deep hurt. I thought to myself, Why would Debby say such a thing? Why would she insult her sister so?

Meanwhile, Debby ran off to show the flowers to my husband. Minutes later she returned and I could see she was on the verge of tears.

"What's the matter, Debby?" I asked.

"I went to show Daddy the flowers and he didn't like them."

"He told you that?" I asked, surprised.

"No, but I can tell he didn't like them." Tears welled in her eyes. "Why would he want me to feel bad after I tried hard to bring something nice?"

I couldn't believe my ears.

"Debby," I thought to myself, "look what you just said to your sister! You were completely unaware of the effect of your words. Yet you were so insulted from something your father only insinuated!"

When I hurt you, it doesn't seem like a big deal. But it becomes a "big deal" when *I'm* the victim. If someone hurts my feelings, I feel he's insensitive. When I'm accused of hurting him, the response differs. "He's just being overly sensitive."

It is fascinating and disquieting to observe in ourselves this capacity to unabashedly justify in ourselves what we condemn in others.

*T*he other day my friend Ahuva was visiting and during the course of our conversation she told me about a big problem she's having with one of her neighbors.

"It's just awful. She made such a major fight over nothing. First she was just unfriendly, but now she won't talk to me at all. The worst thing is that she dragged her husband into this. She told him all these nasty things about our family — and he believed them! How could he just believe her without so much as asking us or clarifying if it's true? He just swallowed everything she told him."

"Really?" I said. "How do you know?"

"What do you mean? My husband told me!"*

We have been commanded not to do an "injustice" when judging. What is meant by "injustice"? Permitting for ourselves what we forbid to others.[4] In a nutshell:

Any defense we use for ourselves, we must be willing to use for others too — otherwise, it's an injustice.

*W*hen she woke up Shabbos morning, Mrs. Blum told her husband it might soon be time to head for the delivery room, and she asked him to come home from shul as soon as possible. He went to shul, but left right after Kedushah of Mussaf to hurry to be with her. As he was taking off his tallis, he saw another man on the other side of the shul also taking off his tallis and putting it away. Can't he stay to finish?

---

*Not only are we forbidden to speak *lashon hara*, we are also not allowed to believe it.

*What's his rush? (so he'll eat his cholent 10 minutes later!) Mr.
Blum thought.*

*When Mr. Blum arrived at the hospital with his wife, they
hurried straight to the delivery room . . . and who do you
think was there?*

You and I are both doing the very same thing. I know *I* have
a good reason. Why doesn't it occur to me that *you* might have
a reason that's equally valid?

*N*aomi and her family moved to Netanya two years ago
and had a very difficult time adjusting. Yesterday, she
*was pouring out her heart to me. One of her close friends from
years ago, Rina, does volunteer work with new immigrants.
She helps them with everything — money, places to stay, pa-
perwork, social adjustment, etc.*

*Naomi had seen her friend at social occasions during these
two difficult years, but never once did Rina ask her about her
adjustment, nor did she ever call to see how things were going.*

*Naomi so much wanted warmth and understanding, espe-
cially from a friend used to dealing with these problems all the
time.*

*Finally, Naomi's hurt and resentment built up to the point
where she decided to call Rina and let her know how she was
feeling. Rina heard her out and then explained that the past
two years had been very hard ones for her too. Her father-in-
law had passed away, her mother-in-law had been in and out
of the hospital, and much of the responsibility had fallen on
her. "Besides," Rina said, "you always looked so happy whenever we met. You gave me no clue that something was amiss."*

*At this point in telling me her story, Naomi stopped and
lashed out angrily at Rina: "She should be ashamed to give
me such lame excuses! In two years, you can find time to
show an interest, no matter what's going on. We all go
through a lot. And what did she want me to look like? Should
I have donned sackcloth to make my point?"*

*So I asked her, "Naomi, if she was such a good friend, why
didn't you call her all those months?"*

To which Naomi retorted: "I had no idea what was happening in her life!"

More than a little shaken by her answer, I wished she could hear what she was saying. I tried again: "It's hard to give warmth to all those who need it. There may even be people in your life who want more of your attention."

"There sure are," Naomi interjected without hesitation. "My mother-in-law keeps complaining that I never call her."

"Why don't you?" I asked. To my amazement, I heard Naomi reply, "There is so much going on in my life. I'm trying to get my life together . . . I just don't have time."

We can be perfectly happy with our behavior and yet see that same behavior in somebody else and strongly disapprove. We use justifications, sometimes *illogical* ones, for ourselves, which we would never accept from someone else.

This double standard mentality — demanding higher standards of others than we demand of ourselves — makes a constant appearance in our lives. Let's look at some common areas of double standards:

✍ I can forget, but you aren't allowed to.

We forgive our own forgetfulness as a matter of course, but that of others often strikes us as the height of insensitivity.

Did you ever make a *simchah* and have to send invitations? Did you ever forget anyone? What might you say for yourself? *Look, I'm only human. You know there are hundreds of people . . . is it really possible to remember everyone?* Most of us have that unpleasant fear of leaving someone out. And very often we do. We feel so bad but . . . we forgot. We hope other people will be understanding.

But what happens when *we're* left out, when somebody forgets us? Do we then understand that "people are only human," and that sometimes people *do* get left out?

Why do excuses sound flimsy only when they're not our own?!

I worked for this really nice family, Dr. and Mrs. Solomon, as an au pair. Yesterday, Mrs. Solomon came home from grocery shopping and the minute she stepped into the house, she remembered that she had forgotten to buy eggs. She asked her daughter Tamar, who was sitting comfortably with a book, to run out and buy eggs, and while she was at it, to get some cake for the guests they were expecting.

Tamar came home half an hour later with a nice assortment of cookies and danishes, but no eggs.

"How could you forget the eggs?" her mother demanded angrily.

I was lax — but you, you were irresponsible.

✎ *I can make a mistake, but you can't.*

The telephone rang at our pharmacy. It was the doctor. He demanded to know why the pharmacist had dispensed medication different than the one prescribed. The pharmacist apologized and there followed a lengthy speech as to how important it is to dispense what was prescribed, responsibility to the public, etc., etc.

Afterwards, the pharmacist sifted through the pile of prescriptions to find the relevant prescription. To her surprise, she discovered that she had dispensed what had been prescribed; the doctor had obviously written the wrong item. Out of curiosity, she rang the doctor and explained the situation. "Oh, well, anyone can make a mistake,'" was his casual reply.

✎ *I'm not a mind reader, but you'd better be one.*

When someone accuses us of not coming through for them, don't we sometimes feel, "Well, how could I have known? Do you think I'm a mind reader?" But when we're in need, we *do* expect people to know.

"She knows I don't have a car — why doesn't she offer me a ride?"

"She knows I'm making a luncheon — why doesn't she offer to help?"

We want and expect family, friends, and neighbors to be "mind readers." We want them to anticipate our needs without our telling them.

*O*ne of my closest friends and her husband had gone on a month-long trip abroad. I had been looking forward to her return, but even though I called to welcome her, I sensed a chill in the air over the next few weeks. Finally, I couldn't take it anymore, so I came right out and asked her what was wrong. I almost dropped the phone when she said, "Why didn't you fill up the refrigerator for us? You knew we were coming home on Tuesday and there'd be nothing in the house!"

I go away on trips too and it never occurred to me to expect someone else to shop for me before I come home. How was I supposed to know that's what she wanted?

We can be incensed that people are living without complete awareness of our needs, and yet would we have the temerity to claim our antennae are always tuned in to those calling out to us?

For me, it's out of character
— but for you, it's who you are.

We often feel that our offensive behavior is not indicative of us as a person. We feel it's out of character, that it doesn't reflect our true personality. We usually explain it as a result of extenuating circumstances or a reaction to something the other fellow said or did. *We* are basically nice people who were caught off guard — "I really don't do things like that . . ."

But when it's the reverse, when others are rude and hurtful to us, we instinctively feel: What a rude person!

Simchos: Sometimes we go to a *simchah* knowing we can only stay for a short time because of other pressing obligations. What happens, however, when it's our *simchah*, and someone comes in, shakes our hand, takes a drink and walks out! Might we wonder, slightly offended, *How come they're running out so fast?*

Thank yous: "I was annoyed when your thank-you note came three months late . . . until I remembered some of mine which had never been sent at all!"

Being on time: I realize I made you wait on the corner for fifteen minutes, but I'd like you to be understanding.

Yet, when I'm standing there waiting for you, I find it difficult to imagine a valid excuse. And when you finally come and tell me what delayed you, it sounds so flat.

Visiting: I was in your neighborhood and didn't visit you, although I knew you would appreciate a visit from me. But it was impossible: I couldn't. I was late for an appointment. Someone else was driving. It would have meant a half-hour stop. I hadn't called first.

But when it happens in reverse and we know a friend passed right by and didn't come in, don't we wonder: *Why couldn't she take the time to stop in and say hello?*

Double (and worse) Parking:

My friend lives in a condo where everyone has an assigned parking space. One day, she and I were coming back from shopping and as we pulled into the parking lot, my friend saw someone else's car parked in her space. I don't want to repeat what she said. She recognized the car as belonging to a neighbor and raced to his door to let him know that it was unacceptable to park in someone else's spot, regardless of circumstances.

A week later, we were again pulling into the parking lot after a day out. My friend had some relatives staying with her and their car was parked in her spot. She turned the wheel and pulled into an empty spot nearby.

"Hey, Bella, didn't you say you can't do that?"

"Too bad," she said as she shut the ignition.

Sharing secrets: When I don't tell you private information, I would like you to understand that there are certain things one just doesn't share. But when I find out that you, one of my closest friends, didn't tell me the news, I feel very hurt. We're such good friends — why didn't you share it with me?

Borrowing and returning: When I ask you to lend me your _____, I realize it's . . . expensive, irreplaceable, new, the last one you have. But I'm desperate, I really need it!

But when you ask to borrow my _____, I'm surprised and maybe a little annoyed (and maybe a lot) that you should ask for something that . . . I might need, is so fragile, I've hardly used myself, is stored away and hard to get to.

Cutting words: I could lash out at you with the most devastating and damaging type of insult, and defend myself with, "But it's true!"

But if you point out even one minor fault of mine, I can't forgive you.

At some time in this discussion you may ask: But isn't there a point where it's time to say that certain actions are simply wrong? Hurtful, harmful, and just plain inexcusable?

Of course.

But let us consider a minute these people who are doing these inexcusable things. Do *they* consider their behavior inexcusable? Notice we say "they," the bad / inconsiderate / unreasonable / wrong ones, as opposed to us, the good ones. Do "they" have an excuse?

You might say, "If people act improperly, who cares if they have an explanation!"

The reason we should care is because at some time or another **we are those people**. We are the people that other people are struggling to deal with.

- I took my son off camp grounds even though it was against the rules. I felt my son needed it. I knew the camp director wouldn't agree, but I hoped he would try to understand. There was really no time to ask and the truth is, we were up and back faster than we could have found someone to ask.
- I know people get very annoyed when I park my shopping cart in a check-out line and then go back to finish my shopping, but I am so pressed for time, I feel I don't have a choice. I understand your point of view, I agree with you, but I can't do it your way.
- I backed up without looking and almost hit the lady . . . and I didn't even get out of the car to apologize. It's really inexcusable. She must have thought that I'm crazy. I really would have and I certainly usually do, but everyone was beeping and I couldn't stop.

I'm know I'm wrong . . . but I'm not crazy.

How often do we hear people who are upset lash out at the offender: "She's crazy!"; "He's just no good." Yes, there *are* evil people in the world, as well as people incapable of rational behavior. (But just because your neighbor wants to build out on property that you *know* is yours, or refuses to move his car — that doesn't mean he's evil or crazy.) We are working with the assumption that the majority of people we deal with are rational, sane, sound-minded, balanced, upright, decent, proper, "okay" people . . . in short, people like *us*.

Sure we have insensitivities that can hurt many who deal with us. We have pains of all sizes, we have fears of all shapes, financial pressures which are sometimes choking — worries and limitations that thwart our ability to come through for others the way we would like to. We hurt people, we infuriate them, and we sometimes cause deep and long-lasting pain, yet we know we are rational, reasonable, and decent. And you know what? The other fellow feels that way too — about himself!

Even when we admit that there is no good excuse for what we have said or done, we usually have one ready: We plead guilty with an explanation.

✎ I forgot / or didn't come through for you and I know you were counting on me . . . but:

"I had a lot on my mind."
"I was under a lot of pressure."
"I'm absent-minded."
"I just couldn't."
"I know I should get to it."
All said with such warmth and goodwill when prefaced with "I."

"I really meant to" — I might judge you by your actions, but I would like you to judge me by my intentions.

✎ I did something extremely inconsiderate . . . but:

"It was the end of a long day."
"It's a bad habit of mine."
"Was it *so* terrible?"
"I'm not the only one."
"I didn't know you'd be that upset."
"I'm only human."
Have you ever used that for yourself? Now try this: "She's only human." How does that sound?

✎ I said something very unkind . . . but:

"I was caught off-guard."
"I had reached my breaking point."
"I usually wouldn't, but she provoked me."
"There's only one way to deal with such a person."
"I just wasn't thinking."
Have you ever tried to understand someone else's behavior with the excuse, "I caught her off guard"?

"As soon as I said it I felt terrible."

"When I thought it over, I realized it was insensitive."

"If I could only take back my words I would."

"I couldn't sleep just thinking how I had hurt you. I meant well and now I feel bad that it came out wrong."

"I'll never say or do anything like that again."

Although we know how bad we felt afterwards, it rarely occurs to us that another person might also regret what he's done. *Why is she acting so obnoxious, unreasonable, or curt?* we ask ourselves, ignoring the fact that she might have sincerely regretted it — as we have regretted our words on countless occasions.

We know how bad we can feel about certain behavior even though we may never apologize. But as for you — if you had those feelings of regret, why didn't you express them immediately?

If I have the capacity to use an excuse for myself, then I have the obligation to share it with you.

*T*he other day, a casual conversation revealed to me that a close friend whom I've known for years was in my neighborhood and did not take the trouble to stop by.

I told myself not to make a big deal about it, but I couldn't seem to push it down. I myself was surprised that it wouldn't go away. Look, I said to myself, there are a lot of logical reasons why she might not have come over. But my heart didn't feel like using them for her.

It took me a few hours before I could move over to the other side of the fence — and I'll tell you what did it. I pictured myself being in a friend's neighborhood and not going in to visit her. I realized that the reason I wouldn't be dropping by was very likely to be one of those logical reasons I wasn't willing to allow for my friend now.

How can I, in all fairness, deny her the excuse that I in all likelihood would gladly use for myself?

We have taken a look at some of the excuses we take for ourselves — the creative rationalizations and justifications we use to defend our own actions and speech — in order to prove that we in fact do know how to judge favorably . . . if we choose to.

Let's not waste these excuses! Let's notice what we take for ourselves and then let's be willing to use these *zechuyos* to make others look good. That's real *ahavah* — that's the meaning of the word כָּמוֹךָ (like yourself) in וְאָהַבְתָּ לְרֵעֲךָ כָּמוֹךָ — caring about others the way we care about ourselves.

Instead of moving through life with a double standard, our goal should be to move towards one standard — the same standard — for me *and* you.

10
Until You Reach His Place

הִלֵּל אוֹמֵר . . . אַל תָּדִין אֶת חֲבֵרְךָ עַד שֶׁתַּגִּיעַ לִמְקוֹמוֹ.
Hillel Said . . . Don't judge your friend until you reach his place (Pirkei Avos 2:5).

One of the most valuable pieces of advice we are given to help us fulfill the challenging and satisfying mitzvah of judging favorably is found in *Pirkei Avos*: If we see someone stumble in word or deed, we shouldn't judge him unfavorably until we "reach his place"[1] — that is, until we have been in the same situation — and successfully passed that test. Until then, we have no right to judge.

When we are upset, we might try to convince ourselves that we really shouldn't be so critical of others. A small inner voice hesitantly suggests: "Maybe you're coming down too hard. You're not in his shoes — how can you judge him?"

"Maybe if you were a principal, you'd also want to admit only high achievers."

"Maybe if you had those kinds of pressures, you'd also be the weak link in the car pool."

"Maybe if you got rich, you'd also snub some of your old friends."

"Maybe if you had been offered a higher-paying job elsewhere you'd also think nothing of leaving, even though the firm gave you your start."

But often we are not convinced. A louder, clearer voice rings in our ears: "I would never do something like that, even if I had been in his place. How can you not invite first cousins?" "I don't care what you say — you don't return a book in that condition!" "It's inexcusable — I would never . . .!"

You would never? Don't be so sure!

"**Y**ou know what really bothers me? It's so upsetting when I'm in the middle of a conversation and the person on the other end asks me to wait while she takes care of something on the stove, takes another phone call, or just wants to see who's at the door. I always feel it's slightly rude and a bit inconsiderate. Anyway, it surely is a pet peeve of mine.

"After that speech, it's a little bit embarrassing for me to continue telling you this. I never thought it would happen, or quite this way.

"I was on the phone when there was a knock on the door. I couldn't just ignore it and I was so glad I didn't, because it was the repairman. I had been waiting for him for three days. Was I happy to see him! And of course I hurried him into the kitchen to explain what was wrong with the refrigerator. It took a while to explain where the leak was coming from, and then he asked me to take the things off the top of the refrigerator so he could move it. All the time I was thinking, my friend is waiting for me — you just can't do this to someone."

There are situations when we say, "That behavior is unacceptable" — and then we cross our own bottom line. We should therefore keep in mind this understanding of Hillel's teaching: We shouldn't judge others until we reach their place.

✒ Passing judgment on ourselves

One of the obstacles to judging people favorably is our certainty that if we would be in that person's place we would never behave that way:

"You'd never catch me doing that."
"I don't care how tired / busy / pressured you are, there's no excuse for . . ."
"No one in my family would ever . . ."
"There are limits!"
"I simply can't understand how anyone could . . ."
"I would never, ever . . ."

To overcome this hurdle we should consider another interpretation of the same Mishnah taught, by the Baal Shem Tov: A person isn't judged in the Heavenly Tribunal unless he first passes judgment on himself. But who would be willing to pass sentence on himself? Therefore, when we are being judged for a transgression, our misbehavior is "shown" to us, but in a slightly different form — with someone else as the perpetrator. Not realizing that the verdict we give will apply to ourselves, we look at the other person's behavior and pass judgment: "That was rude. Selfish. Uncaring. Irresponsible." Our judgment is unequivocal: "A person who would do such a thing should be _____! . . . deserves _____! . . . is a _____!"

Our Sages therefore warn us: Don't judge your friend until you reach his place. "Don't judge" can also mean "you won't judge" — you won't be called upon to judge unless you were in that place. Realize that this disturbing behavior is shown to you so that you can pass judgment on yourself, for you too were in that situation and acted similarly. Know that the verdict you now assign to another, will be the one given to you.[2]

When we try to be more understanding, when the judgment we pronounce is favorable, we are the ones to benefit, because the *zechus* we use to defend someone else will then be used for us.

✑ The magic of remembering

STOP! You were here!

Knowing that a similar incident is there in our past helps us slow down and calm down. Even if we don't know exactly what it is or when it happened, knowing it is there should act as a big stop sign. It should give us the incentive to be kind and lenient judges.

We can take this one step further: If, with Hashem's help, we can actually recall an incident where we did something similar, and then remember what we had to say for ourselves at that time — that's dynamite! The excuses we have for ourselves are always much better than anything we can possibly think of for someone else. When I remember how I felt at the time, how comfortable I was with my excuse, how impressed I was with my reasoning, and how easily I accepted my justifications, and then I use this *zechus* for you...

When my neighbor returned the iron she had borrowed from me, on time, I was pleased. Until she added, as she handed it to me, "I'm sorry, but an inch of the cord was accidentally burned. The iron still works, but I'll replace the cord if you want." I answered that we would tape it, and as long as it still worked, it was fine. But as I turned to put the iron on the shelf, I was thinking: A person should really be more careful with someone else's property.

I closed the closet door, but those words seemed to trigger something in my mind. Slowly, distant memories of a far-away time and place began to return...being careful . . . ten years ago . . .

Ten years ago my husband and I sublet an apartment owned by friends. One day a neighbor and I were standing outside discussing a major community project. In the middle of the conversation I suddenly realized that fifteen minutes before I had left a Corningware tea kettle filled with one cup of water on the fire. Expecting an explosion or worse, I dashed into the kitchen, turned off the fire, and removed the tea kettle. Afraid it would explode, without taking time to think, I put it on the counter.

It left a large gaping hole in the beautiful formica. I felt terrible. What an expense we'd have paying for an entire new counter! We had to face our friends, the owners. It was embarrassing, but what could we do? Mustering up courage, we called them. They were very understanding and even generous enough to tell us to forget about it.

I never had to give the little speech I had mentally prepared in my defense: "I wasn't careless, I wasn't reckless, I was outside, talking to the neighbor about something important, I didn't want the kettle to explode — I didn't see that I had a choice at the moment."

When I remembered, vividly, the excuses I had for myself, it was easier to understand my neighbor with the iron, and my attitude towards her "carelessness" mellowed considerably.

Knowing an incident is there in my past gives me the desire to understand. **Finding** that similar case gives me the insight, capability, and tools to judge favorably.

Malka was having guests for Shabbos and she knew her neighbor was going away. She had done so much for this neighbor over the years that she felt comfortable asking her for a favor. But when Malka asked if she could have her apartment for guests, to her surprise the answer was a flat "No."

Malka was left with a definite resentment towards her neighbor. She felt there was no valid excuse for her refusal. The people she wanted to put in the apartment were reliable, clean, and conscientious. The neighbor was leaving anyway. Why would anyone want to lose out on such an easy mitzvah?

Then Malka started to consider the various reasons her neighbor might have had for refusing. Maybe there were problems with the apartment that her neighbor didn't want others to know about. Then too, when you lend an apartment, you

*have to get yourself together to prepare it. Maybe her neigh-
bor felt she wouldn't have time to straighten up the way she
would have liked. Maybe she didn't like strangers in her
home. In her mind, Malka could list the possibilities, but in
her heart, Malka felt her neighbor had definitely lost out.
With a little extra effort, her neighbor would have had a
chance to return a favor.*

Malka shared her resentment with her sister Yaffa, who
saw how worked up she was and sympathized between
bites of apple pie and sips of coffee. Returning to the table
with a second helping, Malka glanced towards her sister
who was now sitting pensively. "Penny for your thoughts,
Yaf."*

*"Malki," her sister offered earnestly, "I was just thinking.
Did anybody ever ask you to do them a favor and you said
'no'? Did you feel you 'lost out on a mitzvah'? "*

*As she took another sip of coffee, Malka thought back on
times when she had been forced to decline requests. She remembered some of her excellent reasons. As those reasons
paraded before her and each one took a convincing bow, her
resentment seemed to melt away.*

*"You're right," Malka told her sister with new-found clari-
ty. "I didn't look at it as if I had 'lost out on a chance to do a
favor.' At the time, I saw it as something I simply couldn't
do!"*

Malka *did* judge her neighbor favorably. She used the mitzvah of *dan l'kaf zechus* as it should be used; the explanations
she thought of were realistic and logical and could have been
sufficient. However, Malka still retained her complaint: "With a
little extra effort, my neighbor could have come through for
me." Malka's emotions hadn't caught up with her intellect; the

---

* A person who feels the need to talk out his resentment with a third party should
try to conceal the identity of the person being spoken about, as in this story where
it was unnecessary to specify which neighbor. When this is not possible, the
Chofetz Chaim explains that we are permitted to share our annoyance for the purpose of improving our attitude towards a person with whom we are annoyed, even
if we must reveal his identity, providing we fulfill the seven conditions of speaking
lashon hara for a constructive purpose, לתועלת.

resentment was still there. She needed a different kind of an effort to rid herself of her irritation — the "magic" of remembering herself in the same position. As she reviewed those scenes, she saw that "losing out" was not the way she phrased it when *she* had to refuse.

One of the major benefits of finding a parallel in our lives is its use as a tool to lessen resentments. It doesn't always make the action "okay," but it frees me to understand you.

We live across the street from a girls' dormitory, and like many families in the neighborhood, we try to make the girls feel at home. A while ago, we lent our blow dryer to one of the girls in the dorm. She sent it back to us through someone else, and when my daughter tried to use it, she saw it was broken. I was extremely annoyed, as you can well imagine. The girl didn't have the decency to tell me, to apologize, or to offer to pay. I went about my business, but a few times during the day I heard myself saying, "What a chutzpah!"

Something was gnawing at me, though. I couldn't put my finger on it. It wasn't only the girl's irresponsibility; something else was in the back of my mind refusing to come forward.

And then this scene from many years before reappeared:

My friends and I were studying for a test at someone's house. There was a blackout. We lit some candles so that we could continue studying. A few minutes later, my friend screeched, "Look, Esti! The candle!" One of the candles I had lit had fallen onto the upholstery and burned a hole in the couch. I felt terrible. But I never did anything about it. Nothing. I didn't talk to the people, I didn't call them . . . and I never offered to pay. Why? Because I was so embarrassed I just didn't know how to face them. Thinking back, I can hardly believe I did something so irresponsible.

With that memory fresh in my mind I thought sympathetically, I bet that girl is so perplexed that she just can't bring herself to face me — just as I couldn't face those people then.

Don't you think feeling "embarrassed" is a weak excuse? Shouldn't people take responsibility for damage they cause? If so, why did this weak excuse seem to satisfy Esti? It only became meaningful when she recalled being guilty of a similar offense and remembered having used that excuse for herself. Recalling that event, and particularly her reaction, gave her the ability to understand and even sympathize with behavior that would otherwise have been unacceptable.

The justification we used for ourselves when we "were there" may not be as good as others we could and should consider or as good as the person may deserve. But because we used it to clear ourselves, we breathed life into it. Then it becomes powerful and meaningful when we apply it to others.*

*A*lthough her niece's wedding was less than a week away, Dina still hadn't found a dress for her daughter. She called her friend Libby, owner of a children's dress boutique, to see if anything new had come since Dina had last been there.

"Sorry, nothing's come in," Libby answered sympathetically. "But you know what? If nothing turns up, I'll lend you one of Miri's dresses. It's the size you need and it's perfect for a wedding."

"Thanks so much," Dina smiled into the phone. "I can always count on you."

Two days later, Dina was still without a dress. "Libby," she said over the phone that night, "I'm ready to take you up on your offer." An hour later, she was holding the dress in her

---

* Feeling "embarrassed" is only a partial excuse. While understandable, it does not exonerate a person from his responsibility. If the *zechus* I consider only lessens the severity of the wrongdoing in my eyes but does not totally exonerate, then I should be aware that there may be more to say in someone's behalf.

Let's take Esti's story as an example: Esti judged favorably in a way that was meaningful to her. And her annoyance was certainly diminished. But the "culprit" deserved more.

This was discovered the next morning when Esti walked into her daughter's room and saw her blow-drying her hair with the very same blow-dryer she had thought was broken. Why hadn't it worked the day before? Was a wire loose? Had she pressed the wrong button? Was the electricity momentarily off? Was the socket faulty? They may never know.

hand. "It's perfect," Dina gushed enthusiastically. "Thanks a million."

"Not at all, I'm happy to help you out — and again, a big mazel tov. Just do me one favor," smiled Libby warmly. "Please make sure to return it right after the wedding."

The wedding came and went, days turned into weeks, and Dina still hadn't returned the dress. Libby wondered whether she should call or wait a few more days. The problem seemed to solve itself when she bumped into Dina on the street. After catching up on all the news, Libby added, "By the way, do you want me to send somebody over to pick up the dress?"

"No, that's okay. It's on my to-do list. I'll get it over to you."

But the dress never came. The days flew by, with Libby still unsure of exactly how to handle the problem. Then an errand brought her to Dina's house. This is it! she thought. No excuses now.

As she was leaving, she turned to Dina, trying to keep the irritation out of her voice. "Maybe I can take the dress now so that you don't have to make a special trip to bring it."

Dina went to the hall closet to get the dress. She handed it to Libby and confessed uneasily, "I'm really sorry I didn't return it sooner. It has a stain on it, and I wasn't planning to return it that way. I wanted to replace it with a new one. I didn't have a chance to buy it yet, but I will."

Later that day, the incident was still very much on Libby's mind. Okay, so Dina had good intentions. But why didn't she tell me? Why not say to me, "I'm sorry, the dress got stained, I plan to replace it . . ." Let me know! Why put me in a position where I have to think of a zechus?

Her annoyance grew.

As these thoughts were racing through her mind, another one intruded and almost knocked her over with its impact: Mrs. Rosen's book! I had planned to buy her a new one, I simply haven't had a chance yet. Why didn't I just phone and say, "The binding ripped and I'm going to get you a new book"? I didn't call because it was so clear to me that I was going to return it, it was like a fact that was happening. It was *so real to me that I neglected to consider that Mrs. Rosen could not know of my intentions. She might be sitting there thinking the same thoughts about me that I had about Dina!*

*T*wo of my friends caused me a substantial financial loss. I was waiting to hear from them, but they never called, so I finally called them. I told them I wanted to meet with them to discuss what had happened. They never came. The loss of the money was annoying enough, but the fact that they ignored me was even more upsetting. I called them again. Even though I practically begged them, time passed, and still they never came.

A few days before Yom Kippur, I bumped into one of these friends. She apologized for never coming over and asked me to please forgive her, but I said, "No, I will not forgive you. I pressed you to come over and you didn't. And we still have unfinished business." She mumbled something, and before I knew it, she was gone.

I couldn't get the scene out of my mind. A week later I was at my friend Laya's house and decided to discuss it with her.*

"You told her you don't forgive her?" Laya asked.

"If a person owes me money," I answered confidently, "I do not have to forgive them, especially since she refused to even come talk to me about it."

"Well," said Laya thoughtfully, "when she saw you, she did ask for your forgiveness. It seems like she was concerned. Why do you think they didn't come?"

I smiled. "Because they're just not nice people." Our eyes met. I could see I hadn't impressed her with my evaluation.

"You know, that's too simplistic — something's missing," Laya said to me. "Let's backtrack. Start at the beginning: How do you know they owe you the money? Did you ever go to a rabbi and ask if they were obligated to pay you?"

"I most certainly did."

"What did he say?"

---

*This is another example of a situation where we can talk out our concerns without using names; to receive support and advice, the name was not necessary.

"He said they weren't obligated to pay me, but that if they were mentchen, if they had any integrity, they would. And not only that," my voice rose a notch, "I want you to know that if I were in their position, I would have run to pay them."

"Listen a minute, Henny," Laya tried another tactic. "Isn't it true that sometimes a person is afraid to come for a discussion because they know the other person is very worked up and emotional and that once the discussion starts, there are going to be a lot of strong words spoken? Maybe they felt that way. Maybe they felt things would get out of control, and the best thing would be to drop it, especially since halachically they didn't owe you any money."

I saw Laya was trying hard to come up with some kind of logical explanation for the whole thing, but nothing she said changed my mind.

Now I'll let Laya tell you the rest of the story:

I could see my friend Henny was still worked up over the incident and very tense. Even though we had so much else to talk about, she didn't want to leave the subject. That gave me a clue. I remembered learning that if a person is very disturbed by a particular behavior and can't let it go, it may be a signal that he did something similar. So I said, tentatively, "Tell me, Henny, is it possible that you once did something similar?'"

All of a sudden I saw her face grow scarlet! She sat there looking at me, her face beet red, and didn't say a word!

I waited. I saw she was troubled. "Did you think of something?" I ventured.

She nodded. Truthfully, I myself was surprised that my suggestion would have triggered such an immediate reaction. I asked her, "Is somebody waiting for you to come to them to make amends?"

She nodded again.

"So why don't you go?" I asked.

"How can I?" she stammered. "He wouldn't listen — he's irrational about the whole thing."

I took a deep breath. "Henny — maybe that's how they feel about you."

"But," she said emphatically, "I would have listened!"

We sat for a while, each of us lost in thought.

"Henny," I broke the silence, "what are you thinking?" She didn't answer right away, obviously still digesting our conversation.

"I was thinking," she said at last, "that I had been planning to write them a nasty letter, but now I think I'll be able to write something a little more civil."

When we find ourselves strongly condemning and invalidating another person, it should be a signal that we *will* be able to find "that place." Our Sages teach us: *kol haposeil b'mumo poseil*, One who invalidates others does so because of his own shortcomings.[3] There is a saying: When you point a finger at someone else, three point back at you.

Does this mean that every time we notice a fault in someone it means we have a similar flaw? Not at all. Recognition alone does not reflect inner turmoil. It's the *condemnation* of a shortcoming in another that reflects that turmoil. Notice that our Sages do not say: Whoever *sees* a blemish is blemished, but rather, whoever *invalidates* and *condemns* others is in fact blemished himself. When someone is constantly condemning, and especially when he can't let go, he is signaling a shortcoming within himself.

When we find ourselves in this position, it should warn us that there's a lesson to be learned. We can then tune in to our inner selves, coming face to face with our weaknesses and the less-than-perfect motivations behind our actions. This introspection can become a precious opportunity for personal growth, a chance to explore areas that lay deep within us and are usually masked.[4]

In order to understand "that place," we may have to search. At other times, "that place" might leap to our mind immediately. The memory envelops us with understanding and enables us to deal with life's challenges in a better way.

*L*ast year, one sunny afternoon, a neighbor asked me to watch her three-year-old son at the sandbox where my children were also playing, while she popped across the street for a few minutes to buy something in the store. Though I was somewhat preoccupied, I kept my eye on the blond boy in the blue T-shirt, glancing at him sporadically to see him playing nicely in the sand.

Imagine my horror when my neighbor returned to the sandbox to hear a friend tell her how she had just rescued my neighbor's little boy from the roadside. All that time I had been watching the wrong boy!

Shakily, I tried to explain to my friend what had happened. "All this time I was watching this little one," pointing to the blond look-alike. "I'm so, so sorry." I was mortified, and aside from profound gratitude that her son was okay, my overriding feeling was one of "please, please hear my story and judge me favorably. It was a mistake, a potentially dangerous one, but please understand; and if you judge me, please bear in mind I would never, never have been careless on purpose." I am blessed with a good neighbor who understood and forgave me (far more quickly than I was able to forgive myself, I might add).

The incident receded in my memory until a different afternoon when I was at the sandbox together with another neighbor, Raizy, and our children. I had volunteered to go to the store to buy a bag of cookies for all to share. Raizy had agreed to watch my two younger children, including the nineteen month old, who was in her buggy. After a few minutes I returned, mission accomplished, with the cookies, only to find Raizy holding my very unhappy baby. I assumed the baby had missed me. In fact, she had scrambled out of the buggy so quickly that Raizy assumed I had taken her with me to the store after all. Baruch Hashem, another mother had retrieved the baby from the road, unscathed.

It's hard to say who was more shaken by all this, Raizy or myself. Mercifully, my reaction came later. At the time, I was able to reassure Raizy that I understood what happened, and, most important, the baby was okay.

Looking back, I know that had I not gone through the painful experience the previous year with my neighbor's *child, I would never have known how to judge my friend fa-vorably in quite the same way. I would have used harsh words just at the very time when she most needed forgive-ness and understanding. I had so needed my friend to understand my mistake, that I learned how to forgive some-one else.*

✎ The magic of "getting there"

That "place" has power in all directions. Sometimes if we are wise and aware, we can dig into our past and use it to grasp the hitherto incomprehensible. And at other times, it's the future that holds the promise of understanding and forgiveness.

When we find certain behavior so incomprehensible that our minds remain locked shut, that's when we need to remember another lesson from the Mishnah: "Don't judge your friend until you reach his place." One day we might find ourselves in "his place" and then suddenly we will understand his behavior.

The people in the following stories "got there" and then they understood:

Yael was holding a sweater sale and decided to advertise in a local newspaper with a large circulation. When the ad appeared, to her horror Yael read: "Sweaters For Sale — Only $18.00."

"Oh, no," she gasped. "I wrote $38, but the paper printed $18! What are all my customers going to think?! They've been buying my sweaters for $38! They're going to read that ad and be very annoyed with me and I have no way to defend myself. I won't even know who they are, so how can I explain to them?

"And what about all the people who read the ad and come to buy sweaters? They're going to say, 'Where are the sweaters for $18?' And I'm going to have to tell them, 'There aren't any. It was a typographical error — they cost $38.' Are they going to swallow that?

"No one ever thinks that newspapers make mistakes like that. I even felt that way myself. I remember going into a store to buy something that was advertised for $5.00 and when I got there they told me it was the 'newspaper's mistake' and the item really cost $15.00. And I remember thinking to myself, 'Sure. Now she says $15.00. That's some tricky way to trap customers, writing five and then telling them fifteen once they get in the store.'

"I'd like to take back what I thought about them."

D asi was enjoying her Shabbos at the Leifers. They were such a warm family, and their lively home offered a welcome change from dorm life. Her year at seminary was just beginning and she could see it was going to be an exciting one. Just that week they had begun in-depth discussions on judging favorably, and as she shared her new-found enthusiasm with the Leifers, they too were fascinated.

After Shabbos, she called her dorm and asked the girl who picked up the phone if she could please speak with Toby. "No problem," was the cheery reply. Minutes passed as Dasi hung on to the phone waiting for Toby — or the girl — or anyone! — to get back on the line. After 10 minutes of waiting, she hung up, furious.

"I can't believe how inconsiderate some people are. She just walked off and left me hanging!"

"But Dasi," the Leifers protested, "you spent the whole Shabbos telling us about the mitzvah of judging favorably and now you're calling her inconsiderate. Why don't you judge her favorably?"

"Listen," Dasi said defensively, "usually you should, but I live in that dorm and I know what goes on. People answer the phone and then drop it and don't come back. In this case, there's no excuse. It's plain inconsiderate."

What could they say? She had made up her mind and that was it.

A few weeks later, Dasi was on her way to the dorm dining room when the hall phone she was passing started to ring. She picked it up and heard the voice on the other end ask: "Could you please go get Adina?" "Sure," answered Dasi agreeably, and went down the hall to call Adina to the phone.

*As she passed a window, she noticed a heavy rain just be-
ginning. The wash! She raced to take in the laundry — a
whole week's worth — and managed to rescue it before it got
soaked. After putting away what she could and hanging the
rest to dry in her room, she finally made it to the dining room.*

*Two days later, it hit her: "Oh, no!! That call . . . I had some-
body on the line and I never got back."*

When Dasi was the victim, her mind was closed. The only reason she could imagine was lack of consideration. She had to be
in that situation herself to realize there could be other reasons.

As for the girl who left Dasi hanging, this is what happened:

*"I was passing by the hall phone when it rang. A girl on the
line asked me to get Toby, and I happened to know that Toby
was with a bunch of girls in one of the classrooms studying.
I went to get her but when I walked into the room, the girls
were listening to a speaker. Then I remembered we were having a guest lecturer. Some of our teachers were there, and I felt
too embarrassed to walk out. I was stuck. I had no choice but
to take a seat and stay."*

*M*azel tov! Elisheva Hirsch became a kallah. She and her
parents, Baila and Yaakov Hirsch, wanted to make the
wedding before all their friends would go to the mountains for
the summer, which left them only six weeks to make all the
arrangements: band, photographer, hall, etc., etc.*

*It wouldn't be easy, so Mrs. Hirsch got right to it. First on her
list was the photographer. The first one she called was too expensive; the second was unavailable. The third sounded
perfect, but when she called the in-laws, it turned out they
didn't want that particular photographer. What could she do?
She got back on the phone, made some calls to friends who
had made weddings recently, asked neighbors, and finally got
the name of a fourth photographer. She breathed a sigh of relief
when she heard him agree. He could make it that day, the price
was right, and best of all, the in-laws agreed, so they closed the
deal. Now at least the photographer was taken care of.*

A few days later, the phone rang and Elisheva, the kallah, answered. A girl named Shifra was on the other end of the line. "I need a favor," she began. You could almost hear the pleading in her voice. "The photographer told me you hired him for your wedding, and I want to tell you that I'm getting married the same night and I really want this photographer. He's a friend of the family, and he's also a very close friend of my chassan. We've taken him for all our simchohs, so could you please do me this favor and let us have him?"

"Look," Elisheva said, "I'm sure you have no idea how hard it was for us to finally get this photographer."

But Shifra wouldn't take "no" for an answer. "I'd do it for you if I would be in your place. If it was your husband's friend and your family took him for all your simchahs — if someone would tell me that story, I'd do it."

What could Elisheva say? "Just a minute. Maybe it's better if you speak to my mother."

After speaking with Shifra on the phone and listening to her request, Elisheva's mother answered tensely, "I'm sure you can't even imagine what went into this. And this is just one of many, many details we have to take care of."

But Shifra persisted.

We finally got one thing arranged and now she wants us to start from scratch!! thought Mrs. Hirsch as she listened. In an effort to bring the irritating conversation to an end, she said, "Listen, if you can find me somebody else we can all agree on, call me back and we'll talk about it."

That night Mrs. Hirsch tossed and turned in bed. If it's so important to her, let her have the photographer. I'm not going to feel good at my wedding taking this photographer if I know I'm causing such distress to somebody else. But another thought kept interrupting: that girl had a lot of nerve asking such a thing. She turned it back and forth in her mind: maybe Shifra shouldn't have asked, yet maybe she should do her the favor anyway. And with these thoughts swimming in her mind, she finally fell asleep.

When she woke up the next morning and reviewed the conversation of the day before, she realized it wasn't only the conversation with Shifra that bothered her. She was even more irritated with the photographer for having given her name out to someone else. It was improper and unethical. Who wants their name given out so that people can call up and bother them? It's certainly not very professional. Mrs. Hirsch's annoyance escalated. He never should have given out our name in the first place!

Later that morning the photographer called. "Mrs. Hirsch, you may get a call from the . . ." and he mentioned the name of Shifra's family. "They called the studio yesterday and asked for your date. Our secretary was out and her replacement who answered the phone told them the date was taken. They asked who took it. The secretary was too inexperienced to realize that she shouldn't give out names. I want you to know I would never do it, because it's not proper business ethics. I would never give out a client's name and I'm really sorry. You might get a call, but be assured that the date is yours."

Never would have thought of that one, would ya, Baila, she thought to herself.

Meanwhile, Mrs. Hirsch and her husband were busy with all the other wedding plans, and right at the top of their list was finalizing a hall. Together with the in-laws, they narrowed it down to two possibilities. One was nicer, but inconveniently located, so they decided on the second. The manager agreed to hold it for them as long as they gave him a definite answer and a deposit within three days. But by the time they called, on the morning of the fourth day, the manager told them it had been rented a few hours earlier. They had no choice but to take the hall which was so much further from where they lived, making it inconvenient for the family and their guests.

Mr. Hirsch decided to try a long shot. "Let's call the hall again," he suggested to his wife. "Maybe they'd agree to call the people who booked that date, and maybe that family will be willing to let us have it. It may be easier than we imagine for them to take a different hall or day. It's even possible they were considering two halls, and if they knew someone else wanted this one, they might be willing to let it go. We'll even offer to pay the difference."

The whole family applauded their father's ingenuity, until they heard their mother's voice. "Hey, wait a minute," she protested. "Didn't this just happen to us? Even if we ask the hall to call them for us, we'll be putting these people on the spot. And we know what that means — what a commotion it would probably cause in their house."

Mrs. Hirsch could well understand the feelings of people who would be asked for that kind of a favor, having so recently "been there" herself. They discussed it and decided not to call.

Looking thoughtful, Mrs. Hirsch remarked, "Look what we were prepared to do because we were feeling desperate!" Then she thought back to her conversation with Shifra. What seemed, at the time, to be "a lot of nerve," could now, with a new light shining on it, be seen more clearly as "desperation."

Postscript: Two days later the phone rang; it was Shifra. Her voice was teary. "Mrs. Hirsch, I called to apologize. I really am so sorry. I don't know what came over me. I don't know how I could have called you and asked you to do such a thing. How could I ever have put you into such a position?"

I have always believed that parents should train children to send thank you notes. That's the way I was brought up and that's the way I bring up my children. It shows a lack of respect for the people who went to the trouble and expense to give a gift not to recognize their efforts and send a thank you. And it shows a lack of gratitude. I could never understand why people neglected this courtesy.

Then we made a bar mitzvah.

And of course, we reminded our son that he should make a list and write down every single gift as soon as he received it, so that everybody would be remembered.

It all went well, except for the ones —

- *which somehow didn't get written down.(It happens!)*
- *which were received weeks later at a hectic moment and didn't get on the list.*
- *which were put aside for the correct address (and misplaced).*

- *which were never mailed (stuck in the drawer, left in a jacket pocket, etc.)*
- *torn by a younger child.*

I still feel strongly about this matter and continue to stress to the children that thank you notes must be sent. But now, if I don't receive one, I have a new understanding of how it could have happened, because I went through it myself.

I never thought I would have to say this, but I sure hope those people who never received ours will judge us favorably.

When we are told not to judge our friend until we reach *his place*, it can also mean *his position*. As children, we cannot fully appreciate the difficulties parents face until we ourselves become parents. Until we become grandparents and great-grandparents, we cannot expect ourselves to be able to understand their situation. Only if and when we reach the other person's *position* can we say we have reached his place and judge him. And when we do get there, oh, how different we may find the view from our new vantage point!

The tenant has a different view of things when he becomes a landlord. It's unbelievable how, all of a sudden, the landlord's position becomes so much more acceptable. When a doctor becomes a patient, a whole new world of understanding opens to him. A daughter-in-law has so much more insight into her mother-in-law's behavior when one day her own son gets married.

When I was still an unmarried student I used to board with families. It was only when I myself got married and took in boarders that I realized how many things I had done that must have bothered the people I stayed with. I could never have imagined I was doing something that would disturb anybody. After all these years, I wrote a note of apology to my ex-landlady.

The *Sfas Emes* gives us yet another interpretation of the Mishnah: Although we might someday find ourselves in a situation similar to that of another person, we can never be in *exactly* the same place.[5]

For example, a person living in a different era faces different tests. If we are not at the same point in history, we cannot understand what people were up against then, and we certainly cannot judge them. How can we know how we would have acted had we been there? This includes making retroactive judgments, as this well-known incident from the Gemara[6] illustrates:

> *R av Ashi was going to teach his students about the various kings who worshipped idols. He referred to the kings as "our friends," equating himself to them. That night, Menasheh appeared to Rav Ashi in a dream and asked him a question he could not answer. Rav Ashi was amazed, and exclaimed, "You were such a great Torah scholar! How could you have been trapped by such nonsense?" To which Menasheh replied: "Had you been there, you would have picked up the hem of your garment and run after me."*

But even if we are contemporaries, even if he is our "friend," and we feel we know enough about him to judge him, we still must exercise caution. That's why the Mishnah tells us, "Don't judge your *friend* until you come to his place." For, as the *Sfas Emes* says: You will never reach your friend's place — even if he's a close friend. Never — exactly.

Can we ever say we have exactly the same background as someone else? All that goes into making him who he is, the basis for his every action and word, is sometimes a complete blank for us. You know how *you* would understand the situation, and how you'd react. But it's not the way he understands the situation . . . and the way he would react.

You can try to put yourself in someone else's shoes. As hard as that might be, it is easier than putting him in his own shoes. Yet that is the only way to achieve *true* understanding.

For most of us, reaching *his place* is difficult, unless we have the assistance of past remembrances, or the clarity afforded by arriving at that place. Even then "the place" we arrive at can never be *exactly* the same.

However, there are some lofty souls who without ever having *been there* are nonetheless able to project their imagination to feel somebody else's plight. They are able to argue his argument, plead his cause, as if they were in *his place*.

*A*n aide of the Skulener Rebbe, R' Eliezer Zusia Portugal, *once related: Among the many people whom the rebbe had rescued from Europe was a woman who had informed the Rumanian government of his religious activities, which led to his arrest and imprisonment. Why go to such effort and expense to save a person of her ilk?*

"You have no idea how much she suffered beforehand, and how tempting the authorities make it to inform," the Rebbe said with tears in his eyes.[7]

11
Judging the Whole Person

הֱוֵי דָן אֶת כָּל הָאָדָם לְכַף זְכוּת.
"Judge everyone favorably" (Pirkei Avos 1:6).

"Our Kind of Folks"

We have a tendency to excuse those in our own group, people who have our own political leanings, from our alma mater, shul, or country. These people get the "good eye." We are willing to excuse their actions, even when they are involved in less than noble pursuits, while those in the "other groups" can never quite do the right thing. Even when those "others" are involved in worthwhile activities, we sometimes see it in the wrong light.

In truth, in every country, in every city, in every group there are worthy people, and those less worthy. If we want to find fault, we can do so anywhere. Because this tendency is so prevalent, it is important for us to listen to the advice given in *Pirkei Avos:* Judge **everyone** favorably.[1] This is the most commonly found translation of this Mishnah.

There is, however, another interpretation which can help enhance our relationship with others. If the intention of our Sages was only to teach us the lesson of judging *everyone* favorably, it should say: כָּל אָדָם, *every person.* Since, in fact, the Mishnah states, כָּל הָאָדָם, **all of the** person, we are able to derive an extra lesson: When judging, consider all of the person, the **whole** person.[2]

Before we wave a flag of indignation, we are asked to take into consideration all parts of that person. The "whole" of a person can include factors which, although unknown, are vital contributors to the whole. Or there may be a revealed part of the whole, which, while known to us, is ignored or not appreciated.

Eclipses

*M*rs. Kay bought a pink shower curtain. When she got home, she realized she had forgotten to ask for the rings that attach the curtain to the pole. She called the store and asked if they could mail them out and charge her.

The package arrived a few days later. When she opened it and saw the box of rings, her smile turned to a frown. The cover was transparent plastic, so she could see without even opening it that a mistake had been made. The rings were peach, not pink. Oh no, she thought in frustration, now I'll have to exchange it. I thought it would be so simple — pink is pink. That salesman must be colorblind!

As she moved to put the package on the table, it slipped from her hands. The cover fell off, and she watched the pink rings fall to the floor.

Pink? How did they become pink? Or were they pink to begin with?

*They sure were. The plastic cover of the package was tinted.
Mrs. Kay was certain she knew what was inside. It seemed
clear. But when the cover fell off, she was in for a surprise.*

We are confident that our evaluations of others are accurate.
We think we know what's going on, not realizing that our understanding is based on a superficial glance. If we could look
into the inner world of another human being, we would also be
in for a surprise.

But we can't. The cover is always going to be on. And therefore much information that would enlighten us remains inside,
hidden from view. At least part of the whole will always be
eclipsed.

*When we moved into our new home, several of my close
friends came over for a housewarming. These friends
didn't really know each other, but I knew everybody. I knew
their life stories — the ups and downs, private hurts and dis-
appointments, major tragedies, unfulfilled hopes and dreams,
sore spots. And as I listened to the conversation, I saw how
each person could have been misread because of what the
others didn't know. And even I, who felt I knew each one so
well — who knows what I'm missing?*

*Whenever I meet Mrs. B., the conversation turns to "that
subject." Tonight, I excused myself in the middle of her
sentence. She called after me, but I didn't turn back.*

*She had no way of knowing the anguish this subject
evokes. It's hard for people to understand, or for me to explain,
my torment and loneliness. Maybe she meant well, but for
me, she was stepping on twenty-five years of pain.*

A Glimpse of a Thread

Every individual is like a tapestry made up of thousands of
threads. It takes each of these numerous threads to produce a
final picture — that whole person.

The comparison is far too simple, however, when we consider the complexity of a human being, the myriad "threads" that go into producing and influencing a person and are the motivating forces behind his behavior. We can't turn someone inside out to see what those threads look like or to where they connect. Yet, to pass a fair judgment, to make a really fair evaluation, we would have to take into account all these threads.

Here's how one person discovered a "thread":

Channie's roommate Ita used to save rubber bands on the door handle. It bothered Channie because she had difficulty opening the door with all those rubber bands around the handle.

But Ita wouldn't remove them.

One day, Channie happened to be visiting Ita's house and she noticed that there were rubber bands on her mother's door handles too. She was curious, so she asked Ita's mother, "Why do you save rubber bands on the door handles?"

*"Because I saw it in **my** house," she answered with a smile. "And we did it because my grandmother did it too."*

A neighbor who was visiting at the time remarked, "In my house, we were taught to make rubber band balls. My mother remembers the time when people valued even little things. She wanted to pass down this value to her children and grandchildren too.

"My friend told me that her father never travels without a piece of string," she added. "Why? Because almost a hundred years ago his grandfather always carried a piece of string. In those days, people didn't have paper clips, scotch tape, staples, etc., but if you were a mentch," she said, "you carried string."

Channie still prefers knobs without rubber bands. But since that visit, Channie sees rubber bands — and Ita — from a new perspective.

When our Sages tell us to *judge the whole person favorably,* it is a reminder that people are not creations of the moment. Think how much "past" went into creating the present!

Occasionally, like Channie, we *do* catch a glimpse of even one thread, and that alone weaves for us a different picture.

Malki Silver was not doing well in school, especially in reading, which affected all her studies. The school made many attempts to help the child and the family. They gave the Silvers names of professionals who could evaluate Malki, which would be the first step. At first, the family simply refused to become involved in any discussions. Finally, they agreed to go for an evaluation, but afterwards canceled appointment after appointment with all kinds of weak excuses.

Why are the Silvers so stubborn? was the question on everybody's mind. Why are they so lax? Why wouldn't they want their daughter's problem assessed?

The administration's exasperation evaporated when by chance they discovered that Malki has a seriously brain-damaged sister. The fear of facing other problems was paralyzing the family from doing what they themselves knew was right.

I presented my new daughter-in-law with a watch, along with a cute note saying that she should always use her time well.

Instead of a big kiss and the profuse thank you I was expecting, her eyes filled with — was it hurt or anger? I couldn't believe it. I chose that gift so carefully, and spent much more than I had intended. Even if it was not her taste, it was absolutely rude to act that way.

It was many years later, when she was sure of my love and approval, that she felt confident enough to tell me what was behind that look: She had always been known as a big time-waster. She was sure I had found out and was giving her a not-so-gentle hint.

We are at times given an insight into a tiny part of that whole. Then, instead of being so sure in our condemnation and smug in our disapproval, we are humbled into being more tolerant, patient, and forgiving.

*A*t four years old I already felt independent and responsible beyond my years. I remember how important it was
for my mother that I be strong and self-sufficient. But I couldn't
understand why she so obsessively emphasized strength and
independence.

*My parents almost never discussed their war experiences. I
was therefore unprepared when one day my mother unexpectedly turned to me with an anguished face and said, "Mein
kind, I can't forget being forced out into the street of the ghet-
to. I watched hysterical, desperate mothers, women who were
forced to abandon their screaming children." She was quiet for
a moment and then continued, "Those young girls who were
tied to their mother's apron strings dropped like flies."*

*This was the sum total of my mother's unexpressed plea to
hear what she could not say.*

*I was sixteen years old when this incident happened. As a
teenager, I felt confused and unprepared for these messages. It
is only now, years later, as an adult, when I reflect back on
that moment, that I realize the significance of those words. To
my mother, strength and independence meant survival. At
that moment, my mother had given me a glimpse — a key to
understanding her and my childhood.*

Pirkei Avos is a tractate of ethical teachings, containing de-
tailed guidelines on how to relate to others. It is significant that
it begins with the admonition: Be deliberate in judgment (*Pirkei
Avos* 1:1). Be slow and careful, not hasty or impulsive, in evaluating others. It is a warning not to be tricked into misjudgment
based on minimal information. When our judgmental mind demands a quick verdict, let us remember: All the evidence hasn't
been submitted.

"Chapter Three"

In a certain way, every person we encounter is like a book.
When we meet someone, we are entering in the middle of his
life; we are opening up to Chapter Three of a fascinating,

complicated story. Is it possible to understand what's going on in Chapter Three without reading Chapters One and Two?

Many situations in life appear clearly negative. They may appear that way because we are missing the preceding chapters. How can we possibly understand what's going on? How can we draw a clear, true and fair picture if we've just opened to Chapter Three?

*O*ne of my close friends, Alissa, and I agreed that we'd meet later in the day at a luncheon. She asked me to save her a place and we looked forward to spending the time together.

I saved her a place at a table with mutual friends, and made sure to save her a first course when I saw she was late. Everyone at the table knew I was holding the place for her. Suddenly one of the women spotted Alissa entering the hall: "There she is!" We all watched her as she walked in. I smiled a warm welcoming smile and mouthed a "Hello." Alissa smiled in my direction, nodded her head, and sat down at a table near the door!

The hurt and embarrassment rushed in uninvited, and ran through the rooms of my mind unchecked, unlocking the doors of rejection and betrayal.

Perhaps she had forgotten our plans. Perhaps she had thought that the table was full, and didn't want to make a fuss. Perhaps there was someone at the other table whom she couldn't pass by. Perhaps I had misunderstood. Don't make a commotion about this — people have a right to sit wherever they want, I tried to convince myself.

After that evening, our friendship continued as usual, but the incident still bothered me.

Several weeks later, when Alissa and I were both standing outside chatting, a friend of ours came out of the building. Alissa whispered to me, "Who's that?" It was one of our closest mutual friends. Why didn't she recognize her? Turning to Alissa in surprise, I said, "That's Rochelle — can't you see her?" I saw from her pained look that I had touched a sore spot. I stood there awkwardly, watching the tears form in her eyes. "I didn't want to tell anyone," Alissa began with a catch in her throat. "It's caused so many misunderstandings."

Then she confided that her eyesight had deteriorated so badly over the past month that her doctor was scheduling an emergency operation within the coming week. "But please don't tell anyone," she pleaded. "I don't want people to know."

As I spotted Elana walking towards me I made up my mind to ask her where she had bought the outfit she was wearing. She was pleased with the compliment and gladly shared the name of a private party who sells exclusively by appointment in her home.

It wasn't until a couple of weeks later that I found the time to look up the name she had given me. When I saw there were too many "Kaplans" listed for me to know which was the right one, I decided to call Elana for more exact information.

Elana answered the phone, and in reply to my question said curtly that the lady's first name was Miriam and I could look it up again. I thanked her and I asked her if she could give me one more clue, the street name. I was a bit taken aback when she answered with obvious impatience, "Anchor Drive," and hung up.

"Talk about being abrupt!" I was tempted to say something but I decided to drop it.

And am I glad I did. At the end of the week I received a postcard from the shul: "With profound sorrow," it began, and announced the passing of Elana's husband.

At the shiva, while Elana and I spoke, I listened remorsefully as Elana chokingly tried to explain her behavior that day on the phone. "You couldn't have known," she said, "but while other friends were calling about my husband's state of health, you were calling up to ask about clothing!"

My husband and I went to a neighbor's wedding. We made an effort to arrive early so that we could get good seats. I can't enjoy a wedding unless I can see what's going on. I usually pick the aisle seat, about four rows back, so as not to take the seats of family and relatives.

When I got there, the hall was still quite empty. I picked my seat and after a few minutes people started coming. Ten minutes later, when the seats were filling up, a woman came to where I was sitting and asked if I could move down. I thought that was unfair of her since I had come early just to get that seat. But I wasn't going to tell her that, so I just pointed out that the seats next to me were filled.

"Could everybody move down?" she asked, pointing out that there was an empty seat about six chairs down.

Here I had made this big effort to come early to get the seat of my choice and this lady who comes late just says, "Move over"!

I didn't want to make a scene, so I passed the message to the people in the row. No one else seemed to mind, so we all moved over one, and she sat in the aisle seat.

As she sat down, she turned to me and said quietly, "I have to keep an eye on my son," and she pointed to the boy right across the aisle from her. I looked up. She was referring to a boy of about 15 years of age. Who's she trying to kid? I thought to myself. That boy looks old enough to take care of himself just fine. It was one thing to ask for my seat, but to make up such a flimsy excuse — that she needed to keep an eye on her son, who was no baby — took double chutzpah.

She struck up a conversation and asked where I was from, which side of the family I was on, etc. She said she had come as a guest of the bride, who was her son's teacher. Every so often she would bend over towards her son and explain to him what was going on.

And then it hit me. I remembered that this past year the bride had been a teacher for mentally handicapped children. As I watched more carefully, I could see that this boy was a special child. My indignation and her "chutzpah" — both evaporated.

We are told, *judge the whole person favorably,* which can be understood as saying, without the whole picture, we can't help but misjudge. We should therefore judge favorably, based on this understanding: If we *could* see the whole, that disturbing behavior would surely look more favorable.

It's a Package Deal

"Judge the whole person" is advice that can be used productively in many directions. It is extremely helpful in coming to terms with peoples' shortcomings. The "failings" are easier to accept when we are willing to see them as part of a broader picture.

Each person has a core of qualities from which stem both strengths and weaknesses. The very same quality at times appears to be a virtue and at times a liability. When the benefit we derive from the strength outweighs the distress we experience from the weakness, it is an incentive to remember: It's a Package Deal.

☐ Mrs. K.'s husband is charming and witty. That's one of the things she has always enjoyed in his personality and which others enjoy and appreciate. The humor helps in his teaching and wherever he goes he brightens people's lives.
But sometimes she's not in the mood for his jokes.

☐ Mr. L.'s wife is very relaxed, slow-paced, and easy-going. As a consequence, meals in their house are sometimes on a hit-or-miss basis. Mr. L. enjoys his wife's tranquil nature, and he realizes that it is the decisive factor in creating the relaxed atmosphere in their home which is so important to him.

The strengths and accompanying weaknesses are two sides of the same person. Both Mrs. K. and Mr. L. have more pleasure from the positive side of these respective traits than loss from their negative expression. So it's a Package Deal — accepting both expressions of a trait, both when it suits us, and when it doesn't suit us *exactly.*

☐ "My downstairs neighbor is warm and friendly. She's in and out of my apartment throughout the day, borrowing, returning, sharing some news, asking for advice. I'm far away from family and old friends, so I'm thrilled with her outgoingness. There are times, however, when I need my privacy. But I feel that that's the price I pay for this friendship.

"I appreciate the positive aspect of this friendship most of the time and I can't expect her to be a different person the other 10%."

This approach can benefit other relationships as well: Roommates, hired help, children, co-workers, committee members. Their strengths and related weaknesses are part of a Package Deal. If we can focus on the fact that on the whole we are really getting a good deal with this relationship, then we have the recipe for successful living.

When we're annoyed with other people, with their habits or the way they are conducting their lives, when we feel that the path we have chosen is superior — or that we are! — it may be helpful to consider: **His weakness may have a strength in it, while my strength may contain a weakness.**

Accepting a Package Deal is a formula not only for peace but for personal growth as well. Rather than concentrating on the weak link in the other person's strong points, it is much more productive to concentrate on the bright side of their weak areas. Concentrating on other people's failings distracts us from reflecting on our own. The first is usually counterproductive, while the second is our obligation. We should be sensitive to our own failings no matter how minor, yet be willing to excuse or make allowances for even the most obvious faults of others.[3] Hashem created a phenomenon in His creation which conveys this message to us: Everyone has two eyes, one stronger, one weaker. The stronger one is for introspection into our own imperfections; the weaker for viewing others.

We must make an effort not to confuse these functions.

The Last Act

There are times when, logic aside, it's the last act that seems to define the person. Maybe you have a friend, or more accurately, had a friend, a good friend with whom you shared years of happy experiences. All friendships have ups and downs, and this was no different. But all in all it was a good friendship. And then came a disappointment — a big disappointment. And the friendship soured. (How much *lashon hara*, resentment, anger . . .) But what happened to all the good? Where's all that was positive that passed between you? Everything got swept under the rug — forgotten . . . as if it never happened.

Where's our sense of balance? Where's the whole? In all fairness, is this fair? It's unfair not to take the whole person, the whole picture into account.

Let's not waste the whole because of one part.

*I*t had been a beautiful wedding, Ariella reminisced. And it *would have been perfect, if only . . .*

Ariella Pollack and Shula Heller had both married doctors. The distance from California to New York didn't lend itself to shared shopping sprees or dropping over for a cup of coffee, but the two sisters felt as close as ever. They were grateful that their husbands understood and were willing to foot the bill for telephone calls that were frequent and lengthy.

The years passed and both Dr. Pollack and Dr. Heller established successful practices. When the Pollacks' son, David, made the decision to follow in his father's footsteps, it was the East Coast that caught his eye. When he was accepted to a prestigious New York medical school not far from his aunt and uncle, his mother, Ariella, was thrilled.

Her sister and brother-in-law did not disappoint her. David was made to feel like one of the household. He knew he could come over whenever he wanted a good home-cooked meal, a quiet place to relax, or encouragement and advice from his uncle. He came often, and brought friends too.

After four years, David felt almost as much a Heller as a Pollack. Aunt Shula nursed him through a bad bout of flu, entertained his friends, sewed on buttons . . . can four years of care and devotion be summarized in a few sentences? David knew his aunt and uncle were always there for him.

More years passed, and David was starting out as a sur-
geon. He was affiliated with a hospital, and on the side,
opened a private surgical practice. He was counting on his
uncle, Dr. Heller, to help by referring patients.

However, time passed and he didn't get a single referral
from his uncle. Although David threw out hints on several oc-
casions, they were never picked up.

On his calls home, David mentioned to his mother his dis-
appointment.* His mother was puzzled. What was going on?
Why wasn't her brother-in-law helping out? The hints became
stronger, and so did the hemming and hawing. The calls con-
tinued between California and New York. Every time David
complained, his mother's resentment increased. Ariella decid-
ed to speak to her sister openly. She was sure that she could
straighten it out. Shula, however, claimed that her husband
wouldn't let her get involved in medical issues.

After that conversation, things were just not the same. Soon
both husbands saw a big reduction in the telephone bill, until
the sisters hardly spoke to each other. When the Hellers made
a wedding and sent the Pollacks an invitation, the RSVP was
returned with an apology that they couldn't get away.

And now David himself was getting married. The Hellers
found out about the wedding from a family member. They
hadn't been invited.

We should not let years of "good" get swallowed up by one
disappointment, no matter how wrong the person may have
been. How much more so in cases like this, where people
may have valid excuses and are in actuality doing nothing
wrong.

The topic of "favors withheld" and the resulting resentment is
vast. Briefly, the feeling that people *must* come through for us
because
we need it . . .
and they can do it . . .

---

* This is called *rechilus*: *Rechilus,* a Torah transgression, is a statement that can
potentially cause ill will between the person hearing it and the person in whose
name it is being said.

and we feel they owe it to us . . .

is the basis for countless family feuds, broken friendships, and dissension and discord in every relationship.

One of the reasons that the Torah does not allow us to hold on to grudges for favors not done us[4] is because there is often a very sound reason why people cannot come through for us the way *we* would like. We are wrong in not considering the other fellow's point of view. The same energy we put into grudge-bearing can be channeled into understanding the other side of the story. Let's not let the last act draw the curtain on our friendships.

Liking More People More

*M*indy was a housewife living in Queens. One day, she got a call from her Aunt Ella, whom she rarely saw, saying that she had come in from New Jersey for the day. Aunt Ella was staying with her sister nearby, and wanted to visit Mindy and the children. "We'd love to see you," Mindy answered warmly. "When would you like to come?"

"I'm not exactly sure, because I'm waiting for a phone call. But as soon as I get this call, I'll come right over. I hope to be there in about an hour."

"That's good for me too. I'm just running out to do an errand. I'll see you soon," Mindy said cheerfully before she hung up.

Aunt Ella got her phone call and as soon as she finished, she called a taxi and arrived at Mindy's home as she had anticipated, about an hour after their talk. The maid opened the door and said that Mindy wasn't home. She had gone out with the children and she'd be back soon.

"Well, I'm Mindy's aunt from New Jersey. We spoke on the phone and she's expecting me, so I'll just wait here for her to come back, if you don't mind." She made herself comfortable and waited . . . and waited. Fifteen minutes, twenty, a half hour went by. Even the maid started getting nervous. After waiting almost an hour, Aunt Ella left.

Aunt Ella walked into her sister's house with an annoyed

look on her face. After a while, though, her annoyance gave way to worry. Mindy knew I was coming, she thought, so why wasn't she there? I hope nothing happened.

She tried calling, but Mindy still hadn't returned. Her concern increased by the minute. Why isn't she home?

Ten minutes later she called again . . . and Mindy still was not home. Who knows what could have happened to her and the children!

Another quarter of an hour went by, and Aunt Ella called back again. This time, Mindy herself answered the phone.

How do you like that! She should have called me the minute she set foot in the door! thought Aunt Ella with irritation. The maid must have told her I had come and waited and that I've called so many times and was very concerned — why didn't she call me?

Despite her indignation, she felt relieved hearing her niece's voice. Now she was waiting curiously to hear what Mindy would have to say for herself.

Mindy's aunt anticipated some kind of an explanation — maybe some funny misunderstanding, or perhaps an unexpected emergency. But all Mindy said was, "I'm sorry, Aunt Ella, I'm really sorry we missed you. I had planned to come back right away, but I met a friend. We started talking, and I lost track of time."

That was all she said.

Mindy's aunt hung up the phone. What an irresponsible girl, she thought, shaking her head, her mind dwelling on several other times when Mindy had proven to be unreliable. But then she reconsidered. What's the matter with me? Aunt Ella thought to herself. I'm the one who made the mistake. Mindy has disappointed me on so many similar occasions in the past. I should have known to call again before I left to make sure she had come home.

In hindsight, Aunt Ella realized that Mindy's behavior could have been anticipated, even predicted. Mindy had proven time and again that she couldn't be depended upon when it came to deadlines and appointments.

How does one judge favorably in the case of repetitive negative behavior? When a person has proven himself consistently unreliable in a particular area, we are not required to excuse him by thinking that maybe this time there was a change in his regular pattern, or that maybe this time there was a special reason. Keeping appointments, arriving on time, meeting deadlines is a virtue; the opposite, a failing. We are not supposed to give a favorable verdict to improper behavior. In such a case, the favorable judgment is not for the action, but for the person.

The question here is: How do we deal with a person who has a trait that causes us distress or even a loss? *Practically*, we should plan accordingly so that neither we nor others become a victim of unnecessary loss or suffering. But what about our *attitude*? When we feel that a person has a disturbing shortcoming, how can we come to terms with his weakness?

Some people caught in such a situation would be so disturbed by this aspect of Mindy's character that they would invalidate her altogether, letting her drown in a sea of unworthiness. Here is where "consider the whole person" comes to the rescue. So as not to allow one shortcoming to completely color our attitude, it is helpful — and also more just — to judge a person in his entirety, seeing the weakness as one aspect of an entire personality.[5] A person with whom we are dissatisfied usually has many virtues, but we may overlook them because we are so busy concentrating on the disturbing qualities. We don't see that they balance the scale, let alone tip it in his favor.

Mindy may be admired by friends and family for her care in choosing her words, her willingness to help out in communal projects, and her cheerfulness even under stress. She may be a kind-hearted neighbor and a devoted wife and mother. What a pity it would be to miss Mindy's bright side, what a shame to overlook it, to be blinded to her virtues because of her irresponsibility and lack of consideration, as disturbing as they may be.

Why should we be willing to accept weaknesses in others? Because we are all less than perfect. And yet we want other people to accept us and appreciate us for our good qualities. We hope they will overlook our deficiencies as much as possible and/or learn to deal with them and focus on our strengths.

If we feel a person is lacking in a certain area, even something we might describe as essential to proper living, we can "raise them up" in our eyes. We can develop a more positive attitude, and thereby improve our relationships. We can like more people — and like them more — if we are willing to judge them as a whole.

Considering only one part of the whole brings about dissension and disdain. Taking into account the whole person gives us the understanding and wisdom not only to coexist with others, but to acknowledge their struggles with compassion, and to recognize and appreciate their strengths and their worthiness.

In previous chapters, we learned that loving a person leads us to judge him favorably even in the worst of situations. In this chapter, we learned that the opposite is also true: Judging others favorably contributes to the growth of *ahavah*. Considering the "whole person" gives us the impetus to cultivate the care and concern, the love and the unity which is the cornerstone on which the structure of our Torah is built.

12
Misunderstood Messages

I f daily life is full of accusations and condemnations, it's because it's saturated with misunderstandings and misinterpre-
tations, an impressive number of which occur in our daily
conversations. We are all victims of the complexities of
communication — the gap between what is being said and what
is being heard. How many times have we felt hurt, indignant, or
up in arms, all because of a miscommunication of the type illustrated in the following stories. In each case, giving the benefit
of the doubt undoubtedly would have been a great benefit!

Messages received are
not always messages sent

We might be left with a negative impression of a person because we felt he said something which in fact he never said.

*S*aul Friedman headed a large chain of stores. His son, Mordy, eventually joined him in the business. Both were highly successful, each in his own way. Each had his distinct approach to both customers and employees. The executives and secretaries in the office were well aware of their divergent styles.

One afternoon as Mordy walked into the office he heard one of the secretaries say to another, "Mordy's disgusted with Mr. Friedman." The two secretaries didn't seem to notice that Mordy had come in. He sat down in his chair, irritated. *Is she trying to stir up a rift between me and my father? True, my father and I have our differences, but what she said is an outright lie.*

Mordy felt he could not let this incident go unmentioned. It could undermine the good will in the office. He waited for the right moment and called her in.

"I want you to know I overheard your conversation as I walked in this afternoon. Although we've been pleased with your work, remarks like the one you made will ruin morale around here."

The secretary stood there dumbfounded. *What in the world is he talking about?*

Mordy saw from the look on her face that he had to be more specific. "Why would you tell the office staff I'm disgusted with my father?"

"I never said that."

"I heard it clearly."

"I don't know what you're talking about. The only time I mentioned you and your father was when we were talking about the new insurance policy you are considering for the company. Pearl wanted to know if your father had approved it, and I told her that you discussed it with Mr. Friedman."

*H*indy's sister-in-law had just had a baby girl. It was a big simchah for the whole family, since this was the first girl born in several years. Hindy had heard that they were naming the baby on Shabbos and was curious as to what the name would be.

Motzaei Shabbos was hectic, so Hindy said to her little daughter Zehavi, "Call Tante Liba and tell her I'm busy and I can't speak to her now. I'll call her later. But I am curious about the name."

The call was made. A short time later Hindy's phone rang.

*"Hindy, this is Liba." You could hear the anger in her voice. She didn't even give Hindy a chance to say hello. "I want you to know I'm very upset, and I really think you have some nerve. Don't we have the right to choose the name we want? Are you telling me that I have to consult with you first before I choose a name for **my** baby?"*

"Liba," Hindy interrupted, finally able to get a word in, "what in the world are you talking about?"

"What am I talking about? Didn't Zehavi just call to tell me that you're furious about the name?"

I was speaking with my niece Yocheved, who had just begun attending a new school. What do you talk to a five-year-old about but what she's learning in school? I got quite a shock when she answered, "We're learning the dybbuk."

"What? You're learning the dybbuk?"

"Uh huh," my niece answered with a big smile.

"Why?" I asked my pre-1A niece in disbelief.

"'Cause that's what we're up to and that's what the teacher says we have to learn."

You see that? I thought. Each school is trying to outdo the other, just to impress the parents with how progressive they are. But this is just too much.

I went into the kitchen to let my brother know what I thought of his choice of educational institutions. He seemed skeptical and decided to ask his daughter himself.

"Tell me, Yocheved, you're really learning about a dybbuk? Is that what they're teaching you in school?"

"Oh, yes," she answered confidently. "We finished the A book, the B book, and the C book. Now we're learning the D book."

 What you heard is not necessarily what was said.

Messages sent are not always messages meant

Even when we hear the word correctly, we can misinterpret the meaning. He may have said it . . . but he didn't mean what I heard.

✍ I heard the word, but thought it meant something else

*M*rs. Fogel lent her electric nut grinder to her neighbor, Mrs. Brown. Since it was a very delicate machine she warned Mrs. Brown not to wash the machine with water, but only to wipe it off with a damp cloth.

When Mrs. Brown finished using the machine, she was careful to follow her neighbor's instructions. However, there was one detachable part on the top which was particularly dirty, and which needed not a wipe, but a wash. It was made of plastic, so Mrs. Brown was positive that it would be okay to remove it and wash it. But since she had been warned so strongly, she decided to ask first.

"Mirel, please ask Mrs. Fogel if you can wash this," she said as she handed the piece to her six-year-old daughter.

Mirel knocked on their neighbor's door, and when Mrs. Fogel answered, she held out the grinder piece and said, "My mother wants to know if you can wash this."

Incredulously, Mrs. Fogel took the piece and washed it. As she handed it back to Mirel and closed the door, she thought, *What a peculiar thing for a person to do!*

I was chatting with one of my friends on the phone. "You know," she confided, "I can't decide what to do about my daughter. She's eight years old and doesn't read."

I was shocked, to say the least. Eight years old is late to discover a learning problem. This should have been worked on years ago. Where were they until now?

"How does she keep up with her schoolwork?" I asked.

"Oh, she's a smart girl and does well."

That's surprising, I thought.

"You know," I began apprehensively, "if her main problem is reading, I have a cousin who loves to tutor children and her prices are very reasonable. She does remedial reading and maybe she could help. Would you want to call her?"

There was silence on the other end, followed by peals of laughter. With amusement in her voice, my friend explained, "When I said she doesn't read, I meant, except for what she has to do for school, she never opens a book."

*D*anny Klein was learning at a yeshivah out of town and was going through a difficult adjustment period. One day as Danny was walking back to his room, Rabbi Goldman caught up with him. Putting his arm around Danny's shoulder, he struck up a friendly conversation. One thing led to the next, and Danny felt he had found a listening ear. Over the next few weeks, the advice Danny got from Rabbi Goldman was just what he needed.

As time passed, Danny became more confident and made more friends. He felt he had found his place.

One day, he got a message from the secretary in the office which said: "Call Rabbi Goldman." And underneath was written: "Don't give up."

Danny was very hurt. Does he think my situation is so bad I would give up? Is that the way he looks at me?

He tried to call Rabbi Goldman, but the line was constantly busy. After many attempts, he finally got through. It was hard to cover over his hurt feelings, but he did the best he could. "Rabbi Goldman, this is Danny. I want to thank you for all your time and I want you to know that things are really much better for me now."

Rabbi Goldman answered, "I'm glad to hear that, Danny. And I want to thank you for persevering in getting through to me. I know it's discouraging for people that my phone is always busy. I wanted to ask you about . . ."

*Y*esterday afternoon, Miri, one of my daughter's best friends, came over to play. I had just arranged cake platters for a family gathering that evening. The children had been playing for about half an hour, when I saw Miri walk into the kitchen, go over to the table, and take a piece of cake from the middle of the platter. The first thought that went through my mind was, Didn't her mother ever teach her that when you go to someone's home you don't walk over to the table and grab? You wait until you're offered, or at least ask first.

If her mother is not going to tell her how to behave, I decided, someone else should.

"Miri," I said gently, "it would be nicer to ask permission before you take a piece of cake."

Miri looked up earnestly. "My mommy said I'm not allowed to ask for anything."

I know my friend Elisheva is a night owl. Unexpectedly, we had to be in her neighborhood, so I didn't hesitate to drop in, even though it was 10:30 at night. Her daughter Tami answered the door and told us that her mother had had a long day and had decided to turn in early. She insisted that I come in and taste some homemade pie and catch up on the family news. We sat and talked for a while. I called home to check on the children, and then left.

A week later, I was shopping in a department store, riding the down escalator when I saw Elisheva coming up on the opposite side. She saw me too, and waved to me from the bottom. As the stairs brought us within earshot, I called to her, "Elisheva, you know I came by Tuesday night?"

She called back, "I heard."

Maybe she didn't notice my double-take as the stairs took her away, so I never got to ask her the next obvious question: "If you heard I was there, why didn't you come out to say hello? How often do we have a chance to get together?" The stairs carried me down with no desire to seek out a friendship that wasn't mutual.

Did you get it right away? It's not so hard, when you know it's a story in a book on judging favorably. It's easier to catch nuances when we're looking from the outside in, particularly when it's not a statement about *our* friendship. It was painful for Elisheva's friend to imagine Elisheva listening to her voice yet making no effort to come out. (Whether this is a reasonable expectation or not!)

Her hurt was masking a more obvious understanding of "I heard," which might have been followed by, "my daughter told me" if the escalator had given her more time.

✓ We heard the words, yet missed the meaning.

ᕮ *The same word can mean different things to different people*

When we are talking to a person who is speaking in a language which is not his native tongue and over which he does not have full command, there is much room for miscommunication.

☐ However, even when two people speak the same language, there can be misunderstandings which lead to false conclusions and ill will.

We were busy at our computers when one of the secretaries walked in with a big smile on her face. She happily announced her brother's engagement. "The best thing is," she said enthusiastically, "that she lives right around the block from our family in London."

"You know the girl well?"

"I sure do. She's go-o-orgeous."

We were waiting for her to go on, but she didn't say anything else. "Tell us more," we prompted.

"What else can I say? She's just go-o-rgeous!"

I turned back to the screen and thought to myself, How superficial. Is that all she has to say about the girl her brother's going to marry? Apparently I wasn't the only one who felt that way because someone else piped up and said, "Is that all you can say? We understand she's pretty — can't you tell us anything else?"

Our British friend laughed and explained, "When we say 'gorgeous,' we mean that she's **everything.**"

I came to seminary in Eretz Yisrael to study for the year, but after I arrived I wasn't sure that I hadn't made a mistake. I was so homesick! I had never been away from home for any length of time and I really wasn't prepared for this. I couldn't keep phoning home, since Mom said the bills were ridiculous. The other girls in the dorm all seemed happy and well-adjusted. I needed someone to talk to who would understand.

I had become close to our teacher, Mrs. Levinson, and I decided that I would pour out my heart to her. The next day I caught her after her nine o'clock class and asked, "Mrs. Levinson, could I speak to you just now?" I know she is very busy, but I am sure she noticed tears forming in my eyes, and therefore I couldn't believe it when I heard her say, "I'm sorry, but I really don't have time."

I turned away as fast as I could, before the tears spilled over.

I missed all my classes that morning. I spent that time in my room crying and feeling sorry for myself. About twelve o'clock there was a knock at my door. I opened it, and was surprised to find Mrs. Levinson standing there.

"I'm really sorry, Vicky," she said to me. "I was in a big rush when I saw you before, but if you'd like, I have time now."

"Oh, thank you so much, Mrs. Levinson. I was so disappointed when you told me this morning that you wouldn't be able to talk to me!"

"I did?" said Mrs. Levinson, obviously puzzled.

We sat and talked, and I felt much better. Mrs. Levinson helped me a lot. One of the valuable things I learned from our conversation is that outside South Africa, English speakers understand "just now" to mean something like, "at this moment," whereas we from Johannesburg understand it to mean sometime in the near future.

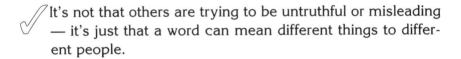 In different countries where people speak the same language words may be used differently.

☐ **In addition, even in the same country, people attach different meanings to the same word.**

My next-door neighbor had told me that she knows how to sew, so when I was having trouble attaching a collar that just wasn't sitting right, I figured she was the person who could give me advice.

To my surprise, she said she couldn't help me. After a little bit of discussion, I realized that "knowing how to sew" meant one thing to her and something completely different to me.

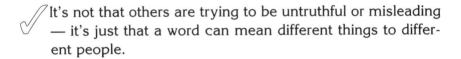 It's not that others are trying to be untruthful or misleading — it's just that a word can mean different things to different people.

☐ **What may appear to be ill will, may simply have been an innocuous comment expressed in an unfamiliar style. It might even be someone's sense of humor that has passed us by . . .**

We were at a family gathering and I needed a ride home, since my husband had left early and took the car. I turned to my cousin who lives not far from us and asked, "Could I have a ride home with you?" adding with a smile, "I hope it's not an imposition."

"It sure is an imposition. But you can come anyway," said my cousin as she put on her coat.

I wasn't sure I had heard right. If I hadn't noticed the broad smile on her face, I would never have realized she was joking.

"I'm sorry," I said, as I accidentally bumped into the girl beside me. She looked me straight in the eye and said, "You should be."

I had a painter working in my house, a friend of my brother-in-law's.

I asked him if there was anything I could get him, and he answered that he had brought along a Walkman but had forgotten to bring tapes. Maybe I had something to lend him.

We had just gotten a set of very interesting tapes by an informative and entertaining speaker, so I offered them.

About three hours later, when the painter was breaking for lunch, he passed by the living room and said with a big smile, "Mr. Davidson, these tapes are great — I could listen all day."

"Oh, no," I chuckled, "I should never have given them to you. Now you'll probably stretch out this job just to hear more!"

"Mr. Davidson, really, I'm working as fast as I can," he answered, obviously hurt at my implication.

*M*y neighbor Mrs. Hess called me to say she was going to the United States for six months. She needed someone to handle her weekly bank deposits, and a few other minor details like taking in her mail and watching her canary. Would it be too much of an imposition to ask me?

We like canaries, and I felt I could handle the rest, so I agreed. She continued to tell me about her forthcoming trip to her children, and went into detail about their families and where each one of them lived. As she was speaking, I thought to myself, Wonderful! — Now I can get the package to my relative.

One of my relatives had been touring and had bought mezuzos, but the cases which had been specially ordered weren't ready when he left. He had asked me if I could pick them up and find someone to bring them. Now Mrs. Hess was going to his town.

I told her the story and asked, "Do you think you could take the mezuzah cases?"

"I'd be happy to," she replied.

"Are you **sure** you don't mind?"

"Well, how many are there?"

"There are twelve. Is that okay?"

"Well," said Mrs. Hess, *"if it's too much, I'll give you back six."*

I thought to myself, She's asking me to do her a favor for six long months, week in and week out — and all I'm asking for is one small favor! What does she mean, "I'll give you back six"?!

It didn't make any sense. Why would she say something like that? Then I figured out that she probably had similar experiences in the past. Someone must have said something like, "I'm just going to send a little envelope," and then they walked in with a large parcel. Perhaps she was concerned that I would send much more than twelve mezuzah cases.

That was it. That was the zechus I found for her.

I was telling the story in a class I attend and one lady said, "Come on — that was just a joke." And right away, all the other people agreed. "Of course. It's like giving a person twelve needles and having them say, 'If it's too much, I'll give you back six.'" Someone else in the room offered, "Of course it's a joke. It's as if you said, 'Could you take this sweater? I hope it's not too much trouble,' and the person answered, 'If it's too much trouble, I'll cut off the sleeves.'"

✓ Some people are very literal, others are witty. If we aren't attuned to a style, we may take as an insult what was only meant as a joke.

■ **Then there's the turn of phrase we've never heard before . . .**

*H*ere I was, coming home from the hospital with my first child, bursting with happiness. Did my bubble burst fast! As I got out of the car with my precious bundle, a neighbor passed by. She came over with a big smile and, of course, wanted a peek at the baby. She took one look and — are you ready for this? — said: "What an ugly baby!"

I walked into the house in tears. Would a normal person say such a thing?

Later that afternoon, my mother called. When she asked me

how the baby was, I burst into tears. She got really nervous. "Is everything all right, Shaynale?"

"Everything's okay, Ma, but would you believe that one of my neighbors said that our sweet little baby is ugly?"

"Ugly?"

"Yes, I met her in the street, she peeked under the blanket and said, 'What an ugly baby!' "

I heard my mother laughing, so I asked her, "Ma, what's so funny about that?"

"Don't you know that's what some people say when they think your baby's so beautiful that they don't want to make anyone jealous?"[1]

This story illustrates a principle that was mentioned in an earlier chapter: The more unreasonable a behavior appears, the more likely that there has to be something we're missing. Here, it was this new mother's lack of familiarity with a style of expression that misled her and caused her unnecessary anguish.

✓ Individuals, families, and cultures have their own styles of expression. Lack of familiarity with a style can lead to conversational confusion and unwarranted grievances.

Messages sent are not always forever

When I sent the message, it was true, but since then, the situation changed, or an exception came up . . .

I said I can't do it . . .

I said I don't do it . . .

I said I would *never* do it . . .

. . . and here I am doing it!

"I was supposed to be invited for Shabbos to a certain family," Simi told Mrs. Davis in a hurt voice. "At the last minute, the wife called to say that she was 'terribly sorry' but she didn't feel up to having guests. That was okay — I made other arrangements. But the next week, one of my friends

started telling me about her great Shabbos at — you guessed it — the same place I was supposed to go to! How do you think I felt?"

"You won't believe this!" Mrs. Davis interrupted her excitedly. "Listen to what happened to me. A few weeks ago my husband invited some neighborhood friends for a Shabbos meal, but since I wasn't feeling well, my husband called to cancel. Considering the circumstances, we knew they'd understand, and there was still plenty of time for them to make other plans.

"A short while later, I got a call from one of my close friends. As soon as I heard her voice I remembered that weeks before we had discussed her forthcoming trip, and I had promised to have her and her family eat with us the Shabbos before she left, and here it was. She called to say that she was all packed and ready to leave right after Shabbos, and so appreciated my invitation.

"What could I say?

"As we were all sitting around the Shabbos table, there was a knock at the door — and who do you think walked in? Our neighborhood friends! They came over to say good Shabbos and to see how I was feeling."

✓ When the message was sent it was genuine and truthfully conveyed. But since then, something changed....

Messages may be sent, but may not be meant for you

Comments that are not directed at you are not *meant* for you to understand — and *that's* why you can misunderstand them.

✒ Overheard conversations

*M*y first year in a new bungalow colony found me facing a scenic lake complete with floating ducks and geese.

I was relaxing in front of the bungalow, enjoying the view, when two ladies from the colony strolled by the lake. I caught fragments of their conversation. Imagine my shock when I heard one of them comment:

"This year, somehow, the gang is just not sticking together. They don't seem to be so friendly."

The other woman tried to take the defensive. "It's still early in the season. It'll take them a while to get close."

I was deeply hurt. We were new to the place. Maybe they meant us. I had wanted to start off on the right foot and had gone out of my way to be friendly, and that's what I got? What kind of a place was this if people spoke that way about each other? I started to have second thoughts about this bungalow colony.

As the pair continued walking by me, I picked up the tail end of their conversation:

"You know, it's really a shame that it takes so long for the new ducklings to warm up to the old ones."

M rs. Abramsky's daughter was rushing to town very late Friday morning to pick up some cakes for Shabbos. As she was dashing out of the building, her sister Gila called down after her, "Don't go to Freedman's bakery — they don't have anything good."

Mrs. Abramsky, who had heard the comment, went over to her daughter and reprimanded her. "It's bad enough to say lashon hara about Freedman's bakery, but it's even worse to scream it from the porch so that all the neighbors can hear."

"What lashon hara?" asked Gila.

"That Freedman's doesn't have good cakes."

"Oh no," laughed Gila, "that's not what I meant! They have very good cakes, so good, that by 11 o'clock Friday morning, they have almost nothing left."

R ivkie got on the train. A few stops later two men got on and sat down in front of her.

"Hey, Eli," one asked the other, "whatd'ya have for supper last night?"

That's a funny question to ask someone, Rivkie thought.

"Frozen pizza? Or something else from the freezer?"

Eli didn't answer. A few seconds later, he asked his friend, "What did you have, Josh?"

"You know we have normal food in our house."

The thought flitted through Rivkie's mind: Hey, that's not nice. You want to wreck his marriage?

Josh continued. "Come on, Eli, admit it — aren't you hungry? What do you eat when you're hungry, fill up on cake?"

This is getting worse and worse, Rivkie thought.

She was almost ready to get off when she heard Josh saying, "I know your wife isn't coming home for a few more days. I'm only going to stop nudging you if you agree to come for a meal."

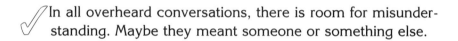 In all overheard conversations, there is room for misunderstanding. Maybe they meant someone or something else.

✎ *Telephone misunderstanding*

---

*A*t the beginning of the month, Mrs. Hoffman called the bank for her monthly statement, as she often did. This time, she was surprised when the man who answered replied to her request in brusque tones: "I'm very sorry. We can't give you that information." Mrs. Hoffman tried to explain that Ruth, one of the clerks, always gave her this information over the phone, but the voice only repeated: "Listen, I don't know you, and neither does Ruth. There is nothing you can do over the phone. You'll have to come down in person."

Mrs. Hoffman had received this information from Ruth dozens of times in the past, with no problem. What's going on over there? she thought with annoyance. She got into her car and drove right over.

She approached Ruth's desk in an indignant huff. "I don't understand why I wasn't able to get the information about my account over the phone this morning like I always do."

Ruth broke into a smile. "Oh, it was **you**, Mrs. Hoffman! You're the customer the manager told me about. He knew he had spoken to the wrong person, but we didn't know who it was, so we weren't able to call to apologize.

"A few minutes before you called, a woman called asking to know her daughter's bank balance. The clerk refused, but she was insistent, so he put her through to the manager. Just then, your call must have come through on another line. When the manager picked up the phone, he thought he was talking to the woman who was asking for confidential information about her daughter's account. Only when he picked up the other line and the insistent mother was on there did he realize what had happened."

*I*t was after the big morning rush. Almost everyone had left for school. Only Shoshana was still at home, but she was half out the door so I decided it would be a good time to call my friend Adina. I had told her I'd let her know if I'd be able to go walking with her.

Her husband picked up the phone.

"Can I speak to Adina, please?"

"Adina, telephone," I heard him call.

There was a long silence. She must be in the middle of something. I imagined her house and pictured her in any one of many places. Meanwhile, I saw Shoshana dawdling by the mirror. I was too familiar with this scene. Soon she'd ask me for a note because she was late.

"Hurry up already," I called a little impatiently. She didn't seem to be moving so I repeated, "What's taking you so long?"

Just then I heard Adina's husband calling impatiently, "Adina, hurry up."

I was surprised to hear his voice. I hadn't realized that he was still on the phone.

"You're calling from out of town?" he was asking.

"No," I answered, puzzled at the question.

Then the light bulb went on.

"Oh, no!" I exclaimed, and rushed to apologize. "I wasn't talking to **you**!"

We hope these stories *do* talk to you. And that their messages are being received.

We have taken a look at the confusion and ill will that can be caused, albeit unintentionally, in our everyday conversations. Judging favorably is an indispensable safeguard against error that leads to condemnation. Whenever we hear or overhear statements that bother us, we should reconsider that what we heard just might be a message misunderstood.

13

More Clues For Unraveling Mysteries

Throughout this book, we have offered clues to assist us in unraveling the mysteries of human behavior. A clue, by definition, guides us in solving anything of a doubtful nature. A good clue points us in the right direction. The following clues have proven themselves time and again to be helpful in judging favorably.

Missing Information

When we catch ourselves judging unfavorably, one of the most helpful clues to remember is that we might be missing information about what really took place.

Often we are missing only one fact, one detail unknown to us which **is** the other side of the story. As we have seen in so many of our stories, it is that one piece of information, that missing piece of the puzzle, which will, when found and placed, make the whole picture clear.

□ . . . **about people and situations**

*M*y cousin, Yossie Weiss, was making a wedding for his daughter, and I arrived just in time for the chuppah. Glancing around at the crowd, I noticed Rabbi Chaim Ebstein, the distinguished uncle of the bride. I was sure this prominent family member would be given one of the honors. But to my mounting astonishment, he was never called upon. How could Yossie have forgotten him? What an oversight!

I decided that I shouldn't stand by quietly and let it pass. If I'd tell Yossie right away, he might still be able to make it up in some way during the evening.

After the ceremony, I walked over to him. "Mazel Tov! Mazel Tov!" I began, pumping my cousin's hand with feeling. Leaning closer, I lowered my voice to a confidential whisper. "I feel I must mention this — you forgot Uncle Chaim."

Yossie looked at me for a minute uncertainly and then smiled. "Uncle Chaim? Would I forget Uncle Chaim? Of course he was on the list. I even called him yesterday to remind him. But just as the ceremony was getting under way, Rabbi Golden walked in unexpectedly. Uncle Chaim came over to me and said that because I hadn't been expecting Rabbi Golden and didn't have an honor for him, he insisted on stepping aside and giving him his place."

*M*y friend Tamar, an old classmate, came over to spend the afternoon. I promised her a lift home. Tamar told me she was going to be picked up at her house at 6:00 sharp, and she needed to get back in time to get ready before her ride came.

We had a wonderful day together. Late in the afternoon, as Tamar and I were in the middle of a conversation, she jumped up suddenly. "Is that clock right? Is it really 5:00? Let's go quickly or I'll be late."

I rushed out with her and drove her home. As soon as we arrived at her block of flats, she jumped out of the car in mid-sentence and rushed towards her entrance. I drove to the end of the block to turn the car around. Meanwhile, I noticed a small store and went in to pick up an item I needed. As I drove back, I passed my friend's building. To my surprise, there was Tamar sitting on a bench and talking to a neighbor, as if she had all the time in the world.

How did she suddenly have so much time? What happened to the big rush?

I wish I had found the solution to this mystery earlier than I did — it would have kept me from a few suspicious feelings. But at least I only had to wait until the next day, when Tamar called. Not knowing that I had witnessed her sitting on the bench, she complained to me how scatterbrained she was becoming. She told me that when she had reached the flat, she discovered that she had locked herself out, and had no choice but to sit and wait outside for her ride.

□ . . . **about prices and quality**

*B*atsheva was talking to her neighbor Chedva about some electrical work she needed done in her house. "My brother recommended someone named Alex," Batsheva commented, "an electrician he's worked with, and I think I'm going to take him."

"I also took Alex," Chedva remarked, "but my neighbor took someone named Uri, and he was much cheaper."

Batsheva mulled that over for a minute. "Well, Alex's prices are reasonable and I like his work. I think I'll stick with him."

The next day, Batsheva answered the phone and it was Chedva. After the hellos and how-are-yous, Chedva said, with a touch of embarrassment in her voice, "I was thinking *about what I said yesterday, and I realized that what I told you really wasn't right. Alex wasn't more expensive. I remembered that he charged more because he installed a special safety device for me — and my neighbor didn't have that."*

When someone says, "My cousin got the *same* thing for half price," it's not always the same thing. It might be a different model, or have different features you haven't noticed. It might have been a floor sample. Maybe it was bought on sale. It might not be the same quality. It is important for us to be careful before giving our evaluations of how others have been overcharged. It's enough for **one fact** to be left out to be caught in an inaccurate and therefore untruthful statement which can cause both resentment and loss.*

I sent my daughter to the farmer's market to buy a jar of honey. Local stores sell a small half-kilo jar for 10 shekels. I asked her to bring home a large one-kilo jar. I figured it should cost less than 20 shekels since the market prices are known to be lower than the local stores.

Was I surprised when she came home with a one-kilo jar and said that it cost 27 shekels! I had thought we would save money; instead, we ended up spending more. What bothered me the most was that "that man" saw a young girl and overcharged her.

Several days later, a friend of my daughter's came over, and during her visit she noticed the jar of honey on the counter. She told us that her father works with honey, and added that although all honey might look similar, there is a very big difference in quality. "That honey on the table," she pointed, "is one of the best."

And when I told her how much we paid, she said it was a bargain at 27 shekels!

---

* This is called *motzi shem ra* (lit., spreading a bad name), defined as slander or a non-truthful statement. This is worse than *lashon hara*, which is a derogatory or damaging statement but is *true*.

□ . . . **about schedules**

*A*s I was waiting for the community library to open a few
minutes before 4:30 one afternoon, another woman
joined me. Both of us were holding the books we were waiting to exchange.

"I wonder if they'll come today," she said, sounding concerned. "I've been here a few times and they never showed
up." Her comment surprised me. I was a frequent user of the
library and my experience was that they were always open
when I came.

Soon the librarians came and opened up exactly on time.
The woman said to the girls working there, "Why have you
been closed so many times lately?"

The girls looked at her in confusion and said, "The library
is open every day."

Suddenly, I had the idea that maybe this woman didn't
know that the hours alternated, so I pointed to the schedule
posted in front of us:

Sunday: 6:30-8:00 p.m.
Monday: 4:30-6:00 p.m.
Tuesday: 6:30-8:00 p.m.
Wednesday: 4:30-6:00 p.m.

She read it and blushed.

"Look at that. I've been here on Sundays and Tuesdays in
the afternoon."

She apologized profusely to the librarians as she returned a
book on being *dan l'kaf zechus*, which, on second thought,
she decided to renew.

□ . . . **about professions**

*M*rs. Lewis was being treated by her family physician for
an ongoing condition. She picked up the phone to ask
the doctor what she felt was a pressing question. Instead of
hearing the nurse's voice, she heard a recording saying that
the doctor was on vacation for two weeks. There followed the
name and number of a doctor to be called in case of emer-

Why didn't he tell me he was going on vacation? I would have discussed this problem before he left if I had known he was going away. How can he do that without notifying his patients?

Mrs. Lewis was unaware that it is not accepted practice for physicians to notify patients of their upcoming vacations.

Our expectations of professionals may be unrealistic. Each profession, business, and service organization has its own code of accepted behavior that is specific to that profession and yet hidden from anyone who is not familiar with the workings of that profession. It's not that we're faulted for not knowing that information — we can't be experts in everything — but we *are* faulted for not judging people favorably.

□ . . . **about media and communications**

*S*hlomo Singer was a pensioner looking for some worthwhile way to use his spare time. He decided to devote himself to helping out new immigrants. Since he was very handy, he offered them his household repair services free of charge. Not only did he give his time on a volunteer basis, he even supplied these newcomers with the raw materials necessary for the various jobs he undertook.

This went on for years. His neighbors got wind of his benevolence and as a result, he was interviewed by a local radio station. The interview took place in his home. The next day, his family and friends gathered around and hung on to every word as they listened to the interview being broadcast.

"And how did you get involved in this?" the announcer's voice was heard asking Mr. Singer, who explained patiently how the idea had come to him. After sharing interesting stories of incidents that happened over the years, Mr. Singer was asked, "And how do the people react to what you do for them?"

There was a pause. "They really don't care," was Mr. Singer's surprising response.

All the people in the room listening raised their eyebrows as Mr. Singer sat dumbfounded.

as Mr. Singer sat dumbfounded.

At the end of the broadcast, one of relatives turned to him and said, "Shlomo, don't the people appreciate what you do for them?"

"They certainly do!"

"So why did you say they don't really care?"

"I'm telling you I never said it. These people can't do enough for me. They're always giving me presents, also for my wife and children. They thank me for even the smallest of favors."

Yet it was hard to deny. They all — himself included — had heard him say it.

What could have gone wrong? he wondered. How could he have maligned those good people with whom he had developed such a strong mutual affection? Then he remembered something the interviewer had mentioned to him before he left:

"We have only a twenty-minute slot and this interview is much longer, so we'll have to splice part of what you said."

I read in the classified advertisements that one of my neighbors was having a meeting in her home for a certain organization. I was shocked to see that she would be involved with such a cause and such people. She herself was horrified when she started receiving calls that she knew nothing about. She called up the paper, and after investigating they told her that they were terribly sorry. The personal information — her name, address, and telephone number — was put together with someone else's advertisement!

Today people are aware of the many mistakes and misrepresentations that appear in the media.

Journalists must work with space limitations and deadlines. Photos are cropped, articles are edited. The wrong caption can appear under a picture. Digital photography now makes it possible for anyone with the right equipment to put into a picture someone who wasn't even there, or take out someone who was. That's why, when we see or hear something negative in the media and we wonder, "How could he say that?" — the answer may be that he didn't!

□ **. . . about technology**

Mashie brought her two children over to my house Friday morning. The previous week she had told me she had to attend a weekend bar mitzvah out of town and asked if I could do her a favor and watch her children. She wanted to know if she could bring them early because she needed enough travel time. I agreed, even though it wasn't going to be easy having her "lively" boys from early Friday morning throughout the entire Shabbos.

We tried to make the best of the situation. My oldest daughter took the children out to play, while the rest of us began to get Shabbos preparations under way.

Late that morning, the phone rang. It was none other than Mashie. "How's it going?" she inquired.

"So far, okay," I answered, quite surprised at the call. It was much too early for her to have arrived at her destination. She had to be calling from home. That takes nerve, I thought to myself. She said she wanted to leave the children in the morning because she had to get an early start, and here it is eleven o'clock and she's first calling to ask how everything is! If she's still home, why did she have to bring the boys so early?

Wait a minute. Why am I thinking she's at home? She must be on the road, and must have stopped off at a service station to make the call.

"Are you calling from a pay phone?" I asked her.

"No," she replied. "We try our best not to make any stops once we're on our way. It wastes too much time so . . ."

She couldn't have gotten there yet. And she's not on the road. If she's really still at home . . .

Mashie's voice interrupted my thoughts, as she continued, ". . . I'm calling from my car phone."

You probably figured out the ending easily, because today everyone knows about car phones. When the story was submitted, however, car phones were not as widely used as they are now. Although the suspense might be gone, this story is still valuable for the lesson it teaches: Whatever is new in technology is, at the outset, an "unknown" to most people. By the time it finally becomes popular, it has already been replaced by countless other "unknowns."

One person knows about honey, another about computers. This man knows about electrical repairs and another about publishing or financing. We all know about some things and are missing endless information about so much else that is going on in this big and complex world we live in.

 CLUE: Other people have information that we are missing, just as we know things they don't know. These information gaps are a frequent source of erroneous judgments about others.

Entering "in the middle"[1a]

It can be confusing to walk into a play during Act II. Yet, although the dialogue may not make sense, we're not upset because we know we entered in the middle.

In order to interpret behavior fairly, we have to be familiar with events that led up to it. When we witness certain disturbing situations, we should approach them as we would that play and realize that we might be walking in in the middle of a story. Since we didn't see the last scene, we're not able to understand what's going on. We wonder, *Why is he doing that? Why would she say that?* If we are puzzled, it may be because we came in on Act II.

I went to the park with my three-year-old son, Avi. It was a glorious day. I found a spot on the edge of the sandbox and watched him climb the slide. My eyes turned to two little children (who looked like brother and sister) who were in the middle of building a castle. Not an average castle, mind you. It had tall towers and tunnels decorated with stones, flowers, leaves, sticks, and anything else within reach. I was fascinated with their patience and realized how long it must have taken them to make it. Somewhere along the line, the little boy turned to his sister and I heard him say, "Let's go home to get a drink," and off they ran.

As they scampered away, Avi ran over to me and asked playfully, "Mommy, can I stomp on it? Can I break it down?"

"Oh, Avi — think of all the work they put into it! Why should you break it?"

Avi reconsidered and I guess he agreed, because he ran off to the swings. A minute later, a little boy came running over. He eyed that castle with obvious glee, circled it, and then, without warning, jumped on that beautiful castle and demolished it. Before I could open my mouth, the little boy had come and gone. What a shame, I thought.

"Mommy, can I stomp on it now? Can I?" It was my son eyeing the remains.

"I guess so, Avi. Not much to stomp on, though."

But Avi was already busy having a wonderful time, stomping and kicking and jumping on what was left of that once-marvelous castle.

I sensed movement and looked up to notice someone running. It was the brother and sister. They had come back with their mother, to show her their magnificent castle.

She and her children shot us two angry looks — one for me and one for my son — and then three angry faces turned around and walked away in disgust.

Here's a second look at the frustrated uncle we met earlier in "Voices" . . .

*M*y uncle was checking in his baggage for an overseas flight. The man in front of him was taking forever. He kept demanding special consideration — and getting it! The ticket agent told him there were two very good seats for him. But this man wasn't satisfied. He insisted that two weren't enough — he needed four (!) so that he would be comfortable and well rested. They finally agreed to that and began checking in his luggage.

My uncle watched as the man insisted that one of his large

change during the flight. And they gave in. There were a few more points he wanted clarified and he insisted on speaking to a supervisor, who was called over and listened patiently and agreeably to all he had to say.

Now it was my uncle's turn. He stepped up to the counter and all he asked for was an aisle seat. The ticket agent said he was sorry, but there were no aisle seats available. After having witnessed the service given to the man in front of him, my uncle muttered under his breath, I'll never use them again! He glared at the ticket agent and demanded to see a supervisor.

After a long wait, the supervisor arrived and my uncle said with obvious irritation, "How can you give such unfair and unequal treatment to customers? How come you gave in to everything the guy in front of me wanted?"

And this is what he heard:

The previous passenger had somehow been sold a first class ticket on a plane which had no first class. He really could have made a big tumult, so he was actually doing the airline a favor by only demanding four seats and a few other conveniences that were coming to him.

 CLUE: Sit down and relax. You came in in the middle — and there's a lot going on that you can't understand.

Misreading Intentions

How many times have we felt unnecessarily hurt, angry, or humiliated because we read into statements or actions more than was really there?

☙ *They were just trying to make conversation*

*A*s Mina walked into a lecture, she met her friend Etta, whose first words were, "What are you doing here?"

Mina thought to herself, What does she mean by that? What does she think I'm doing here? The same thing she is!

Etta, however, might say, "I didn't mean anything at all! I was just trying to be friendly."

Rena Fried was out shopping when she met an acquaintance, Mrs. Deutsch, who was bustling down the street, laden with packages. Rena greeted her. "It looks like you did a lot of shopping — what did you buy?"

They chatted for a few minutes before continuing their separate ways.

After they parted, Rena felt awkward. I'll bet she feels I am a real busybody, standing there and asking her what she bought. What business is it of mine what she has in her packages?

It was on her mind, and the next time she met Mrs. Deutsch, she immediately began to apologize.

"Please don't think twice about it," Mrs. Deutsch smiled. "I knew you were only trying to make conversation."

And the truth is, that's all it was.

CLUE: Don't read into these kinds of comments more than was intended. They're just "openers," a way of being friendly.

They were reacting to something else — it wasn't you

At times, we are pleased with the response we receive from other people. The interchange is pleasant and there is mutual understanding and respect.

At other times, we are not prepared for the response we get. Seemingly for no reason, the other person lashes out at us with an angry tirade. Or, at the other extreme, he fails to give us the attention, warmth, or time we'd like. In the middle, there are other responses of every shape, size and intensity, to which we might take offense. People seem grouchy, nervous, impatient, brusque, unfriendly . . .

- You call on the phone — and there is an edge to his voice.
- You knock on the door — and they are abrupt.
- You walk over to the host — and she barely greets you.

When we feel insulted, we assume that an insult was intended. It certainly *seems* that the other person's behavior was a response to something we said or did. However, it might well be that what we felt was a reaction to us, was really triggered by outside factors that have nothing to do with us.

While there always is a chance that their behavior *is* a message to us, it is equally possible that it is not. For instance, many times people are struggling with anger over some other matter. Right then, we come along, and those pent-up emotions are let out on us innocent bystanders.* Because, as the Chofetz Chaim tells us,[2] outside factors are so often the cause, an intelligent evaluation demands that we give at least equal consideration to that possibility.

We should get into the habit of asking ourselves: What else could it be? Consider any one of the following:

- He may be angry or upset —
  he was just criticized;
  he just got a parking ticket;
  he just heard sad or shocking news;
  the customer before you unnerved him.

- She may be preoccupied —
  she is concentrating on finishing the job at hand;
  she is wondering what to serve the guests;
  she is in the middle of looking for a lost item or person;
  she is responsible for making arrangements and there's a
      snag;
  she's wondering how she'll pay for this affair.

- They may be busy —
  they are just sitting down to eat;

---

* This *zechus* should be used to understand others, but not as a justification for our own improper behavior.

they are just sitting down to eat;
they are on their way out, or in a rush;
her husband just walked through the door, or the children
just came home;
they still have other guests.

- They may not be up to socializing —
  it's the end of a long day;
  they had a lot of visitors or company before you came;
  they needed a quiet time to think.

- She may be experiencing physical discomfort or pain —
  the air conditioner is blowing on her;
  a smell is bothering her;
  she's been sitting too long;
  there's not enough air in the room;
  she may have a backache, toothache, headache, or some
  other pain.

- They may be under stress; they are experiencing anxiety about financial pressure or deadlines; they are feeling over-whelmed by business, social, or household obligations; they are worried about children or suffering from a loss . . .

Of course, this is only a sampling of why people might not give us the response we would like, or one they would like to give. You can surely think of many more.

Since such factors play a continual role in almost everyone's life, they should be one of the first places we look for clues to solve the mystery of strange or disturbing responses. They offer us an alternative route for reevaluating other people's intentions.

Many times we are needlessly hurt because of a perceived blow to our self-esteem. If we can attribute the other person's response to something unrelated to us, and not to an intention-al slight, it sheds light on that troublesome reaction and helps us judge others favorably.

⟹ **CLUE:** Don't take it personally — it might not have been you. Some outside factor could be causing the response

He's Really Right[3]

We are often positive that the law is on our side. We're sure the other fellow doesn't have a leg to stand on.

But he might.

L ast week I had a fight with a cab driver.

My wife and I were on vacation. We were in a cab on our way from one hotel to another. We were trying to travel light, so each of us had only a large suitcase and one carry-on. When we got out, the driver asked for two shekel extra for each bag. Believe me, the number on the meter was already high, and I wasn't going to pay a penny more. And I didn't.

We took our bags and walked into the hotel. I turned to my wife, and we said almost simultaneously, "What a nervy guy."

As we stood at the desk checking in, I saw the driver coming towards me. It looks like he didn't give up so fast, I thought tensely.

Just to prove to myself that I was right and he was wrong, I asked the clerk at the desk what the rules are about paying extra for suitcases. They told me that the Ministry of Transportation regulations say two shekels for each suitcase.

M oshe Bloom wanted to sell his apartment. One of his neighbors, Yosef Frimmer, heard about it and mentioned to Moshe that Dov Ziskind wanted to buy one. Moshe acted upon Yosef's suggestion and began a business transaction with Mr. Ziskind. In the end, Mr. Ziskind bought the apartment. Yosef was not at all involved in any of these dealings.

A few days after the deal was completed, Moshe called Yosef to thank him for making the suggestion, to which Yosef replied, "You owe me a $500 commission for sending you the customer who bought your apartment." Moshe was astonished. How could Yosef ask for a commission? he wondered.

He's not a real estate broker and he made no effort whatsoever to see that the sale would be completed. He surely doesn't deserve a commission, and it takes nerve on his part to even ask!

Yosef, though, was persistent in his stance that the money was coming to him. The two of them decided to go and ask a rav. They were told that even a non-professional who only makes a suggestion, or offers information which eventually leads to a sale, is entitled to a commission.

Moshe had been sure he was right, and had condemned Yosef for asking, but justice was really on Yosef's side.

I bought a used car several years ago. Where I live, cars have to undergo a yearly test for mechanical and safety defects in order to have their registration renewed. Each year I first bring my car to a garage to have it fixed so there won't be any last-minute delays that will hold things up.

A few days ago I brought the car to my regular garage for the yearly check-up. I wanted to leave it overnight so that I could take it the next day to be tested. That way I would be without the car for a minimum amount of time.

The manager, who knows me well, was willing to do me the favor and agreed to stay after hours so that it would be ready by morning.

The next morning, true to his word, the manager had the car ready. But when he presented me with the bill, I was shocked and angry. In each of the previous years, the bill had come to two to three hundred shekel at the most, as the car was generally in good shape. Now I was presented with a bill for over two thousand shekel!

He saw the look on my face, so he went over the bill item by item. But I was asking a different question. "Why didn't you get my permission before undertaking such an expensive repair job? After all, it's an old car and maybe I would rather have replaced it than go to such expense."

He reminded me that I had told him to do "whatever was necessary" to pass the test; besides that, by the time he realized the extent of the repairs, it was too late to call.

He also said that at each stage of disassembling the car, he replaced the faulty part and only when that was done was he able to see that further work was necessary. Since he couldn't just leave my car on the lift, he had two choices: The first would have been to reassemble it, without going ahead with all the rest of the necessary repairs, which this year were more numerous and serious than I had expected. If he did that, I'd be left with an unrepaired car and the bill for labor would still be considerable. If it turned out later that I did want those repairs, it would necessitate taking everything apart again. Then I'd have the added expense of taking the car apart and putting it back together a second time and the bill would be even higher. His other choice was to go ahead.

While his explanation sounded reasonable, I was extremely suspicious of having "been taken." It still seemed to me that the right thing to do would have been to get my approval before proceeding. I felt that he had forced me to undertake a major expense.

So I went to ask my rabbi, quite sure of what the outcome would be. I wasn't expecting the answer I got: If I had indicated that I needed the car to be put into shape and would agree to any repairs necessary for that purpose, then I was obligated to pay. Much to my surprise I learned that the garage manager was within his rights to act as he did and that the halachah supported his actions.

$\implies$ **CLUE:** judging favorably means: even when you're *sure* he's wrong, it pays to reconsider.

He's Really Wrong

Judging favorably clears people of undeserved suspicion and helps us see them in a more favorable light. At times, we can explain behavior in a way that the suspected party is cleared of wrongdoing altogether.

And at times we can't.

If a person acted improperly and his behavior is clearly

wrong, he cannot be completely cleared. Nonetheless, we might still be able to make him look *better*. Since a person's reputation and honor is very dear to him, this too is considered a valuable accomplishment.

When we see someone transgressing, we should bring it to his attention — if we can and if it is appropriate.[4] Irrespective of that decision, the Chofetz Chaim tells us we can judge others favorably by keeping in mind that it might be that . . .

✍ They know it's wrong to do such a thing, but didn't mean to do it[5]

---

*A*s I passed the water cooler I bent over for a drink, and then I stopped suddenly in the middle of a gulp. How could I have forgotten that today was a fast day?

*W*e were having dinner with one of our friends and I told them proudly that our daughter was class valedictorian. A second after I said it, I remembered how much difficulty they have been having with one of their children. I wanted to bite my tongue.

⇨ **CLUE:** It was a mistake.

✍ They didn't know it was wrong[6]

The Torah contains numerous laws and guidelines for successful daily living. We must study them continually in order to know all of them and their many details.

Many of us are unfamiliar with or uninformed about one facet or another of these laws. Some of us know that:

- we are not permitted to speak against people for no constructive purpose even if what we say is absolutely true;

but might not know that:

- we are not supposed to hold a grudge if someone refuses to do a favor for us.

Another person might be aware that:

- not only does food have to be kosher, but so does clothing,

while another might not know that:

- borrowing without permission is a type of stealing.

⇨ **CLUE:** When we see a person doing something clearly wrong, we should consider that he may be lacking knowledge in this matter, just as we may lack knowledge in some other area.

They may know it is wrong,
but do not realize how wrong[7]

The Chofetz Chaim explains that some people are unaware that faulty character traits such as anger, arrogance or jealousy are serious transgressions. People may know that these behaviors are incorrect. However, if they knew with what gravity and severity they are described in the Scriptures and the words of our Sages, perhaps they (and we!) would make a greater effort to avoid violating them.[8]

⇨ **CLUE:** They may not realize the severity of the violation.

They may not realize it is an obligation,
but consider it an extra stringency (chumrah)
practiced by only the most pious.[9]

People may be in a position to give interest-free loans and yet refrain from doing so because they are unaware that it is mandated by the Torah, and that great reward is promised for this kindness. They consider it only a praiseworthy action[10] but don't realize it is a mitzvah, no less important than others such as *succah, lulav* and *tefillin.*[11]

⇨ **CLUE:** They thought it was preferable but not obligatory.

They might feel bad and regret their behavior, even though they never told you. [12]

Mrs. Solomon and three-year-old Goldie were walking out of their building on their way to the supermarket. A little boy was sitting on the entrance steps playing marbles, blocking the way. As Goldie and her mother began walking down the stairs, Goldie slid on the marbles and fell.

Heart thumping, Mrs. Solomon raced to the bottom. Goldie was screaming, and her mother could see, even before she got to her side, that her nose was bloody. She picked her up, trying to both comfort her and see how badly she was injured. After a few minutes, Goldie quieted down, and it seemed that the only damage was the bloody nose. Now Mrs. Solomon turned her attention to the child with the marbles.

How does a mother let her children play in the middle of the stairs? she fumed inwardly. And with marbles, no less!

Goldie in hand, Mrs. Solomon marched back up the stairs and went straight to Mrs. Katz, the mother of the culprit. Her anger mounting with each step, she banged loudly on the door.

Mrs. Katz had barely opened the door to see who was there, when she was hit with these angry words: "Do you think stairs are the place for children to be playing marbles? Take a look at Goldie! She slipped on your son's marbles. It's a miracle that it was just a bloody nose."

Mrs. Katz looked at her and Goldie and answered: "Where else do you want them to play?"

Mrs. Solomon could not believe her ears. She shot Mrs. Katz a look, but before anything else could be said, Mrs. Katz closed the door.

What kind of a response was that? Not a word of sympathy? No apology? Mrs. Solomon stands there, holding a child with a bloody nose, and she gets the door closed in her face. She placed her complaint in the complaint department, and it was rejected. Her valid criticism was not only not accepted, it was met with a hurtful, illogical response. How could Mrs. Solomon judge her neighbor favorably after that?

One way is by reconsidering the scene. If she had, she might have realized that when Mrs. Katz opened the door, she was unprepared for what was coming. Her first reaction was defensive: "Where else do you want them to play?" When hit with an unexpected criticism, no matter how valid it may be, people are quicker to defend themselves than to apologize.

When we offer a valid criticism and the reply we receive is unsympathetic and non-understanding, it would surely bother us as it did Mrs. Solomon. We would rather hear the accused say, "I'm sorry" and "I'll take care of it." However, criticism often prompts disturbing responses, especially if it is not given sensitively. Keeping this in mind, one can be better prepared for this eventuality. It might have helped Mrs. Solomon better understand her neighbors' words.

Moreover, there was no way for Mrs. Solomon to know how Mrs. Katz felt behind her closed door. She might have been ashamed of her first reaction and regretted it, but, like many of us, might have found it hard to reopen that door and say what should have been said.

Apology aside, what about the "I'll take care of it"? What about concern that steps be taken to correct the situation in the future?

This may very well have been a one-time occurrence. If Mrs. Solomon had reason to believe it would repeat itself, she certainly had the right and perhaps even the responsibility to see that marbles aren't lying near staircases in the future. This should not preclude an energetic attempt at making Mrs. Katz look better by thinking, for example, that away from angry glares with a few moments to think, Mrs. Katz might be taking the criticism to heart. Even without "owning up," she might regret not only her response, but also her negligence, and plan to see that it doesn't happen again.

▱ **CLUE:** She was wrong. Her response was improper.
But she might have regretted it.

✑ *They're wrong. But they're trying hard . . .*
even though you might never know it

I was standing in the bank towards the front of a long line of impatient people. It was the end of the day for all of us. An older lady in a flowered dress moved forward, finished her business, and was trying to collect her things and leave. She was juggling her papers, her change, her glasses and her pocketbook, but was having a hard time getting herself together. Before she finished, the next person in line moved up to the window and put his things down. This turned out to be a wrong move, and the lady let him know it — in resounding tones.

In a different line stood a middle-aged woman with a boy of about ten. When he heard the lady in the flowered dress berating the man, the boy called out: "Be quiet!" in a voice loud enough for everyone in the bank to hear.

Already upset, this set her off. She turned to the insolent boy, gave him a piercing look, and then turned to his mother. "Is that how you bring up your child?" she bellowed. "That's how you let him talk? Absolutely shameful."

I was watching the boy's mother. For a second she stood there facing the lady in the flowered dress. I could see the shock and hurt in her eyes. She was beginning to shake.

*"Shame on me?" she said. "How can you say such a thing? How can you throw something like that into someone's face without . . . without knowing **anything?**"*

She might have said more, but my mind stopped at those words. I thought about some of the times in my life when I was criticized in a way which showed no understanding or recognition of any effort on my part: criticism from my boss about being slow, even after I took work home to finish on my time; knowing looks and comments from relatives about my expensive taste, even though I spent half of what I used to. It hurts to get "D" for effort after expending all that mental and physical energy, after all that struggle and exertion.

My mind came back to the scene I had just witnessed in the bank. Who knows what kind of effort that mother put into her son? Who knows how much she was controlling him, and how much he was controlling himself? Was all that effort the "anything" the lady in the flowered dress was accused of not knowing?

We might look down at a person for his difficult nature or disturbing habits, while in Heaven he is beloved. Considering the load he was given to shoulder (his very difficult nature), he is doing quite well.

On the other hand, we might admire a person, while in Heaven he is being censured. He was born with an easy nature, good character and other virtues. If he had capitalized on these gifts, who knows how far he might have gone!

That's another reason to judge people favorably. We can never know what it took for that person to be where he is today.[13] Maybe he is doing more with what he was given than you, who are criticizing him!*

It is helpful to realize that sometimes a failing is as disturbing to the owner who cannot conquer it as it is bothersome to others who deal with him. That person may have a deep desire to change and might be making an attempt to improve, albeit unsuccessfully.

We don't see the efforts, yet we judge the results.

⟱ **CLUE:** A person may not only regret his actions, but may actually be taking steps to improve. Just because we don't see that effort clearly, it doesn't mean it's not there.

---

* If we are in a position or have the ability to assist other people in improving their behavior so that we, others, and they themselves can benefit, it is a kindness to do so. The Chofetz Chaim tells us that whatever we can do to help another person become more pleasing, acceptable, and beloved in the eyes of others is considered fulfillment of the commandment to love and care for others as you love yourself.

may actually be taking steps to improve. Just because we don't see that effort clearly, it doesn't mean it's not there.

Whoops! It's me!

In a mystery, we're always looking for the culprit. Sometimes, we don't have far to go.

✒ *We remembered incorrectly*

We are *so* sure that:
someone told us
someone didn't tell us
we said something
we didn't say something
We're so sure, but . . .

*B*efore beginning a job as a kindergarten teacher, I searched for material that would be useful. Another teacher in my community was happy to lend me whatever I needed. At one point, she lent me a batch of books, but asked me to be particularly careful because they were out of print and irreplaceable. I was very nervous about having such books in my possession and made sure that I went through them quickly so that I could return them to her as soon as possible, not wanting the responsibility longer than necessary.

Some time later, I found I needed those books again, and I called to ask if I could borrow them. "I don't have them," she said. "You never returned them to me." The whole scene of my giving them to her (in my lounge) was ever so clear to me.

"Don't you remember?" I told her. "When you came here I gave them back to you." She did not remember. Very calmly, I asked her if she wouldn't mind looking again in her house.

worried about the disappearance of her books and so was I. But after all, it was "her problem." It was just before Pesach and I said sweetly to her that no doubt the books would reappear in the process of cleaning (by her, of course!)

What can I say? While cleaning the bedroom I found the whole pile neatly stacked behind our bedroom door. I am in the habit of putting things there that need attending to so they are all in one place without being an eyesore. Now, the whole story came crashing down on me. By my putting them behind the door, it was as if I had taken care of it. The whole incident was so clear to me that I actually "remembered" giving them to her in my own house!

You can well imagine how I felt when I had to call her up and admit to the "crime."

*H*as it ever happened to you that you know, you just know, that you're right? That you are definitely, positively, absolutely-no-doubt-about-it-100% right?

Well, last week I went to a little clothing store in my neighborhood where a very sweet, soft-spoken woman works. I wanted to pay a debt of 215 shekel, as well as pick up a few more items. I walked in, said hello, and told Mrs. R. that I wanted to pay what I owed. She opened up her little notebook and said, "You know, I see that there's also a 60-shekel debt from a while ago that you probably forgot about."

"Oh, I'm so sorry. I really don't remember that at all!" I was rather chagrined to find out that I'd have 60 shekel less now in my wallet. I had taken 660 shekel out from the bank that morning, and I hadn't counted on having to fork over an additional 60. I counted out 215 shekel and put it out on the table, then took out another 60 and put it next to the 215, and said, "I'm just going to pick up a few more things." After about twenty minutes, I went to pay for the new items, and Mrs. R. said, "So I'll leave the 60-shekel debt for next time?"

"Oh!" I exclaimed. "I put 60 shekel down next to the 215." Mrs. R. looked confused and uncomfortable and said, "No, I don't think you did."

"Yes," I said, "I'm positive I did! I put down a 50 shekel note and a 10 shekel note. Maybe you put it into the cashbox?"

Mrs. R. opened up the cashbox and there was a 50 shekel note, but no 10. "Anyway, this 50 is from another customer," she said.

For a fleeting moment I thought, Why is she doing this? I'd never dream Mrs. R. was the type to steal!

"Wait!" I said excitedly. "I had exactly 660 shekel in my wallet. Now all I have to do is remember how much I spent in town before coming to the store, and then we can add it up and see that I did indeed pay the 60 shekel!" I tried to remember where I had gone and what I had bought before coming here, and I came up with the approximate amount of 100 shekel, but I was so upset, that simple addition and subtraction were beyond my mental capacity.

Then Mrs. R. said, "Listen, you gave me 215 shekel for sure and now you paid another 180 for the newest items. That's 395 shekel that you gave me. You said you spent about 100 before coming here, that makes 495 altogether. Let's round it off, and say that so far you've spent 500 shekel. Now, how much do you have in your wallet?"

I opened up my wallet and there inside were three bills: a ten, a fifty, and a hundred, making a total of 160 shekel. I was shocked. I stood there with my mouth open. 500 + 160 = 660. I did not pay her the 60 shekel! I felt my eyes filling with tears. "I'm so sorry. I was so positive. I **saw** the 60 shekel on the table next to the 215!"

Mrs. R. was very sweet and said, "Maybe you put it down and, without realizing it, put it back into your wallet."

"I guess that's just what I did. But I have no recollection of doing it at all! All I remember is seeing the 60 shekel next to the 215 right here on the table. Please forgive me for being so stubborn about it."

Mrs. R. and I continued talking about it — about the "lucky" fact that I knew, with the help of Hashem, exactly how much I had in my wallet, and that I remembered how much I had spent that morning, What if that hadn't been the case? I can't stress enough how absolutely positive I was that

I had paid that 60 shekel. But my wallet proved otherwise: beyond any doubt, I was absolutely wrong.

⇨ **CLUE:** Has it ever happened to you that you know, you just know that you're right? That you are definitely, positively, absolutely-no-doubt-about-it-100% right? Well . . .

✐ We made an unreasonable request

Did you ever ask for a small favor, prefacing your request with, "Could you just . . .?" — and nonetheless your small request was refused?

For example, we ask a friend / acquaintance / relative / neighbor who is a professional for advice in his field. For us, it would be a big favor; for him, it would only be a slight inconvenience, only a few minutes of his time.

Or so we think.

A friend approached me and asked if I would just listen to her three-year-old daughter speak for a few minutes and tell her if the child's speech was appropriate for her age. Since I am a speech therapist, the mother wanted my opinion as to whether professional help was advisable. What she's not aware of is that in order to give a responsible answer, more than a few minutes is required.

It takes time to garner from the parent information regarding the child's general development and specifically speech development; for example, when she said her first words. Time is also needed to observe the child in play to see if her speech behavior correlates with her general behavior. Then the therapist has to evaluate speech reception: Does the child understand instructions to questions at the three-year-old level? Finally, the professional examines different aspects of the child's speech: Does the child speak spontaneously? Does she repeat? Does she answer questions correctly? How long are her sentences? Does she use proper syntax? Are there articulation errors? What kind — omissions, substitutions, distortions? Is there a pattern in the errors?

As a professional, I cannot give a reliable opinion about a child's speech by just listening for a few minutes without taking into consideration all the above factors.

When you ask a "small favor" — and are refused — give the other person the benefit of the doubt. You don't know what size that favor is for him.

A doctor was asked an involved medical question in a hospital elevator by a non-professional hospital staff member. The person who made the request didn't understand that it would be considered medical incompetence (and potentially litigious) to offer a diagnosis of such a nature "on one foot."

As an architect, I often have people approaching me for favors. They ask for just a few minutes of my time to go over their plans. Advice on a proper orientation of their home or apartment. Best layout. Pluses and minuses of various aspects of the building. Inevitably, the few minutes turn into an hour or more. When people ask me if I could "fix up their plans," or "do a sketch," they don't realize that it could entail a morning's work. They probably think, "What could be so complicated about drawing a few lines?"

Whether or not they choose to fulfill a request, professionals, for their part, should judge the ones asking favorably. Laymen are unaware of what "could you just" involves in a specialized field.

When my children were small, I wrote a little story for them. I wanted to teach them some ideas about sharing. I wrote it up nicely in a notebook, and then I realized that children need pictures.

I immediately thought of my friend, who is an professional illustrator. Although I would never impose upon her to do real illustrations, I asked her to do a few stick figures. I figured that with her talent, it would only take her a few minutes.

When she handed the notebook back to me, I couldn't believe my eyes. She had drawn beautiful illustrations, just as she would have done for a professional book. I said to her, "Ilana! I never expected you to do something like this. I just wanted you to make some stick figures."

I was surprised by her explanation. "When I do any work, it's hard for me to give it less than my best effort."

I wouldn't have thought of that before she explained, but once she did, it made sense.

Professionals should bear in mind that people approaching them for advice or favors are often unaware of the amount of time they're asking for. Nor do they realize how much money the professional time they're asking for is worth, and that they are actually asking for free services!

There is another way for professionals, up in arms because they feel imposed upon, to judge "askers" favorably. That is to remember those times when they themselves did the same thing — asked for "small favors" — from professionals in other fields.

"Could you just" also applies to favors asked of anyone, professional or non-professional. When we preface our request with "could you just," the implication is that there's hardly anything being asked . . .

Early one morning, Deena knocked on her neighbor Rivka's door. She was rushing to work and got right to the point. "Will you be home this morning?"

Rivka smiled an early-morning smile. "Yes," she nodded.

Deena continued, "A delivery man is coming. Could you just take my key and let him into the house when he comes?"

"Fine," Rivka agreed. Deena handed her the key and dashed off. Rivka turned back into the house and closed the door. Once inside, she realized what she had committed herself to. Her "yes" really meant, I don't have anything special planned outside the house this morning. Now she realized she

would have to forfeit her morning. It meant four hours of being available, no napping, no bathing the baby, not doing anything that would take her away from the door.

Later in the day, Deena came to take back the key. Her parting wave was accompanied by a small thank you, proportionate to the small favor she thought she had received. After all, how long does it take to open a door?

Rivka found herself thinking, If I myself didn't know what "could you just" meant when I gave my yes, she surely could not have realized that the "five-minute favor" she was asking of me meant donating my entire morning.

Have you ever asked:

If you're going to be in that store anyway, could you just return this for me and get credit?

If you're going to the zoo, could I send my son along?

Would you mind just dropping this off on your way?

⇨ **CLUE:** If we sense hesitation, or actually receive a refusal to our seemingly small request, we should judge favorably and think: Could there be more to what I am asking than I realize?

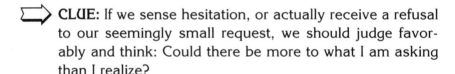

⌇ We pushed first

I was at a wedding, standing with a group of friends. We were discussing clothing, shoes, bags, and getting ready for a simchah.

R. admitted, "It took me two hours to get ready for this wedding."

I piped up, "Two hours! I could never spend two hours to get ready."

"Well," commented R., "that's why I look like this and you look like that."

I turned and walked away, not knowing where to put myself or what to think. Why would she have said something like that?

After replaying the conversation endless times in my mind, it suddenly dawned on me that R. must have felt insulted and lashed back at me for what she felt was an insensitive comment directed at her. Seeing her comment in the context of a response put it in an entirely different light.

In judging favorably it is helpful to recognize the part we play in triggering other people's responses. When people feel verbally attacked, they often strike back. We often don't see our comments as provoking, until someone lets us know — and in no uncertain terms — that they felt provoked. We realize that we are reacting to others, but do we realize others are also reacting to us? *I* know *I* said what I said because of her. But *she* might have said what *she* said because of me! We feel it when we are being pushed, but not when we're doing the pushing.

Questions can also be a "push." After being asked, "How much did that cost you?" or "Who did you vote for?" a person may let you know, not so gently, that it's none of your business. You feel their response wasn't called for, but it is helpful to understand that he may have felt the same way about your question.

There are endless possibilities where it is appropriate to judge favorably by realizing: "Maybe she's . . . because I'm . . ."

⇨ CLUE: That hurtful statement may have been a defensive response to your verbal push.*

～ Them is Us

We're so busy blaming others. "Who took the keys? WHO TOOK THE KEYS?!"

"Who saw the phone book? I know you had it last!"

It's so embarrassing when we discover that . . . "them" is "us."

We went on vacation, swapping apartments with a family in another part of the country. When we came back, I was missing a pretty glass plate I had recently bought. I

---

*This is an example of a *zechus* that doesn't completely clear the person, but does make him look better.

called the woman who had stayed in our apartment, Mrs. Stern, to ask her about it, but she said she hadn't seen it while she was here. I looked high and low for it — even checked the floor for glass splinters — but to no avail. I even bothered her a second and third time to ask. I had no choice but to leave the mystery unsolved.

Some time later, one of my neighbors, who was packing up her belongings to move, knocked on the door and handed me my glass plate. Very surprised, I asked, "Where did **you** get it?"

"Don't you remember bringing us some slices of your anniversary cake?"

A few days before we left on our vacation, my husband had gotten a big cake to celebrate our first anniversary. Since neither of us really needed to eat so much cake, I had brought some to the neighbor — on my new glass plate!

*B*etween the morning chores and preparing lunch, I remembered I had to make an important phone call. I picked up the phone and dialed. When I put the receiver to my ear, I heard a child's voice.

"Could you please call your mommy?" I tried encouragingly. The child answered with a loud, definite, "NO." Oh, no, I thought, now I'm in trouble. I'll never get that lady on the phone. Annoyed at my predicament, and groping for some constructive strategy, I thought, When I finally get that mother on the phone I'm going to tell her what happened so she can give it to that kid. If he is old enough to answer in such a clear, definite way, I reasoned, he can also be taught other things.

As my mind returned to the receiver, I heard the child chattering on the other end. "CALL YOUR MOTHER!" I yelled into the receiver. As I listened for some adult sounds, the babbling suddenly sounded more and more familiar. And then it hit me — I had never connected with the other party. It was **my** two-year-old talking on the other extension.

*Z*vi Goldman checked his coat in the coat room of the convention hall, inadvertently leaving his cellular phone in the pocket. At the end of the evening, he went to get his coat and the phone was missing. He was very upset, and blamed the hall for being negligent and hiring dishonest people. The management said that the hall had an impeccable record. Nothing had ever been stolen, and their employees were all honest. They suggested that Zvi might have left the phone in his car or at home. He checked both but to no avail. As the week went by, he became more upset, and threatened to report the incident to the proper authorities.

I heard the whole story from Zvi the following week as we were riding home from work together.

"You certainly seem pretty calm about the whole thing now," I commented to Zvi. "I guess time cures most everything. And I see you replaced your phone," I said, noticing one on the dashboard.

Zvi looked at me and smiled. "There's more to the story."

"Okay, I'm listening."

"I hadn't worn my coat since the night of the convention," Zvi continued. "Yesterday it started to drizzle, so I took my coat to work. As I walked towards my office, I felt something banging against my knee. It started raining harder. I put my hand in my pocket, where I found a hole, and walked faster.

"The flash of lightning in the sky must have lit up something in my brain, and all of a sudden I realized that the knocking at my knee was the phone. It must have slipped through the hole in my pocket into the lining of my coat," Zvi finished sheepishly.

Miriam and her son Moshe Chaim were shopping in a large supermarket. They were casually walking up and down the aisles, as Miriam checked out the sale items. I'm low on softener, was the last thing she remembered thinking before she felt the powerful blow to her calves. "Wounded in action near the soap detergents," the headlines would read, was her first thought. As she held on to the shelf for balance, her second thought was, Who was so careless with her cart?

From the corner of her not-so-steady eye, she vaguely saw the form of a child behind her. Now she was even angrier. Why do mothers allow their children to maneuver difficult-to-control shopping carts when they are obviously too young to hold on to them properly? Her next thought was, Okay, the kid hit me. It was surely not intentional. But where's an apology? How come no one is calling out, "Oh, I'm so sorry"? If the child doesn't understand any better, how about the mother, who must be somewhere in the vicinity?

Within seconds, though, Miriam was already more in control of herself and was judging the mother favorably. She reasoned that the mother must be so embarrassed that she was probably just standing there dumbfounded at her son's clumsiness. Miriam just knew that when she turned around to meet this mother face to face, she was going to see one contrite, penitent shopper. So Miriam turned around, full of magnanimity. And who was standing there, holding the offending shopping cart? None other than her own Moshe Chaim.

We are all asked to be master detectives, searching not for culprits, but for *zechuyos*. If one clue doesn't lead to the answer, we tirelessly follow another until we know, not "whodunit" but "why he dunit" — and why we should judge him favorably.

14
Why Don't People Speak Up?

J ust because there's a mitzvah to judge favorably, may people do things that look suspicious, objectionable, or improper, relying on the fact that others have an obligation to judge them favorably? May one say to oneself, "As long as *I* know I'm doing the right thing, why do I have to be concerned with what others think?"

The Torah answers: "You shall be clean before Hashem and Israel."[1] It is not enough that *we* know we are blameless — we have an obligation not to arouse suspicion in others. Although in Heaven we may be "clean," acting in a way that causes others to suspect us of wrongdoing is in itself a transgression.[2]

The Torah's warning not to arouse suspicion in others applies specifically to those times when a transgression is suspected, e.g., stealing, lying or damaging property. There are other instances when although what we are doing is not objectively wrong, people might disapprove. Here there is no violation of the admonition to "be clean." Nonetheless, it is preferable (a *midah tovah*) whenever possible and appropriate to avoid behavior that is offensive to others. As it says in *Mishlei* (3:4), we should want to "find favor and good understanding in the eyes of Hashem and man."[3]

While it is certainly preferable to avoid situations where we will be under suspicion, there will be occasions where we cannot avoid giving the impression that we are doing something undesirable. In such instances, we can clear ourselves by speaking up. By explaining and clarifying, we can absolve ourselves of culpability. Peace and good will are restored, and again we are "clean."

If people would only explain themselves, there would be less need for others to judge them favorably!

However, while people *should* explain themselves, the fact is, they often don't. And because they don't, we assume they have nothing to say in their own behalf. The Chofetz Chaim teaches us that this is an incorrect assumption with this example:

Reuven is yelling at Shimon. He is accusing Shimon of a serious offense, and Shimon is not defending himself. The onlookers intuitively feel that if Shimon were innocent, he would speak up. His silence is viewed as a tacit confession. Still, explains the Chofetz Chaim, we cannot accept a person's silence in the face of criticism as conclusive evidence that he is guilty. Furthermore, even if we know him to be the type of person who usually would speak up in his own defense, yet this time doesn't, his silence is still not proof of his guilt.

Why *would* a person choose to remain silent even when he's innocent? The Chofetz Chaim answers this question with two valuable insights into human nature:

People have a tendency to feel that if someone is willing to accuse another to his face, especially in front of others, it's a sure sign that the accusation is legitimate; otherwise he wouldn't have the audacity to do so publicly. Knowing this, the accused, though innocent, might size up the situation and decide that it's futile to speak up. He senses that any denial on his part will be doubted.

Secondly, he may decide that it's just not worthwhile to get involved in a noisy quarrel.[4]

Let us look at some other reasons why people might not excuse themselves or might consider it inappropriate to explain.

People choose not to defend themselves even when they know their behavior raises eyebrows and elicits scowls . . .

BECAUSE . . .

I work as a secretary in a small office. Over the years, I have been given an increasing amount of responsibility and I know my boss, Mr. Green, counts on me. So when he gave me a project with a two-week deadline, I gave it my best. On Tuesday, the day before the deadline, my boss left early. I was sitting at my desk, working feverishly to finish, not even stopping for a cup of coffee, when I realized that I needed to clarify a major point before I could continue. Although I don't like to bother Mr. Green at home, this was one of the occasions when I knew he would want me to pick up the phone.

I dialed and Mr. Green answered.

"I'm trying to finish this up, but I ran into a problem. Do you have a minute?"

"No, I really don't."

"Mr. Green, you know they're coming for this tomorrow. I just need a few minutes of your time."

He hardly responded. As a matter of fact, he didn't even seem to be listening. I tried again.

"Mr. Green," I continued, *"without your input, I'm not sure I'll be able to work through some of this information. It'll just take a few minutes."*

"Sorry," I heard him say. *"I can't."*

Hey, I thought, this is for you, remember?

"Try to figure it out," he said. And the next second he was no longer on the line.

I did the best I could . . . and went home fuming.

The next morning, still annoyed, I left for work. I had plenty to say to my boss when I got there.

As I approached the office, I heard a lot of noise. When I opened the door, there seemed to be some kind of a celebration. The secretaries were all sitting around, cakes and drinks on the table, and on the wall there was a big sign: Mazel Tov! It took another minute for me to find out that my boss, Mr. Green, had just become a father. The night before, his wife had given birth to a baby boy.

Why didn't Mr. Green speak up? One possibility is that at the moment his secretary called, his mind was elsewhere. He was so nervous about this long-awaited event that he couldn't focus on office problems at that moment. Or maybe he and his wife were waiting for the doctor to get back to them and he wanted to hang up quickly.

Another possibility is that he *chose* not to tell. Perhaps to him, the information was personal. In any discussion of what is considered private or personal, there will be differing opinions. What to one person is *not* open for discussion, may be the everyday conversation of another. Other people might have been more forthcoming. Maybe you feel you would have been too. Everybody has a different understanding of what he wants to share with others — and when.

Do you remember the story about the lady with failing eyesight?* Because she kept her condition secret and her friends were unaware of the situation, many misunderstandings and hurt feelings occurred. Do you agree with her decision to keep this information to herself? Perhaps yes, perhaps not.

We weigh the disadvantage of looking bad against the need for privacy, then we make our decision as to which consideration outweighs the other. We know we'd look better if we spoke up, but sometimes we choose to remain silent because OF PER-SONAL OR PRIVATE REASONS.

---

* See "Judging the Whole Person"

OR BECAUSE . . .

*L*ast week, I almost didn't leave the house. I canceled all my appointments, didn't attend any functions, and only went out when absolutely necessary. One of my front teeth had been knocked out in an accident, and the dentist told me it would take a week to replace it.

I had walked out of the dentist's office feeling uncomfortable and hoping I wouldn't meet anybody I knew. As I came out of the building on my way to the parking lot, who did I see coming towards me but my friend Ilse Fine. She flashed a big smile and waved. I quickly turned and crossed the street. I don't know what she thought, but I knew there would be no way to avoid a conversation, and I was too embarrassed to face her.

*T*he wedding was lovely. It was the first time in a long while that the family had been together. Everybody was walking around having a good time, but I stayed glued to my seat. Family and friends kept coming over to me and saying, "Rose, what's the matter with you tonight? You okay? Come on and get up and socialize." I just smiled.

No one knew that underneath the table I was hiding two unmatched shoes that had somehow found their way onto my feet in my rush to arrive — and were only discovered under the bright lights of the hall.

I knew people were wondering why I wasn't getting up, but what could I say? Nothing — because *I WAS TOO EMBARRASSED.*

OR BECAUSE . . .

*M*y daughter Shiffie came home from school and announced that the teacher said all the girls needed white blouses for the play they were putting on. "Uh-oh," I moaned, "where will I find a white blouse now?"

I went through closets, searched and found, washed and ironed — and Shiffie had her white blouse.

The next day Shiffie came home from school with this information: "The teacher says it's not a good white blouse."

Oh, who has time for this? I thought. White is white. What could be good or bad about a white blouse? Why is this teacher being so difficult?

Somehow I found another white blouse, but was I annoyed.

The day of the play, mothers arrived with smiles on their faces and big expectations. The girls were delighted, whispering excitedly about the surprise for their mothers that they had been holding on to for weeks.

"Now you'll see, Mommy," whispered Shiffie, who couldn't help but run over to me for a minute. "Now you'll see." And she ran back to her place.

The curtain rose, the play began, and soon we were all oohing and ah-ing as the ultra-violet lights shone on our daughters, reflecting a dramatic and colorful scene as the girls moved on stage.

When the play was over, Shiffie ran over. "See, Mommy? See why we needed a different white blouse?" But I still did not understand, until I overheard the teacher explaining to a mother who seemed to have been as confused as I: "Under the lights, some white materials have rich purple tones, and some white materials appear as dull grayish-beige. I worked so hard with the girls to prepare this surprise for the mothers. A big part of their fun and excitement was keeping the secret. I hoped you'd be patient and understanding without my having to explain and give it away."

The teacher felt that even if it was a bit of a bother to get the right kind of white blouse, it was well worth the effort. She reasoned that soon all would be clear and the mothers themselves would be so pleased that any inconvenience would be forgiven.

Think back to those times when you wanted to surprise someone or someone wanted to surprise you. Did you feel all the confusion and misunderstanding was worth it?

The point of judging favorably is not necessarily to bring us to agree with the decisions of others, rather, it is to try to focus on the fact that they may have had good intentions and even our benefit in mind.

*D*ay camp was over. The boys were sitting around the table eating supper. I heard them talking about what a crazy camp this was. The Director made them turn off all the lights because there was no money to pay the electric bill; they were to recycle the paper cups because there was no money; and the bus could not come to the entrance, but stopped in the parking lot because it cost extra to have it drive up to the building. I told them that maybe the camp was working on a deficit rather than a profit. My husband is a teacher in the learning program, so I asked him what was going on.

"How come the camp is being run so poorly?"

My husband gave me this funny look and quietly told me, so the kids shouldn't hear, "They're breaking out Color War!"

I had a good laugh, and I didn't say anything to the boys except that they should be dan l'kaf zechus.

The next evening when they came home, I said, "Nu, what happened today?"

They answered with bright smiles, "Ma, did you know? Did you know there was gonna be a Color War?"

I just smiled and thought to myself, I sure did, but . . . *I DIDN'T WANT TO SPOIL THE SURPRISE.*

OR BECAUSE . . .

I had switched to a new dentist and had an appointment for 11:30 Thursday morning. I arrived at 11:25 and asked a woman sitting in the waiting room what time her appointment was for. She said 11:00 so I realized the dentist was already running half an hour late.

I went over to the receptionist to let her know I had arrived. She checked the scheduled appointments but seemed to have difficulty finding my name. What an inefficient office they run, I thought. She went in to speak with the dentist, then came out saying, "Everything is okay. It'll just be a few more minutes."

Soon a woman in a blue dress walked in and I asked her what time her appointment was. When she said "11:30," I thought: This dentist really tries to pack them in — two patients both scheduled for 11:30! I hope waiting in this office isn't always going to be like this.

After I announced that I, too, had an 11:30 appointment, the lady in blue seemed undecided about what to do, and finally said she could do an errand and would return soon. A short time later I was called in, treated by the dentist, and was soon on my way home.

Later in the day, my husband and I were talking when suddenly he interjected, "Hey, I think it's my mother's birthday today. What's today's date?"

I went to look at the calendar. My eyes widened and my jaw fell.

"What's the matter?" my husband asked.

I told him what had happened at the dentist's office that morning, adding, "My appointment is for next Thursday at 11:30!"

The dentist's office tried to be accommodating, even though the mistake wasn't theirs. Since they were able to handle the situation, they didn't think it was important to point out that it was the patient's mistake. They didn't speak up because THEY DIDN'T WANT TO EMBARRASS HER.

OR BECAUSE . . .

"For five weeks we've been asking him when they're going to bring the new computers, and he keeps pushing us off."

"I think we should give him an ultimatum or he'll keep stalling."

Aaron Zucker, manager of the department, was sitting in his office. He knew he had a problem. His staff had been pestering him for over a month about upgrading the computers. He realized they couldn't understand his reluctance to go ahead since the purchase had already been approved. But he knew what they couldn't know — inside knowledge about a forthcoming merger which he couldn't tell them because HE WAS NOT AT LIBERTY TO REVEAL THIS INFORMATION.

OR BECAUSE . . .

"**M**rs. Goldstein called me up to ask me if I would be able to sit at the door and sell tickets for next week's benefit concert. I knew she needed a "yes." It's a worthwhile cause and selling would be fun too. Even so, I had to refuse. Mrs. Goldstein kept pressing me, but all I could say was that I was very sorry. I think she was waiting for an excuse, but I didn't offer one. I felt my explanation wouldn't satisfy her, especially since she's one of the main organizers and feels everybody should do all they can for this important community project."

We *do* have reasons that justify our actions, but we may hesitate to offer them. Even though it's right for us, we realize it won't necessarily sit well with others.

Even when we feel we have a legitimate explanation, we might not offer it because WE FEEL OTHERS WON'T ACCEPT OUR EXCUSES OR OUR PRIORITIES.

OR BECAUSE . . .

One party to a dispute may hurl verbal abuse and condemnation, while the other side remains quiet. This may occur in an argument between family members, a disagreement between parents and school, a dispute between business associates, or a quarrel between neighbors. People aware of the differences assume: If they (the reticent side) had anything to say for themselves they would speak up! Based on what we learned from the Chofetz Chaim at the beginning of this chapter, we should rethink this assumption, not allowing silence to confuse us into suspicion. Even though a person knows his reticence may be taken as a sign of guilt, he opts for silence because HE'S NOT WILLING TO PAY THE PRICE THAT AN OPEN BATTLE WILL COST HIM, and sometimes, because HE CANNOT COMPETE WITH THE POWER AND IN-FLUENCE OF THE OTHER SIDE.

When a divorce is in process, or even after the settlement, one side may be blackening the name and reputation of the other, while the second side remains quiet. It is important to keep in mind that silence is not a proof of guilt. Their silence may not be a result of having nothing to say, but because OF A DECISION NOT TO STOOP TO SUCH TACTICS.

OR BECAUSE . . .

I needed a new watch and decided to buy it from my neighbor Abe Baum, who has a small jewelry store. The next day after work I drove over. After a long day, I'm really exhausted, but my schedule is full and there was no other time. Abe was helpful and in no time I found exactly what I was looking for. I was eager to pay and get home. But when I asked Abe for the price, he told me he'd be with me in a minute — he just wanted to finish up with another customer.

I really wanted to get home, so I walked over and asked him how much I owed for the watch. He smiled and said he'd be with me in a few more minutes, and continued with the customer. What's the big deal? I almost said out loud. Tell me the price and let's just finish this up. Instead I said, "I'll give you a check if you don't have time to take cash, okay?

"Okay, Abe?" I said more emphatically and impatiently. I didn't hear an "Okay, a check is fine," as I had hoped to hear, but I saw the other man was finished and Abe was taking his check. Hey, wasn't I here first?

The man left, and Abe turned to me. "Sorry, Moish. I'd like to give you a twenty-percent discount — but I didn't want to say it in front of the other customer."

Often we would like to speak up but can't because IT'S THE WRONG TIME TO GIVE AN EXPLANATION:

- we're in the middle of something important and we can't take the time to explain;

- it's too long to go into, and saying part is worse than saying nothing;
- we're on our way out the door;
- other people are around.

We have been discussing some of the many reasons why people choose not to speak up — even when they know they look bad, and even when they have a reasonable excuse to clear themselves of suspicion.

In addition there are times when we might look bad and we would want to speak up, but we can't . . .

BECAUSE . . .

- I would have liked to have said something, but I walked in late.
- Before I had a chance to explain, the elevator door closed.
- You asked me to make that call, but you forgot to leave me the number. I would have liked to at least leave you a note explaining, but my ride was waiting and . . . THERE WAS NO TIME.

OR BECAUSE . . .

We enjoyed my in-law's recent visit. But one incident almost ruined it all.

It was the morning of my in-laws' return trip. I left early for shul; my father-in-law was coming later. We planned to meet after shul to say our final farewells.

"Good-bye, Dad, and have a safe trip," I said. My father-in-law just nodded. "Thank you for coming to visit us, we really enjoyed seeing you," I continued. All my father-in-law did was shake his head. Perplexed, I tried again. "And thank you so much for the gifts you brought us." He mumbled something barely audible under his breath. Why isn't he answering *me? I wondered. What could I have done to cause such a re-action, and on the day he's leaving! Doesn't he want to part on good terms? My ride was honking, so I couldn't stay around to find out the answer.*

Calm down, I thought as I closed the car door; everything was just fine the whole time. Maybe he hadn't finished dav-ening? Maybe he's too emotional to say anything and can't talk? Maybe he developed laryngitis? (You're pretty funny for eight o'clock in the morning, I said to myself. But I wasn't laughing.)

I heard the rest of the story from my wife when I came home that evening. Her father had come home from shul looking a little green. Everyone was rushing around pre-paring for the departure, but my wife, taking one look at his face, quickly sat her father down for a cup of tea. Once he felt a little better, he got up to finish packing. As he was walking to the door, he turned to her and said, almost as an afterthought, "By the way, please apologize to David for me. He was saying good-bye to me, and it was all I could do to keep from practically falling on my face. I woke up this morning feeling miserable. I must have caught that virus you and Mommy had last week. I know David was in a big rush so he probably didn't even notice, but apologize anyway."

How many times have you felt too tired to answer, too ill to smile? Not only aren't you up to a big speech, but sometimes it's hard to get out even a few words.

Sometimes we can't excuse ourselves because WE ARE SIMPLY NOT UP TO EXPLAINING.

OR BECAUSE . . .

Chavie taught algebra in high school. Chaviva worked in a bank. But they had a lot in common. They were both a year out of school and they were twins. Identical twins? Identical enough to be mistaken for each other time and time again.

That's exactly what was happening on that Tuesday morning when Mr. Feldman, the principal of the high school where Chavie taught, walked into the bank where Chaviva worked.

Here's how he tells the story:

"There she was, sitting at the desk figuring out some statement, when she probably should have been teaching algebra in one of my classrooms!" he began. "And to think I believed her those times she called in 'sick.' They probably just needed her in the bank.

"I wonder what kind of arrangements she's made, I thought to myself as I waited on line. She sure is a smart girl to juggle two jobs, but not smart enough not to get caught. I can imagine the look on her face when she sees me now.

"But Chavie surprised me. When I greeted her with a "Good morning, Miss Schwartz," she didn't even bat an eyelash. She just looked up at me with a faint smile, her eyes devoid of any sign of recognition. She probably doesn't know where to put herself — caught red-handed. I needed to speak to the manager, but there was a long line. At least, I thought to myself, she might want to ingratiate herself by giving me a little 'pull.' But, oh no, Miss Schwartz just asked me to sit and wait for the manager — at the end of the line!

"A half hour passed. I was sitting there with a lot of time on my hands to consider how to handle this when I got back to school.

"Finally, the bank manager opened his door and called out, 'Chaviva,' and who should come running but Miss Schwartz.

"It was then that I got the first inkling of what was later substantiated: the algebra teacher wasn't doing anything wrong at all! I was the one who had made the mistake — and had come up with the incorrect answer."

Twins can attest to these types of misunderstandings. Since they can't go around wearing name tags, they have to rely on the fact that there is a mitzvah to judge others favorably.

I was on my way to shul erev Shabbos, just before sunset. As I turned the corner, I saw a car pull into a driveway. A man jumped out and dashed for the door. It was Leib Siegel, the shul's caterer.

It's not that I don't understand. I do understand. Don't you think it's hard for me too? The scene is only too familiar. Friday afternoon. Just one more call — one more client — one more sale. Then you miss the train, or the traffic is so heavy that you slide into home base moments before Shabbos, jump into the shower, throw on your clothes and race to shul. That's what business can do to a person, unless you care enough about Shabbos to set limits.

I'm not saying he was desecrating Shabbos. But is that the way to bring in Shabbos? If he's willing to take the chance and cut it so close for an extra buck, wouldn't he be as likely to compromise on kashrus if it were a matter of losing money? I started to think of all the simchos I ate at that he had catered.

I felt this was information that the shul board of directors should have. Let them decide what to do. It was with these thoughts that I walked into shul.

After Ma'ariv, a crowd started gathering around Tuvia Leifer, who was talking a mile a minute. I walked over, and from the bits of information I picked up, I understood that right before Shabbos there had been an emergency in the house next to the Leifers. A child was choking. They called Hatzoloh and in minutes help arrived. Tuvia had been there, and now, to the approval of his audience (me included) he was describing how our own Leib Siegel had performed so heroically.

As the rest of us prepare leisurely for Shabbos, Leib Siegel and others like him are called upon to leave their families and their preparations in order to save a life. They are part of that dedicated team of Hatzoloh workers who are on call 24 hours a day, 7 days a week, some in ambulances, some in private cars, all without fanfare and without signs.

I had an acquaintance, a girl named Aidel, who always chewed gum. Whenever you would see her — at a store, in the street, at home — she'd always be chewing. Not only that, but always with her mouth wide open. Let's not elaborate on *some of the thoughts that had passed through my mind and probably the minds of plenty of others concerning Aidel's "aidelkeit."*

Many years later, I happened to be speaking to Aidel, and in passing she mentioned that she had a severe allergy that she had been trying unsuccessfully to treat for years. Her doctor had told her that it was very important for her to breathe out of her mouth. He advised her to chew gum vigorously — that way she'd have her mouth open most of the time.

This story is brought as an example of any of the many physical conditions which cause people to act in ways that might be described as questionable, if not worse! These conditions are often not up for discussion — and there's no way we're ever going to know what's really going on.

*A*s we walked through the airport I was feeling more like a heel with every step. Although everyone was rushing, more than a few people gave us a look. It wasn't hard to imagine what they were thinking. I myself was embarrassed — it didn't look very good.

Here I was, walking along like I didn't have a care in the world, while my wife, juggling the baby and the diaper bag, was pushing the cart with all our luggage. As we emerged from the baggage area, a hundred eyes were staring at us. I noticed people holding up signs, and I wanted to hold up one of my own:

"MY DOCTOR SAID NO STRAINING OR LIFTING FOR SIX WEEKS."

Does that mean that every time you see a person not offering assistance, when it seems to you he should, you should assume he is post-operative? Obviously not. We hope you've found other possibilities to consider in the pages of this book.

There are so many situations in life that either preclude or do not lend themselves to an explanation. In order to "be clean" in these situations, we'd have to be constantly explaining, but WE CAN'T GO AROUND WEARING A SIGN.

OR BECAUSE . . .

It was two in the afternoon, and I was exhausted, having hardly slept the night before. I couldn't wait to fall into bed. The grocery delivery I had been waiting for had just come and I finally crawled under the covers. Then the doorbell rang. I continued lying in bed, just hoping that whoever it was would forget about the whole thing and go away. But they didn't, and they rang again. Everybody knows that two to four o'clock is resting time. How come this person didn't?

I put on my robe and went to the door. "Who is it?" I asked tensely. I heard a voice saying something about "salesman." "Sorry," I said between clenched teeth. "I can't open the door." From the other side of the door I heard, "It's important."

I thought to myself, There's nothing more important between two and four than sleeping. I heard the salesman saying something else, but I was too annoyed and too tired to listen. On the way back to my room, I heard the bell ring again and I was really beside myself. Just go away! I tried to lie down again, but I couldn't fall asleep, so I decided to get up and finish the lunch dishes.

On the way to the kitchen I passed the front door and saw something scribbled on a piece of paper that had been stuck under the door, halfway in and halfway out. I picked it up, and read:

"Sorry. I just wanted to let you know that your keys are in the door."

We're not always speaking from behind a closed door. More often, we're trying to explain face to face — but it can sure feel like there is a door coming between us. We're trying to explain, but the person we're speaking to doesn't seem to be listening.

The reverse might also be possible: When we feel ourselves wanting to say, "Well, why didn't you just *say* so?" we should first consider that MAYBE HE HAS BEEN SPEAKING UP, BUT WE WEREN'T LISTENING.

*A*s we were driving down the street last week, we found ourselves stuck behind a bus that had stopped to pick up passengers. As we sat in the car waiting, a car behind us started honking at us impatiently.

"This is ridiculous," my husband said. "He doesn't expect me to pass a bus, does he?" But the man in the car kept honking and motioning. My husband was getting more and more upset at the second driver's aggressive manner. "It's such a narrow street — even if I wanted to, there's no room to pass a bus." The impatient driver kept edging closer and closer, gesturing and honking incessantly, until he was almost alongside our car. Then he opened the window and shouted, "Mister, you have a tool on the roof of your car."

"Oh, no!" exclaimed my husband, slapping his forehead. "I must have forgotten to put it back when I changed the tire yesterday."

And then we watched as the "impatient driver" quickly rolled up his window and eased back into the lane.

Why don't people speak up? Sometimes they do. They *are* explaining their behavior, but we're not getting the message. WE'RE LISTENING — BUT WE DON'T UNDERSTAND WHAT THEY'RE TRYING TO SAY.

Sometimes we don't speak up. Sometimes we can't speak up. And sometimes we are not aware that our behavior looks amiss. We would speak up . . . if we realized that we should.

---

*M*r. Abrams and his son Avi were guests of Mr. Berger, Avi's father-in-law. That Shabbos morning, Isaac Berger was happy to be able to introduce his mechutan to his friends at shul. Of course, Mr. Abrams and his son sat next to Mr. Berger, who was a very prominent member of the shul and had seats right near the front.

Krias HaTorah was almost over, and it was time for the Rabbi to speak. For Mr. Abrams, this was going to be one of *the highlights of the Shabbos, since the Rabbi was known to be a very gifted speaker.*

As maftir was ending, Mr. Berger suddenly noticed that his mechutan and his son-in-law had picked themselves up and moved over to the other side of the shul. His surprise turned to anger, especially when his friend sitting behind him tapped him on the shoulder and asked jokingly, "Hey, Isaac — what happened to your mechutan? Is he mad at you?"*

Embarrassed and annoyed, Mr. Berger thought, I don't know if he's mad at me, but I'm sure mad at him.

Mr. Abrams and his son were captivated by the Rabbi's speech, but Mr. Berger didn't enjoy a word. After shul, he made his way to the door, and Mr. Abrams and his son quickly followed after him.

"Gut Shabbos," beamed Mr. Abrams to Mr. Berger as they walked out together. Mr. Berger was silent. Mr. Abrams kept up a steady stream of comments. As they walked home, Mr. Berger was still so distracted and annoyed that he almost missed hearing his mechutan say, "It was a good thing that I remembered at the last minute to change my seat. I'm deaf in one ear so I had to move over to the other side of the shul to be able to hear the derashah from my good ear."

And it's a good thing I kept my mouth shut, thought Mr. Berger, as he smiled back at his mechutan.

Sometimes we act on the spur of the moment with no time to think how our behavior might be viewed. But even when there is time, we wouldn't imagine that anyone would interpret our actions in a negative way — especially when *we* know we're not doing anything wrong.

O*n her way home from work, Mrs. Ross remembered at the last minute the three tubs of cheese she needed to make a cheesecake.*

That afternoon, as they were mixing the batter, she asked

---

*This is a transgression of *rechilus* (relating information that can potentially cause ill-will) and *ona'as devarim* (causing pain with words). It is compounded in severity by the fact that it was said in shul.

her daughter Yehudis to taste it. Yehudis tasted and wrinkled her nose. "Oh, Mommy — you put in salt instead of sugar!" Mrs. Ross laughed, realizing that it wasn't sweet enough for her daughter's sweet tooth, so she added more sugar.

Yehudis tried again, but from her face, her mother could see that there was no improvement.

Maybe more vanilla? She decided to taste it herself. It was awful — the cheese was simply spoiled.

But she had just bought the cheese that morning! The store she shopped in lets customers return spoiled cheese. So she sent her daughter back with the remaining one and half containers.

The next day, Mrs. Ross went to pick up several items she needed from the grocery.

As she was checking out, the storekeeper commented, "Mrs. Ross, I hope you don't mind my asking, but is it necessary to eat one and a half containers of spoiled cheese before you return the rest?"

Mrs. Ross explained and they both had a good laugh.

The next day, when Mrs. Ross was retelling the story, her neighbor interrupted excitedly. "That's the answer! I'm so glad you told me this story. Two weeks ago I was out shopping and I heard them complaining in the store about a lady who returned a container of cheese half eaten, claiming it was spoiled. I was thinking to myself, couldn't she tell after the first bite? Why did she have to finish half a container?"

OR BECAUSE . . .

Was there a time when you were waiting for information and didn't get it? Or found out someone close to you knew information that was important to you and never told you? If you would ask them: "How come you never told me Ella Farber opened a store?" They might answer with a shrug: "I didn't know you knew her."

Sometimes we make an assumption that it is unnecessary to speak up. We think to ourselves: I didn't realize I should say something because:

- I was *sure* you knew the reason I was acting that way.
- I assumed you knew that information.
- I figured you'd find out anyway and I didn't realize you wanted to be told before everyone else.
- I didn't think it was my place to tell you.
- I didn't think the information was meaningful to you.

We don't speak up because WE DON'T REALIZE WE SHOULD.

In the previous stories we have given a sampling of reasons why people under suspicion do not speak up to clear themselves. We found that people may choose not to speak up, can't speak up, or may not even be aware that they should, and yet can still be deserving of *zechus*.

⬤ Now let us consider a different case: Even though you hear him talking, he still didn't really speak up.

In this case, the person under suspicion *does* explain himself. He does defend his actions, but you think his excuse is a poor one. You don't accept his reasoning. You just "don't buy it." You feel, "Look, I heard him out, but he didn't clear himself. He said his piece, but he still looks guilty. His explanation only confirms for me that he really doesn't have anything to say for himself."

Although you *think* he spoke up, it might be that he really didn't say what he *could* have said to clear himself. Even though he gave a reason, there may be another reason — the real reason — that can't be told.

I hired a babysitter, the daughter of a good friend. As the days went by I noticed she was speaking to the children in a way I don't approve of — using language I didn't like — and I felt she was too impatient with the children. I mentioned it to her a few times, yet she continued. I felt I had to look for somebody else, but I knew if her parents were to hear the real reason for my letting her go, they'd be hurt and suffer not a small amount of shame. Fortunately, at that point, the babysitter raised her fee. I really didn't want to pay the extra money, and attributed my decision to that.

Her parents were annoyed. They felt that I could afford it and couldn't understand why I was making a big deal about such a small amount.

The given reason may not be as good as the real one, and certainly doesn't make us look as good as the real reason would. But, as in this story, we're willing to use it to spare someone else's feelings.

If you are dissatisfied with an excuse given you, and therefore the person remains "uncleared," there is a chance that you only heard the given reason and not the real one.

We have looked at situations where people did not speak up to defend themselves, or chose not to defend themselves as well as they could. Our suspicions seemed justified, and yet, as the stories presented here illustrate, judging favorably would have brought more understanding, good will, and peace into the lives of all the people involved.

✍ Now we are going to look at a case where it would seem that judging favorably surely could not apply. Remember this story?

---

*M*rs. Beck arrived promptly for her scheduled x-rays — four in all. She sat in the waiting room until her name was announced. After the x-rays were taken, she was told she could wait outside until she was called. When the technician finally called her over, though, it was not to hand her the x-rays, but to apologize. She was sorry, she hadn't put her in the right position and now she would have to repeat two of them.

Mrs. Beck felt her muscles tense. Because of this technician's incompetence I have to be re-x-rayed!

The technician took her back into the room, and prepared her once more for the repeats. Already annoyed, Mrs. Beck was fit to be tied when the technician clumsily pushed her up against the screen.

Again, she asked her to wait outside until called.

The technician finally opened the door and came over to Mrs. Beck. She told her to come back in a week for the results. Mrs. Beck was surprised. "I always get them on the spot," she said.

"No, I'm sorry. You must come back," was the reply.

This is too much: incompetence, such clumsiness in taking the x-rays, changing the rules so arbitrarily and making it so difficult.

She left before she said something she might regret.

A week later Mrs. Beck returned to pick up her x-rays and bring them over to her doctor.

"Here you have the best hospital in the city," she blurted out as soon as she sat down on the chair in his office. "The most modern equipment. How could they hire such an unqualified technician?" and she told him what had happened. *

When she finished, the doctor leaned back in his chair and began slowly. "That technician has been with us for 20 years. Not only is she the best around, but she is also a very compassionate human being." He paused for a minute and then continued, "She pushed you up against the screen because this machine gives a more accurate reading if the person being x-rayed is right up against it."

As Mrs. Beck sat there dumbfounded, she heard the doctor add, "She looked at the first x-rays and saw something worrisome. She showed them to the radiologist, who told her to repeat them. She didn't return them immediately, because she wanted the top man to check them.

"Because she didn't want to worry you, she made it seem as if it was her fault."

Mrs. Beck certainly had no doubt that the technician was incompetent. The evidence looked conclusive. In fact, the technician actually accepted the blame.

---

*Discussing someone's shortcomings or misbehavior is permissible for a constructive purpose, i.e. in order to protect ourselves or others. The Chofetz Chaim lists conditions which must be fulfilled in order for a statement to qualify as having a constructive purpose (*Sefer Chofetz Chaim* ch. 10).

Not only Mrs. Beck, but most of us, would feel that in such a situation there is no point in giving a person the benefit of the doubt. Where's the doubt? She admitted her guilt! It seems conclusive enough, and yet, as we see here, the person still may be guiltless.

Even when the evidence seems indisputable — even when a person actually admits his guilt — there may still be room to judge him favorably.

During our stay in this world, we manage to pack our hand luggage full of suspicions. What's more, we feel quite self-righteous and certainly justified in our condemnations.

In a mounting crescendo of certainty we insist:

- "Well, if he had something to say, why didn't he speak up? Isn't that a proof that he has nothing to say in his own defense?"

  And we continue:

- "Okay, he did speak up. But that flimsy excuse is proof that he has nothing to say for himself."

  And finally, we present our conclusive evidence to prove that in this case there simply is no room for the mitzvah of judging favorably:

- "But he actually said he did it!"

While people should explain themselves, the fact is, they often don't and frequently can't. We hope the above true stories have helped explain why.

15
Familiarity Without Contempt

F amiliarity, some claim, breeds contempt — but it doesn't have to. We should be busy cultivating other things besides disapproval and displeasure for those close to us.

True, the more frequent our contact with others, the more possibilities there are for misunderstanding and the more opportunities we have to become aware of shortcomings and weaknesses. Pirkei Avos exhorts us to "acquire a friend and judge him favorably." Although we should judge everyone favorably, we need an extra measure of *limud zechus* with "friends," meaning people who are especially close to us.

Which brings us to those closest to us, our family. Although some challenges and issues in the home are not easily solved, much minor friction can be prevented when we become skilled in judging favorably. Especially in the home, *limud zechus* is a useful tool to keep handy.

*A*s I was finishing my supper, I caught snatches of my wife's phone conversation with her sister Rachel. This is what I overheard:

"Kayla got the job? Fantastic!"

(pause)

"Kayla will be terrific at word processing. I'm so glad. It will be so good for her."

(pause)

"You realize, of course, she's not the best secretary."

That last forkful of chicken remained in mid-air. What's going on here? I frowned. Why would my wife ruin it for my sister Kayla? I knew Kayla had applied for a job in the office Rachel's husband manages. It sounded like Kayla had landed the job. Why would my wife comment so negatively on her secretarial skills?

When my wife got off the phone, she came into the kitchen. One look at my face told her something was bothering me. "What's the matter?"

There was no point in pussyfooting around, so I came right out with it. "Why would you speak that way about Kayla?"

"What way?" she asked. "What in the world do you mean?"

I didn't mind refreshing her memory. "Didn't I hear you say that Kayla isn't a good secretary? What do you know about her secretarial skills anyway?"

She looked puzzled. I heard her reviewing the conversation to herself: "It's a good job . . . word processing . . . so happy for her . . . it will be good for her . . .

"No," she insisted, "I never said a word about her not being a good secretary." Then I saw her face uncloud.

"I know what you must have heard me say." She glanced in the direction of our four-year-old daughter, Chayala, who had just walked past the kitchen door. "After Rachel told me all about the job, she said to me with a laugh, 'Do you know I called yesterday and left a message with Chayala? I suppose you didn't get it.'

"I answered her, 'Well, after all, she's not the best secretary.'"

Overheard telephone conversations are fertile ground for misunderstandings any time, but the emotions they evoke are probably stronger in the home. Within the family circle we are generally more involved with the people, both those speaking and those on the other end, and have more of a vested interest in the persons and events being discussed.

Overhearing one end of a telephone conversation is a perfect example of how problems arise when we don't hear the other half of the story.

> We were getting ready to leave after a two-day visit with my folks. I was dressing the baby, while my husband carried out the luggage and the car seat. I took another look around the room to see if we had forgotten anything, and then went downstairs to say good-bye to the family.
>
> As I opened the front door to leave, the heat hit me. What a scorcher. It was midday and the sun was beating down. I hurried to the car, anxious to get the baby inside, out of the strong sun. I pulled on the handle and bent to settle the baby, and then I saw that my husband had thrown in the car seat backwards. He could have spent the extra minute to put it in place and save me the trouble, I thought. What happened to his usual consideration?
>
> Just then my husband came out with the last bag. He saw me trying to adjust the seat with one hand and hurried over to help. "You can fry an egg in this sun," he commented as he put the seat in place. "I didn't want to put the baby into a hot seat," he added, as if reading my thoughts. "That's why I turned it around — so it wouldn't be facing the sun."

We have learned that the mitzvah of judging favorably is to interpret a person's actions in light of his usual behavior.* This is especially applicable in family situations where we witness behavior on a continual basis. If we see a person who is usually

---

* See Chapter One

considerate acting out of character, we are obligated to assume he has not veered from his usual path. If we are asked to find merit even when we're not familiar with a person, how much more should we do so when a person's usual record gives us every reason to believe that this disturbing behavior has an alternate explanation.

Another major aspect of family life is requests and favors.
"Do you have time to bring in my shoes for repairs?"
"Please write down all messages clearly."
"When the maid comes, could you remind her to polish the silver?"
"I'd like you to turn off the sprinkler now."

When we ask a favor of a family member, our expectation is that our request will be carried through, especially when they give us their word.
"Put them in the car, and I'll drop them off."
"No problem."
"I'll make sure to tell her."
"Okay. I'm going right out."

And then, when we see that they let us down, we step on the gas and travel down the road of disappointment at 90 m.p.h.:
"The shoes are still in the car!"
"I don't see one message written down."
"I was counting on you to tell her."
"Didn't you say you'd do it right away?"

We think they've let us down — until we hear them say:
"He said they're not worth repairing."
"Nobody called."
"There was no polish."
"I did. Somebody else must have turned it back on!"

When our mind goes in the direction of: "If you were more responsible," and/or "If you cared enough . . .," instead of zooming down a bumpy road of suspicion and blame, we can make a U-turn. Judging favorably means taking an alternate route and realizing there are other exits.

I *had an important envelope to deliver to a Mrs. Tucker, who lives close to where my sister Shayna works. Monday evening, I asked her if she would have time to deliver it when she went to the office the next day. Despite her tight schedule, she agreed.*

When Shayna came home after work, I was anxious to know if she had found the Tucker's house easily. She apologized and said that she hadn't had a minute to go over, but assured me that she'd fit it into her lunch break the next day.

Wednesday afternoon, Shayna got home before me. When I walked in, I saw the envelope on the table. Exasperated, I looked her straight in the eye and said, "I'm sure you had a very good reason for not bringing over that envelope today."

"I did," she said matter-of-factly. "Mrs. Tucker moved."

S *ince I am the photography buff in the family, my uncle gave me an expensive camera for my seventeenth birthday. A few weeks later, my brother Yussie, who's a year younger, wanted to try it out, so I lent it to him for the afternoon.*

The next day I was on my way out and went over to the drawer to get my camera — but it wasn't there.

I knew I shouldn't have trusted him! I thought angrily. I warned him to put it right back. That's the last time I'm giving him anything. I stomped out of the house without the camera.

I came home late that evening. Yussie was in the kitchen heating up some pizza in the microwave.

"Yussie, you know how many great shots I missed today because of you?"

"Huh?" grunted my brother.

"Where's my camera? Why didn't you put it back? You can forget about asking to borrow anything again."

"Take it easy. I did put it back."

"Then how come I don't see it?"

"Follow me." Yussie led the way up to our room. I walked over to the dresser, pulled open the drawer and showed him the empty box.

Yussie pointed to the shelf over the desk. And there it was.

"Why didn't you put it back where it belongs?"

"I thought that was where you wanted it. When you handed it to me, you took it down from that shelf."

Blame is a frequent visitor in the home. We air our suspicions quickly and freely, hurling accusations with force. That's because we are sure of our target. Yet often we find that we're aiming in the wrong direction.

"My keys were on the table. Who took them?"
"I saw you put them back in your bag."

"Why'd you return the sweater dirty?"
"You gave it to me with this stain."

"Look what a mess you made of my papers!"
"If I hadn't shut the window they'd be all over the room right now."

"Hey! I told you not to touch my bike."
"Dad told me to move it. It was blocking his way."

"Why did you burn the potatoes?!"
"You told me *you'd* shut them off."

"You said you'd wait for me outside."
"If I hadn't moved, we would have gotten a ticket."

"Why would you ask Grandma to sew your pants? You know she doesn't feel well."
"I didn't! She insisted."

Sound familiar? Take an average day and listen in to your own conversations. As you move through your day, notice how the tendency to blame often causes us to attack innocent people. By nature of their proximity and the amount of time we spend together, those closest to us get it the hardest.

As we journey through life together with our family members, blame and recrimination can create tension and friction. While serious accusations can cause major upsets, even the minor ones mentioned here make the road needlessly bumpy. Giving the benefit when there is a doubt makes the ride that much smoother.

And let us remember that judging favorably applies to our children as well . . .

My teenage son, Elie, is an amateur electrician. Even without any training he seems to have an innate talent in that direction. He's always looking for something to fix, and when we have an electrical problem in the house, he's right there to help me out.

However, I am not as enthusiastic as he. I'm always afraid of the danger, but he is so confident and so successful that it's hard for me to say no.

When the vacuum cleaner wouldn't start last week, I knew Elie would want to try his hand. I thought it looked like something for an expert, but he was sure he could fix it so I gave in. In no time at all he had it back together again and said that it was working fine. "Just a blockage that was easily fixed." Company was coming that evening and the rug needed to be vacuumed so I was thrilled that he had come to the rescue.

By the time I got to the rug, it was late afternoon. I plugged the vacuum cleaner into the socket and pressed the button, but it wouldn't start!

I knew it! Why did he insist when I told him it needed an expert? We should have just taken the machine to the repair shop! Our company will be coming soon. What am I going to do now?

One of the other children was watching my frustration. As soon as he realized the problem, he interceded. "Mommy, try another socket. Don't you remember? That one doesn't work!"

When I put the baby to sleep in the afternoon I usually put up a sign asking people not to knock loudly.

One afternoon when the baby was sleeping, I, too, managed to lie down for a nap. As I was resting, I heard knocking. Not average knocks, though, but hard, repetitive knocks which got louder and louder. I became concerned; it sounded urgent.

I opened the door, and there stood my little nephew Shia, a sweet smile on his face, holding a package from my sister who lives down the block. I looked at him in bewilderment. It's hard to be annoyed at such an angelic face, but still, I felt I had to say something. "Shia, don't you see the sign?" I pointed to it and read it out loud:

Please do not
knock loudly!

"I'm sorry," said my three-foot-tall nephew. "I only saw the bottom line."

Sunday morning, Mrs. Shor dived into pre-Pesach cleaning. Hoping to accomplish a lot that day, she decided to tackle a shelf loaded down with dozens of loose pictures and half-filled albums. Mrs. Shor did her best to place as many pictures as she could in the albums. Seeing that it was going to take more time than she had right then, she put the rest of the pictures neatly in a box. To ensure that the children wouldn't pull out pictures again, she reassigned the albums to a higher shelf and issued a stern warning to the little ones not to touch them without permission.

Later that day, as she passed by the dining room, she did a double-take. There was her eight-year-old Meir sitting with the albums and pictures spread out in front of him on the table. "I don't believe this," she moaned. "All my work down the drain. There's no hope, they just can't listen."

Meir opened his mouth to say something, but Mrs. Shor cut him off. "There is nothing to say! I warned you all not to touch those albums without my permission. Do you know how long I spent getting that organized?"

By this time Meir was close to tears. Just then, Mrs. Shor's oldest daughter walked into the room. "Mom, what's the matter? I thought you would be so pleased. Meir was bored, so I *gave him a half-empty album and the rest of the pictures to put in. He was so excited thinking how surprised and happy you'd be."*

Most parents and educators have found themselves accusing a child of doing something he never did. When the truth surfaces, it's hard to tell who feels worse. What can we do to smooth over that unjustified charge? The words of our Sages offer a perfect salve: "A person who wrongly suspects his friend of wrongdoing, should apologize and bless him."[1] This is sound advice for healing the hurt that can be created through false accusations.

Although this principle is applicable in all situations of unfounded accusation, it is particularly useful at home. A sincere apology coupled with a heartfelt *berachah* helps restore rapport and makes both the accuser and the accused feel better.

There is an added factor to take into consideration with a parent-child relationship that does not exist with most other relationships: our obligation to educate.

My niece was graduating from eighth grade. Mothers, grandmothers, aunts, cousins, and sisters slowly filled up the hall. Many more people came than were expected. Since there weren't enough seats for everyone, the young girls who had been sitting stood up to give their seats to the adults.

From where I sat I looked over and saw my daughter Atara sitting in a chair against the wall. Why doesn't she get up and offer the chair to one of the adults standing? I thought. I was surprised and embarrassed at her lack of consideration.

I tried to catch her eye, but she was too engrossed in all the activity going on to notice my signal, so I got up and walked over to her.

"Atara," I whispered quietly, "don't you think it would be nice to give someone your seat?"

"I only took it because I knew no one else could sit on it."

"Why not?" I asked suspiciously.

"It only has three legs."

Even though it turned out that Atara had done nothing wrong, it was certainly in place for her mother to say something. When we see negative behavior in our children we have a responsibility to act upon it. This raises the question: If we judge our children favorably, will it not deter action? Might we not mistakenly whitewash behavior that warrants correction?

As in other cases where inaction might involve a loss, judging children favorably does not preclude appropriate action or reproof — it precedes it. The advantage of judging favorably is that we act and speak with more deliberation and consideration.

Children, like adults, have their reasons. We don't have to agree with or accept their reasoning, but our willingness to understand what's going on in their minds, what's motivating them, will help us decide how to guide them. When we reserve the possibility that we might be missing information, or misunderstanding intentions, then our approach will be more positive and therefore more effective, and can only improve our role as educators. In this way, judging favorably enhances and does not detract from our educational efforts.

*O*ne morning at about 7:45, after the children had left for school, the phone rang. A man's voice on the other end said, "Good morning. Is this Aryeh's mother?"

"Yes."

"This is Sender Epstein from the day school. Is your husband in?"

"No."

"Do you know what time he will be back?"

"He should be home from shul any minute but he leaves for work right away."

"I'll try calling back, but in case I miss him, can you please give me his phone number at work? It is very important that I speak to him as soon as possible."

I gave him the number, but my stomach started doing somersaults. What "important matter" could it be? The children had recently received report cards. Could it have something to do with that? But Aryeh's grades had been good. And my son had also mentioned that he got along well with his teacher. In fact, the teacher had told us what a fine boy he was. What could have happened?

Ten minutes went by and the phone rang again.

"Hello, this is Epstein. Has your husband returned yet?"

"He should be here any minute. Is there something I can help you with?" I asked anxiously. There was a moment's silence.

"Do you know if your husband wrote a note to me stating that after checking your son's notebook, papers, and tests he feels that your son deserves a higher grade on his report card?"

"No, I don't know anything about it. But I don't think so."

"Well, I have such a note here in my hand, signed by your husband. I'd like to speak to him concerning other matters as well."

"I'll give him the message," I said weakly.

A few minutes later my husband returned. I asked him if he had written such a letter to Aryeh's teacher. He said that he had not. Then I became worried and asked, "Do you think that Aryeh wrote the note?"

My husband was much calmer than I. "I don't think so. It doesn't sound like something he would do. Let's not come to any conclusions until we speak to Aryeh and see the letter ourselves. We need to check this out."

"What needs to be checked? His teacher called us about him. He was holding a letter in his hands which was brought to school by our son, signed by you," my voice was getting louder and higher, "but you didn't write or sign such a paper!"

My husband was late for work and had to leave. My stomach was in complete knots thinking about how Aryeh could have written a letter and signed his father's name. Perhaps we should be spending more time with him. Maybe someone is having a bad influence on him. My whole morning was filled with such thoughts, and I felt sick.

At about 11:00, the phone rang once more. By now I was tempted not to answer, but I did. It was my husband calling from work.

"I thought I'd let you know that I just spoke to Aryeh's

teacher for about twenty minutes," he said. "I thanked him for phoning. Then he explained the situation to me. After listening, I mentioned to him that something seemed strange. The story he was telling didn't fit with our child. I asked him if he had the letter handy. He told me he had it right there in front of him."

My husband then told me how the rest of the conversation went:

" 'R' Epstein, would you please read me the entire letter?'

" 'Yes,' he said, and began reading:

" 'Dear R' Epstein,

" 'I am writing this note concerning my son Aryeh Stern —'

" 'Excuse me, did you say 'Aryeh Stern?' I'm Aryeh STEIN's father.'

"There was a moment's silence.

" 'I can't believe I made such a mistake. Of all the parents to call! Your son is one of the best boys in the class. Please excuse me.' "

Listening to my husband's words I felt the tension of the morning disappearing. I even managed a little smile as my husband repeated R' Epstein's final words of apology: " 'I must have mistakenly taken the wrong number from the class list.' "

Judging favorably means zeroing in on the strengths of people and the advantages in situations and not focusing on the negative, i.e. looking at life with a "good eye."[2] In a discussion of *limud zechus* of children, this surely should be brought to the fore.

We all need and want to be seen in a good light. We instinctively shrink from people who concentrate on our faults. Children, no less than we, are anxious to be seen in a good light! They look to their parents to note and reflect back to them the best that is theirs. When we allow that light to reach them, then they, like all growing things, blossom.

As the home expands and new people join the family, the mitzvah of judging favorably helps keep the family friendly.

*M*y parents-in-law came to town to visit us, as well as my sister-in-law Michal and her family. We live near each other, but since Michal has a larger home, they stayed there. The day they arrived I went over with some homemade potato knishes. We had a lovely time and planned to get together the following day.

The next day, my mother-in-law and I spent the afternoon shopping. I guess I must have been waiting for a compliment, but none was forthcoming. I assumed that she just didn't like what I had sent, so she chose not to say anything. I was hurt that nothing at all was mentioned, not even a thank you for my efforts.

Later that evening, the phone rang. It was my mother-in-law. "How thoughtful of you to send over those delicious knishes," I heard her saying. "Michal prepared so much food that we only just now tasted what you sent. They were so delicious I had to call right away to let you know how much everybody enjoyed them."

I remember an incident that involved just a few words, but caused us untold distress. Last summer, our oldest daughter, Yaella, married Avrum Goodstein. Seven months later, a week before Pesach, our second daughter, Mindy, became engaged. You can well imagine that it was a hard time to invite people to a vort (engagement party). We cut things to a minimum and went ahead making plans. We sat down with a pen and paper and divided up the jobs. One person was assigned to call the caterer, two other people worked on drawing up the list of people to invite, I was to go with Mindy to find a dress, etc. After fifteen minutes, I felt relieved to see that we had a good division of labor.

The evening came. Somehow we had made it. As people started coming, I suddenly realized that I had forgotten to invite the Goodsteins! That was unpardonable. How could I forget the mechutanim? What would they think when they'd hear we made a simchah and didn't invite them?

Just then, who do I see walking into the room but the Goodsteins. I was very relieved. Someone more level-headed *than I had remembered to invite them. I noticed my daughter talking to a friend on the other side of the table and called over to her: "Who invited the Goodsteins?" She just smiled. I realized she had saved me the embarrassment.*

It was a wonderful evening. The children made a lovely couple. Everyone was in good spirits except for my machateinesta, Mrs. Goodstein. She hardly greeted me and sat with a sour look on her face. Then she and her husband left without even saying good-bye. What could have been bothering her?

Mrs. Goodstein had misunderstood the meaning of that question — which had been spoken a bit too loudly.

We get letters from both my mother and my husband's mother. My mother writes only infrequently, and quickly dashes off a letter, short and to the point. My mother-in-law, on the other hand, writes regularly. She faithfully sends long letters, always responding to our questions, always full of compliments and nice words. The contrast is obvious.

One day my husband commented, "Why doesn't your mother write letters like my mother's?"

Comparing is unfair. Every person has his own style. Families have their own style too. In your family, it may be normal to comment appreciatively after each course in a meal; in your spouse's family, it may be accepted to comment after the whole meal has been served. One family plays up birthdays and anniversaries, while others let them slip by. In some families, the bowl of fruit is put on the table, offered once, and then guests are left to help themselves; others repeatedly encourage guests to accept refreshments. Some people need a personal invitation, while others don't mind at all being invited via another family member. There are people you can call up at the last minute and ask to come over; other people expect more notice. Most important is that neither side feels they're doing second best; for them, it's first choice.

Instead of comparing, and looking askance at unfamiliar

ways and mannerisms, it's better to try to understand that there's more than one way to do things.

In this chapter we took areas of conflict and misunderstanding which apply to interactions in general and spotlighted them in the family setting, concentrating on how misunderstandings flare up in the family circle.

In all families, much wisdom and proper guidance is needed to live together peacefully. Sometimes the answer is more communication; other times, to seek advice. Sometimes, the best choice is to look away; other times, to compromise; at times, to give in.

A prerequisite for all is to judge favorably.

Our Sages tell us that no matter what material advantage we have, if we lack peaceful relationships, especially with those closest to us, we won't be able to enjoy these blessings.[3] The purpose of judging favorably, as the *Sefer HaChinuch* explains, is to help people live together more harmoniously. Let us bring this mitzvah and *midah* into our lives, into our friendships, and especially into our closest relationships, looking to excuse rather than accuse, explain rather than complain, and keep the familiar friendly.

As long as we don't let ourselves or others suffer as a result of a favorable judgment, cause anyone a loss, teach incorrect behavior, or absolve ourselves from our educational responsibilities, judging family members favorably can only be a plus in the home.

Limud zechus is one of the most useful tools to have around the house. Keep it handy and reach out for it whenever negative thoughts need fixing.

16
Why Guess? Why Not Just Ask?

Why Guess? Why Not Just Ask?

I f judging favorably means imagining untold stories, why not ask and get the real story? Why should we have to be mind readers? What is wrong with asking, 'Why did you do that?' and getting an explanation straight from the source?

In my son's kindergarten there was a "good behavior" chart hanging prominently on the wall. Every time a child did something good, he received a sticker next to his name. I watched the chart day by day when I came to pick up my son and saw that he had only two stickers while other children had three, four, and five stickers. I thought to myself, Can't the teacher find anything good to say about my son? and wondered about the quality of her teaching methods.

After a week, I noticed that one or two children had nine to ten stickers while my son still had only two. I could not understand what was going on. At that point, my husband encouraged me to do the obvious: Ask the teacher.

The next morning, when I brought my son to kindergarten, I asked the teacher about the chart. She told me she hadn't used it for several weeks, and that's why my son had only two stickers. I said that I noticed that some children had almost a whole line of stickers. At that she laughed and said that several children (mine included) had gotten hold of the box of stickers and had generously given them out at random to their classmates!

This mother went to clarify a sticky issue. She was able to solve her problem and not remain with negative feelings.

In many cases, asking *is* in order. However, there are times when asking for an explanation may not be appropriate or advisable. A request for "clarification" will often be viewed by the person on the receiving end as a veiled accusation. Even a level-headed, calm request for an explanation runs this risk. When we approach a person, our intention may be to get a better understanding of what's going on, but the question alone, "Why did you do it?" is charged with condemnation and complaint, and can easily offend, alienate, and sour a relationship. People can feel indignant that anyone would even *consider* them capable of "that!" The fact that someone suspects them and may be harboring resentment itself generates resentment. It goes like this:

Step 1: We ask for an explanation.
Step 2: The other fellow gives his excuse.
Step 3: Now we're okay.
Step 4: But they might not be.

If we decide not to approach a person because of the risk that we may make things worse, then what should we do about the suspicions or ill will that still remains with us?

This is where judging favorably can help us. If we can think of a satisfying *zechus,* we never have to bring our problem to anyone's attention. By reflecting and considering, by working it out, we might be able to remove the suspicion from the other person without ever having to let him know that we suspected him in the first place!

If we aren't able to come up with anything helpful on our own, there still remains the option of getting help from someone else. Discussing it with another person can often help us see things from a different point of view.

A relative of ours was getting married. A few days before the wedding we still hadn't received an invitation. Finally it hit me that we weren't going to be invited.

True, we're on the West Coast and they're on the East, and we wouldn't be able to make the trip, but an invitation was certainly in order.

I was peeved, and shared my annoyance with a close friend who usually gives me sound advice. Could there be any reasonable explanation? That's what I wanted to know. We went over all the technical mishaps — the invitation got lost in the mail, or it arrived but was misplaced, unopened, somewhere in the house, etc. Then I was surprised when I heard her say: "Some people don't send invitations to people who they know are surely not coming." And when I asked why in the world not, she added: "So that it shouldn't seem like a request for a gift."

That was a new one for me.

Did you ever hear of that? Even if you have, you might not agree with this reasoning. Judging favorably means resisting the temptation to condemn when there is an alternate explanation that is reasonable, even if *you* wouldn't do it that way.

This friend offered an alternative explanation that made *everybody* come out looking good. Once the West Coast relative understood that the invitation might never have been sent out of consideration rather than neglect, then her East Coast relative looked better and she herself had her ego restored.

There is a storehouse of accumulated wisdom among our family and friends that is within our reach. Why not take advantage of it? These people are close enough to care about our problems, yet less involved and so more objective than we. If we are successful in having the other side of the story explained, it may negate the necessity of our having to say anything further.*

There will surely be times, though, when we are going to have to get something clarified; when we can't solve the problem on our own and others can't help us either. For example, there are ongoing situations that need correction; events in the past which require restitution; or behavior which according to the laws of rebuke** requires us to bring it to the person's attention. Such cases require direct discussion.

If we are going straight to the source, we might think there is no longer a necessity for judging favorably. This would be an error, because judging favorably is not only essential to clarification, it is an indispensable prerequisite.

Before we approach a person, it is important to put ourselves in the proper frame of mind. If we can attribute to him better intentions than appeared at first glance, it will help us remain calm and will also keep us from adopting a recriminating, condescending attitude. This frame of mind will help make the encounter a successful one.

If, in addition, we can manage to relay in our message that we realize there may be more than meets the eye, we will transform a potential "accusation" into a "clarification."

"You may have already taken care of this . . ."

"Perhaps you tried to get through and the line was busy . . ."

"Maybe you didn't have time, but . . ."

"It could be you were there and I missed you . . ."

"There may be something here I don't understand . . ."

"I might not have noticed this when I gave it to you . . ."

"Maybe I misunderstood . . ."

"I'm not clear about what happened; can we run through it again?"

*C*haya was collecting money from her classmates for an end-of-the-year gift for their teacher. Like many collec-

---

* See footnote page 132.
** See Rambam, *Hilchos Dei'os,* chapter 6.

tions, the money came in slowly and only after many reminders. Finally, everyone's share was in, except for Matty's. How many times can you ask a person? Chaya thought to herself. What was especially annoying to Chaya was that Matty was the one who had suggested collecting in the first place!

That evening, after she checked her lists again, Chaya called up Matty to let her know how she felt. Without too much of an introduction, she voiced her complaint. "You know what it means, Matty, to have to collect money from thirty girls? You were the one who said how important it was to buy a present and now you're the only one who didn't contribute! Where's your —"

" — I left it in your mailbox two days ago," interjected Matty tersely.

Chaya hadn't received the money. In her mind it followed that Matty never gave it. But if Chaya had left open the possibility that some information might be missing, she could have clarified without accusing.

By using the techniques of judging favorably, instead of giving the impression, "Aha! I caught you in a mistake," we can leave open the possibility that we're the ones who might be making the mistake (since this is often the case!). This can save both parties potential hurt and embarrassment.

Sometimes we can't ask for an explanation because it is neither appropriate, feasible, nor advisable. In those cases, judging favorably becomes a prime tool to rid ourselves of negative thoughts and feelings. Even when we do choose the direct approach, we should remember to adopt a positive frame of mind and the effective verbalization to remove the accusation from our query.

In both instances, judging favorably is an indispensable tool and a skillful technique for ensuring the successful interactions to which we aspire.

17
The Accused
Takes
The Stand

No matter how many stories we will hear or read, the "wow!" is always bigger when the story is our own. Listen to someone tell his own story — "You'll never believe it," he says enthusiastically. "In the end, I found the invitation two months later!" — and watch his eyes light up.

Although our own stories may be less dramatic than someone else's, the shock of having our own suspicions evaporate is jolting. Recognizing how mistaken we can be is an eye-opener. It wakes us up to the pitfalls of misjudging with an intensity that cannot be duplicated when hearing someone else's story. It is our own experiences that can make the big difference in appreciating the importance of judging favorably.

Of our own experiences, there are two types. The first is when we suspect others, only to discover, usually to our astonishment and often to our embarrassment, that our suspicions were unfounded.

While this type of story is convincing, there is a second kind of story which is even more powerful: when we are the one under suspicion.

I came out of the drugstore in a rush to get home, but I forgot exactly where I had left the car. Since it's not a common model (and it's been through ten years of car-pooling) I'm always able to find it eventually. This time, too, after some searching, I spotted it.

Somehow, the key didn't want to go into the lock. I began banging the car door, trying to open it. Suddenly, out of the corner of my eye, I noticed someone glaring at me. I tried to be more inconspicuous and stopped banging. I continued to fiddle with the key, but with no success.

And then it came to me, as I turned meekly to the owner who was now standing beside me. This was not my car!

I love shopping in malls. It's so convenient having all those shops together. My friend and I go almost every week.

On one of our trips I decided to take a blouse I had just bought so I could find a skirt to match it.

I was browsing with my friend in a shoe store, one of those that has aisles where you help yourself. We were standing in the corner of the store, and it must have been near an air-conditioning vent because I was very cold. I thought to myself, All I need is a chill, but it was summer and no one would think of carrying a sweater in such heat. So, necessity being the mother of invention — I didn't want to interrupt my friend who was in the middle of trying on a pair of pumps — it struck me that the blouse I had brought would serve my purpose well. I pulled it out of the bag, tag still attached, and threw it over my shoulders.

I realized that it wouldn't look too good walking around with a blouse still tagged.* So I quickly took the sleeve and

---

*See "Why Don't People Speak Up!" concerning our obligation not to arouse suspicion in others.

tugged at the tag, which was a bit reluctant to let go. At that moment, in that secluded part of the store, a salesman walked by, looked at me, gave me an all-knowing stare . . . and walked on.

This story may not convince you of the importance of judging favorably and not jumping to conclusions, but it certainly was an inspiration for this shopper.

The best way to become convinced about the importance of judging favorably is to be the one suspected. Being in a position where onlookers assume we are doing one thing, while we know something quite different is happening, teaches us how a person can look clearly guilty yet still be innocent, and how easy it is to draw wrong conclusions. We learn, hands on, what it means to be unfairly suspected.

At a time when we are the one being misjudged and we need other people's understanding, that is when we really begin to appreciate the value of the requirement to judge favorably.

This episode, which happened to me personally, taught me a lesson I shall never forget.

We were on vacation and I went into the local supermarket to pick up a few things we needed. My husband was waiting in the car, so I went up and down the aisles as fast as I could. I was wearing a sweater and felt a little warm, so I put my sweater in the cart, too. I checked my groceries through with the cashier, she bagged them, and then I put them back into the cart and wheeled the cart out to the parking lot where my husband was parked.

As we were putting the bags of groceries into the car, I picked up my sweater and there was a jar of coffee and a can of herring, worth about $10.00, in the cart. Apparently I had not noticed them under the sweater and had not put them on the counter to be checked out.

I walked back into the store and found the cashier. I held up the herring and the coffee and said, "I'm so very sorry. I found these under my sweater and I never paid for them."

While she was ringing up the items, the checkout girl

looked at me and smiled. *"You didn't see those two ladies behind you, did you, ma'am?"*

"Two ladies?"

"Yes, they were standing behind you, whispering and laughing about you. I didn't know what they were laughing about, but it sure makes sense now. They must have seen those things peeking out from under your sweater."

These women had already left the store and never saw me come back to pay for the forgotten items. I don't know who those women were, but they surely thought they were witnessing a crime with their own eyes. How humiliating to be mistaken for a thief.

Now if somebody comes and tells me a story, even if they say, "Of course it's true, I saw it with my own eyes," I know it still may not be the true story.

For those people who have complaints about contractors, I can offer plenty of excuses. This is not to say they are always in the right, but there are reasons why they might "never call back," or promise to come and then don't show up, or don't have the work finished when promised. As the wife of a former general contractor, let me tell you his side of the story.

People would call all day. When my husband would get home he'd have to be in touch with his suppliers and contractors, the architect, hired help, etc. By the time he got off the phone, the hour was too late to call people back. Or he was too exhausted (and that was when he'd finally sit down and eat his cold supper). I haven't even mentioned spending a few moments with the children or helping his wife.

Why hasn't he come to fix the thing he promised to fix ages ago? He's a contractor, which means his hired help does the work — whether it's the painting, plumbing, carpentry or electrical work. If they don't show up when they promise, then he's the one who looks bad. He's only as dependable as his sub-contracted laborers, and unfortunately, responsible and dependable workers are hard to come by (they can offer their own excuses).

Many times a job isn't finished on time as promised because the homeowner changed his mind several times in the middle of the job, or added extra items to what was originally agreed upon.

I'd also like to point out that people shouldn't leave complaints with the wife. It causes her a tremendous amount of stress to receive phone calls such as, "Tell your husband I'm annoyed . . ." or, "Just let your husband know how angry I am that . . ." The wife didn't do it, she can't fix it, and she can't defend her husband because she doesn't know the details of this particular situation.

When my husband first went into this business, I would get very upset when these gripes were unloaded on me. From the way people presented their complaints, it sounded like my husband hadn't acted responsibly. As time went on, I learned more about how this business works. It certainly sounded different when he'd tell me his side of the story.

And how grateful we are to people who understand us, especially when we are in a position where we know we look bad but can't defend ourselves.

*I*t had been a hectic Friday morning. My 1½- year-old son was acting his age and I just couldn't seem to get my daughter off to kindergarten. As the morning wore on, the chances increased that she, too, would get bored and join in "troublemaking." I began to wonder when I'd get started on my erev Shabbos preparations.

"No, Yossi!" I shouted in exasperation as he reached for a bottle of oil on the kitchen counter. Too late! No sooner had I finished cleaning up the mess than the telephone rang.

"Hello?"

"Hello, is your husband home?"

"No," I said shortly, still annoyed at little Yossi.

"I guess he won't be back until the afternoon?"

"That's right."

"Hmm . . ."

When was this caller going to finish already? Yossi was in the kitchen again and mischief was in the air.

"He won't be back at all this morning?"

I glanced nervously towards the kitchen in time to see Yossi reaching for a jar of jam on the counter, about to tip it into the sink.

"NO!" I screamed (at Yossi).

In my excitement, I slammed the receiver back down into its cradle. Fortunately, I managed to rescue the jam jar before it smashed into the sink. Once I'd recovered from this crisis, I began to moan over the phone call. That man must be thinking, Not only was she rude, but she even shouted and hung up on me!

When my husband got home, I poured out my tale of woe. Fortunately, he figured out who the caller must have been. I begged my husband to explain the whole story with my apologies. The next day, when my husband met the caller, he began to explain what had happened, but was interrupted immediately: "I realized right away that she must have been talking to a child."

Often we can't explain because we don't even know that someone is watching. We can only hope that people know about this mitzvah — and use it.

I used to work in an office in Jerusalem right near the main depot of the inter-city taxi service to Bnei Brak. One morning, my husband was going to Bnei Brak at the same time that I had to go to work, so I accompanied him to the taxi stand.

As he got into the taxi, he realized that he only had a big bill with which to pay the fare. He called to me and asked if I had small change. It was awkward to pour out my change in the middle of the street, so I got into the taxi and started to look through my bag. I handed some change to my husband, got out and continued on to work.

Later that morning, as I was sitting in the office typing, my boss walked in. He took one look at me and said in a surprised tone, "Are you back from Bnei Brak already?"

"Bnei Brak? No, I've been here all morning."

"I saw you going into a taxi with your husband this morning."

"You must have seen somebody else," I replied.

Suddenly I remembered getting into the taxi to hand my husband the money.

For my boss, the evidence was crystal clear. There I was on an ordinary morning when I should have been going to work, climbing into a taxi with my husband, obviously heading for Bnei Brak, a two-hour round-trip. I explained what had really happened and the incident was forgotten. But I learned a terrific lesson on the importance of judging favorably.

How many times have we found ourselves in a situation where an onlooker would be likely to draw the wrong conclusion? We are caught looking bad, and yet we know we have something to say in our defense. This should serve as a powerful persuader that the other fellow may have something to say for himself too.

Our own stories afford us an unusual opportunity. They give us a chance to stop and contemplate, to realize how many mistakes can be made in judgment. We shouldn't let them pass without capitalizing on them. It is our own personal experiences which can transform judging favorably into more than an intellectual exercise. For then our heart joins our mind, and we realize with our whole being how a person can appear to be very guilty, yet in truth be clear of the charges against him.

18

Working
It Out

"**B**efore hearing about judging favorably, I didn't know we had such a 'muscle.' But now that I've learned to flex it, I wonder how I functioned without it!" The woman who made this statement expressed the sentiments of many others.

It is exercise that gets muscles into shape. The more we exercise, the stronger our ability to judge favorably will become, and the easier it will be to meet some of the challenges life will present to us.

The following are exercises in judging favorably. Pictured here are situations typical of everyday life: telephone annoyances, bounced checks, friends and relatives slighting or disappointing us, favors refused, and dishonest sales practices. All were presented to various audiences for open discussion. Here's how they worked them out:

"Why isn't he returning my call?!"

1. He can't because . . .

- [ ] you only left your first name and he can't figure out who called
- [ ] he misplaced your number and can't find the phone book
- [ ] you never gave him your number, and you're not listed

2. He's tried calling many times, but can't get through because . . .

- [ ] your line(s) was continually busy
- [ ] you didn't respond to the call-waiting signal
- [ ] your phone was temporarily out of order
- [ ] the ringer was set too low for you to hear
- [ ] you shut the ringer to take a nap and forgot to turn it on
- [ ] the receiver wasn't replaced properly
- [ ] no one was answering the phone: you claim you were waiting the whole time, but you forgot about those few minutes when you stepped out

3. He wants to return your call but he didn't get to it yet because . . .

- [ ] it's an especially busy time for him:
  - "Until these reports are done, I'm putting everything on hold"
  - "I don't have a minute until registration is over"
- [ ] he knows the call will take more time than he has
- [ ] physically, he's not feeling up to it right now
- [ ] by the time he got to it, it was too late to call you
- [ ] it slipped his mind (do you think this is a lame excuse? Go back to chapter nine, "The Double Standard")
- [ ] he's still trying to get the information you are waiting for

4. He <u>did</u> return your call, but you didn't find out about it because . . .

☐ he didn't leave a message
  - a person who couldn't take a message answered: a non-English-speaking maid; a two-year-old child (the same one who didn't put the phone back on the hook)
  - the answering machine wasn't on, or was broken
☐ he left a message you never got
  - the person who answered couldn't find a pen and thought he would remember but didn't
  - they posted it, but you didn't see it
  - they put it on your desk, but it got lost in the clutter
  - he thought he reached your house, but in fact dialed the wrong number. Because the names happened to be the same, the message was taken anyway
  - the message on the machine got erased
  - he dialed the wrong number and left his message on somebody else's machine

I had come home late from carpool and when I got home I noticed that there was a message on my answering machine. I listened to the message as I was quickly putting a lunch together for my younger daughter whom I was about to take to play group. The message was from someone I didn't know who wanted my advice about something. I was in a hurry to get my daughter to her play group, so I planned to replay the message and write down her name and phone number when I returned home. However, by the time I got back, someone else had erased the message — and there was no way for me to retrieve it.

5. He would <u>rather not</u> return this call because . . .

☐ your phone call is putting him in a position he doesn't want to be in:

"I knew what you wanted and I felt I couldn't come through for you. I didn't want to have to say 'no.' I chose the lesser of two evils. By not calling back, I knew you'd be upset. But if I did call back, I felt it would be worse."

This may be a matter of style. Some people feel they owe an answer, no matter what it is. Other people shy away from having to give an answer that will disappoint or hurt. Refraining from giving an answer is their way of saying "no."

☐ he knows what you want, and he doesn't want to discuss it because:
- He was asked not to speak about it
- He's not *allowed* to speak about it

Not every *zechus* suggested here will satisfy everyone. What is a reasonable and likely excuse to one, may not be so to another. The goal is to come up with a *zechus* that makes sense and is satisfying to **you** and clears the person in **your** eyes. Some of the *zechuyos* suggested here only partially clear the "accused." This is a step in the right direction. Our goal is to do the best we can to make other people look as good as possible.

"Why didn't she return this urgent call when she said she would?"

You need a telephone number urgently. You call a friend who has the number. She says she'll look for it and call you right back . . . but it's fifteen minutes later and she still hasn't called. Why not?

☐ you may not have conveyed the urgency
☐ something / someone needed immediate attention: a worker just came and needed instructions, or a child needed care
☐ she got another call that she couldn't cut short
☐ someone else in her house needed the phone for an important call
☐ you didn't hang up your phone

☐ her mind went blank. She couldn't remember what she was in the middle of doing!

Why not just call back and find out what happened? By all means. These attempts at excusing are not in lieu of a repeat call. They are addressed to the thoughts we have while waiting, and will affect our tone when we make that call.

"Why Is She Making Me Wait While She Prattles?"

You go to visit a friend. She answers the door and invites you in. You ask her if she has a few minutes. She says yes, but adds that she's on the phone and asks if you can wait. You agree. You sit down and she goes back to the phone. She continues her conversation, but you, who are sitting there, hear that she is talking about trivial and inconsequential matters. *Can't she call back?* you wonder. You sit there, waiting, but not patiently. Ten minutes go by. You are restless and irritated. What *zechus* could you think of for this friend?

1. What is "trivial" and "inconsequential"? To you, her conversation may sound trivial, but to her it may be important. It might even be a business call, although it may not sound like one. For example, recipes can wait — unless you're writing a cookbook.
2. Maybe she can't hang up on this person.
   ☐ Perhaps she is speaking with someone who would be insulted if she interrupted the conversation
   ☐ This may be a "peace call" after a misunderstanding and can't be interrupted. It would add insult to injury for her to either cut the conversation short or even suggest she'd like to call back
   ☐ She may be speaking to an older or distinguished person and it would be disrespectful to ask to end the conversation

3. It may be a conversation with someone who is hard to reach.
4. The person on the other end just told her that she's been trying to reach *her* for days. Your friend can't hang up on her now when she finally got through.
5. Maybe it's a long distance call and she can't "just" call back.
6. Remember: *you* were the one who said you could wait! You have not given her an accurate message. She thinks you don't mind waiting.
7. The word "wait" is unclear. To one person, waiting means winding it up in a few sentences. To somebody else, it means finishing in a few minutes. To another, it means you have agreed to wait until she finishes what she has to say.
8. Some people have very casual, easy-going personalities. They wouldn't mind waiting and they assume you wouldn't either — especially since you *said* you wouldn't mind.
9. Take a minute to consider if you have ever done something similar. Have you ever asked anyone to wait while you gave your attention to something you realized they felt was trivial? Try to remember the excuse you had for yourself at that time and see if you can use it to help you better understand the present situation.
10. Instead of being annoyed, try to see the positive in the seemingly negative, the strength in the apparent weakness. What might first appear to be lack of consideration — *Why is she keeping me waiting?* — could be seen as social grace and a healthy measure of consideration for the person who had her attention first.

We certainly haven't covered all the annoyances that crop up in our daily use of the telephone, but we have touched on some. We hope that these will serve as an example of the direction in which we should move when a disturbing thought gnaws at us. Imagine a stop sign: "Danger! Negative Thoughts at Work!" Make the U-turn, and see how many excuses you can pit against the accusation.

"Could there be any reason other than dishonesty or irresponsibility for a check to bounce?"

Although the proper and responsible manner of banking is never to write a check unless we are sure that there are adequate funds in the account to cover the check, nevertheless, there may be reasons why a person's check bounced other than an attempt to evade payment.

For example:
1. He counted on an expected deposit from a third party that didn't come through yet.
2. He deposited a check from a third party in an amount to cover, but *that* amount bounced.
3. He had a long-standing agreement with the *former* supervisor never to bounce a check.
4. His wife had written a check on the same account which depleted the balance and he didn't know.
5. Someone embezzled funds from his account, and the fraud has not yet been discovered.
6. A physical illness incapacitated him and he was unable to get to the bank to make a deposit.
7. He tried to call you and warn you that the check wouldn't go through and to wait a bit, but couldn't get through.
8. He post-dated the check and forgot to make sure there were sufficient funds to cover it when it came due.

Some of these *zechuyos* only partially exonerate; what they do show, however, is that the guilty party was not totally irresponsible.

Perhaps it wasn't his fault at all. Maybe the fault lies with us . . .
☐ We deposited it before the date he told us
☐ We held on to the check too long, and by that time his funds were depleted

Or perhaps it was a bank error . . .

☐ He wasn't credited for his last deposit, or for the total amount of that deposit, because of a computer error

A check I received from a certain woman was returned from the bank. Since she was quite a respectable person, I was really surprised. Then I saw the check was stamped "Account Closed." I thought, Okay, that's the zechus. For whatever reason, she must have had to close that account. It's not as though she bounced her check because she didn't keep track of how much money she had in her account, or wrote checks on money she didn't have. My problem, though, was how to ask her what she wanted me to do with the check, i.e., how she wanted to handle the repayment. I certainly didn't want to embarrass her. When I had the opportunity I mentioned the check as delicately as I could, and right away she apologized.

"I am so sorry. I've been meaning to call you. Let me tell you what happened. I have two checking accounts, one I haven't used in a long time. That day I couldn't find the checks to my regular account so I wrote checks from the account that hasn't been used. It only took a few days for me to realize there was a problem — when people started calling and complaining about my bounced checks. So I called the bank and found out that the bank, on their own initiative, without letting me know, closed that account since it hadn't been used in such a long while. You don't know how much embarrassment this has caused me with the people I wrote checks to from that account!"

Although she is positive that the bank never notified her, it certainly is possible that she received a notification and forgot, or misplaced it, or it was sent and never arrived, or that she had forgotten to notify the bank of her change of address.

I wanted to be one hundred percent sure that I had enough money in my account to cover a check I wanted to write. Just to be absolutely certain there wouldn't be a problem, I

withdrew $5,000 from a savings account in another bank and deposited it in my checking account.

The following day I wrote out that check, assuming it would clear. A week later I got a letter in the mail notifying me that my check had bounced. Needless to say I was very annoyed and could not imagine what had gone wrong.

I called the bank to complain. After an investigation on their part and a little input from me, we put together the pieces of the puzzle. A little while before, the bank where I have my checking account switched branches and changed some of the account numbers. When I made the deposit, I still wasn't sure of my new account number, so I went to one of the tellers who checked the number and wrote it on the deposit slip. However, the well-meaning teller made a small error. My father has an account in that same bank. Instead of writing the number of Leib Fine (me), he wrote the number of Sol Fine (my father), which appeared underneath, and the $5000 was credited to his account. My father was $5000 ahead, and I was way behind.

After finally getting the whole story clear, I felt I had learned an important lesson. There could be a million reasons why a person's check might bounce and it might not be his fault at all!

"How could she not have told me!"

*M*y good friend went on a vacation and never said a word to me about her plans. We are so close and share so many things. I'm sitting here not knowing what to think. I know if I don't stop myself, I'll be furious.

Saying to ourselves, "Isn't this one of those situations where *dan l'kaf zechus* is called for?" helps us change direction. The question alone calms us down, puts us in a better mood, empowers us, and gives us control over our reactions to people and events.

Consider how this can be worked out:

- ☐ She thought she did tell you
- ☐ She tried to tell you (see above section about phones)
- ☐ She was sure you knew
- ☐ She knew if she told you, you'd feel obligated to offer to help (with the family, picking up the mail, watering the plants, etc.) and she didn't want to overburden you
- ☐ She knows you'd like to go too but can't, and she didn't want you to feel bad
- ☐ She couldn't tell you because her husband asked her not to
- ☐ If she told you, she'd have to tell someone else whom she couldn't tell so she decided not to tell *anyone*
- ☐ Last time she made a big announcement and it was embarrassing for her when the plans fell through
- ☐ It was a last minute decision
- ☐ She *did* tell you — and you forgot

"Why did she tell her and not me?"

My sister-in-law Estie just bought a new house. How did I find out about it? Not from Estie!

One day I was sitting with my friend, Mrs. Leifer, and I heard her saying, "So, Mirel, when is Estie moving in?" I wondered if she noticed how I almost choked on the coffee. Trying to keep a smile on my face and interest in my eyes, I listened to her describe the lovely corner house with the beautiful landscaping that my sister-in-law had just bought. I tried to be as vague as I could, not wanting her to know that this was the first time I was hearing about it.

Why did I have to hear that information from someone else?

When we get caught in a family intrigue, it's important to look for logical and reasonable excuses for the "betrayer," before the flame of anger blazes into a conflagration. Smother it by uncovering a likely explanation.

Perhaps:

☐ Estie told Mrs. Leifer during a chance meeting. She didn't realize that the news would get back to Mirel before she had a chance to tell her herself.

We know that all occasions and news in the family require a hierarchy of whom to tell first. For various reasons, it doesn't always work out that those we really want to know first are told in that order.

☐ Another possibility is that Estie never told Mrs. Leifer in the first place.

- Estie may have had to call Mrs. Leifer because she needed some information about the house before she could close the deal. Mrs. Leifer put two and two together, without ever having been told by anyone
- Mrs. Leifer heard it from the seller, or from the agent, but not from Estie
- No one told Mrs. Leifer; she *overheard* it

In fact, Estie hadn't told *anybody* because she really wasn't happy with the purchase. She had so many misgivings, she almost hoped the deal would fall through. This is a *zechus* which can apply for many different occasions and purchases. Although to others there may seem to be a reason for great joy and for sharing the news, there may be unknown doubts and misgivings which cause a reluctance to make announcements.

☐ It was an oversight. Estie herself would agree that she should have told Mirel. When she becomes aware of it, she will surely regret it. But she made a mistake!

☐ None of us have complete sensitivity and understanding of what's proper, considerate and polite in every situation. *She's* always good with thank-yous; *he's* on top of it when it comes to remembering birthdays and anniversaries; *they* always remember those who have to be invited; and so on. But most of us are not she, he and they in all circumstances.

☐ Another possibility is that it may be a matter of a different style of interacting. There are people who have a list in front of them and make sure everybody finds out news on the same day; there are others who give the news when an opportunity arises. The realization that this could be a personal style and not a deliberate slight can help us avoid potentially explosive family conflict.

☐ Mirel might want to consider whether anybody had ever felt insulted because *she* hadn't notified them first. If she can remember her behavior, which was devoid of an intention to hurt yet was misinterpreted, it might give her insight into her sister-in-law's behavior.

One day soon, Mirel is going to be speaking to Estie. Now is the time to prepare herself for that conversation. Taking from this list of *zechuyos* any that make sense to her, she's going to listen in a happier frame of mind when she hears Estie telling her the news.

"He really could have done that favor for me!"

We needed more shelf space in the den, so when I saw the do-it-yourself shelf unit on sale, I grabbed it. That evening I opened the box, took out the directions and rolled up my sleeves. Half an hour later, I still had the directions in my hand. The job was turning out to be more complicated than I thought.

Instead of wasting more time, I decided to go across the street to my neighbor, Dov Fuchs. Over the years he's shown me various projects he's put together around the house, so I was pretty sure he would be able to help me out. I rang his bell, and when he came to the door, I asked if he'd have a few minutes to come over and help me assemble the shelves.

"Sorry, Zev, I'd really like to help you," he said, "but my back has been out of commission."

> *I spent the rest of the evening fumbling around until I decided that I'd better take the unit back to the store.*
>
> *The next day, as I pulled out of the driveway, I saw Dov walking out his front door carrying a huge carton.*
>
> *It's not that I feel people can't refuse to do a favor, but how could he blame it on his back and then lug that big box?*

The greater our expectations and demands of others, the more hurdles will appear on our horizon. Even though we feel our demands are reasonable — the person we ask is usually capable of doing it, we don't feel it's a great imposition, and in addition, we've often done favors for him — we can be disappointed in the reaction we get. When the Torah warns us not to bear a grudge, it is referring specifically to those times when we've put forth a request and were refused. Our minds might remind us that we're not allowed to bear a grudge, but our hearts are often pounding in frustration and resentment. That's when *dan l'kaf zechus* can help us out. In the incident above, Zev understood that neighbors can't always come through. He had a different complaint: "If he's got a bad back, how come he can lug that big box?"

- ☐ "Huge" isn't necessarily heavy. The box could have been empty or filled with lightweight material.
- ☐ The request might have sounded like one of those "could you just" favors, but Dov knew it would take longer than that. While he wasn't up to an extended physical effort, carrying out the box was a short run.
- ☐ A person might overextend himself for a parent, a job, or to fulfill his own family obligations.
- ☐ Maybe there was another reason — the main reason — that he couldn't reveal, and his poor back was only a minor factor.
- ☐ Many physical conditions fluctuate — there are good days and worse days. Zev may have caught Dov on an off day.
- ☐ It looked as if it were Dov carrying out that box, but it wasn't.

"He's a crook!"

"*I've heard these stories about judging favorably, and as far as I'm concerned, most of these stories are in the category of gray, meaning, you can find a zechus if you try. But the story that I'm going to tell you is black and white,*" Mrs. M. stated emphatically. "*The other day, I asked my grocer to give me two kilos of bananas. When I got home and opened the bag, I saw that some of those bananas were inedible. When he was weighing them, he must have put all the nice yellow ones on top, and hidden the inedible ones underneath. This is clearly a case of dishonesty. You see,*" she concluded, "*there are some stories where there is no zechus . . .*"

Or is there?

What does Mrs. M. consider "inedible"? Two people are served soup. One says there's too much salt and the soup is inedible. Someone sitting beside her takes a spoonful, wrinkles her nose, and asks for the salt. It's the same soup.

We don't know what Mrs. M. means when she says the bananas were "inedible." She might not want to buy a banana unless it's perfectly yellow, but not everyone feels the same way. Some people prefer to buy them green and have them ripen at home; others like them speckled. Instead of assuming that the grocer gave her "inedible" bananas, Mrs. M. might want to consider the possibility that to someone else, those bananas would not only have been perfectly okay, but perhaps even preferable. It's not fair to call the grocer a thief because of personal preference.

The grocer may know that many of his customers prefer to buy a mix of bananas, one bunch riper than the other, so that they won't have all twenty bananas getting ripe at the same time. Realizing that the grocer might have thought he was doing her a favor will help Mrs. M. reconsider her negative opinion of him.

What if the "inedible" bananas were riper than speckled? What if they had turned brown? If that were the case, instead of jumping to the conclusion that the grocer was trying to sell her inferior merchandise, Mrs. M. can turn her thoughts in a more positive direction. Perhaps he didn't even charge her for those "inedible" bananas. Imagine if she had made a big commotion when all the fellow did was give her some free bananas!

The fact that Mrs. M. felt the bananas were "hidden" contributed to her suspicions. But just because they were underneath the others, why assume that he "hid" them? The grocer may feel, "That's hiding? I put them on the scale and weighed them. They weren't wrapped up in a package with a knot. If you didn't want them, you could have said something. Maybe you didn't notice, but don't call that hiding."

Although Mrs. M. seems to be upset about the bananas, her reaction may be exaggerated because of some other, unrelated issue. By asking herself, *Is it only the bananas or is something else bothering me?* Mrs. M. might find that her irritation with the grocer is lessened.

If this grocer is innocent of a deception, we can only gain by judging him favorably. And if he is guilty, we also don't lose out. Giving a favorable judgment is not whitewashing wrong actions. There can never be anything right with deliberately deceptive sales practices. For example, the Torah does not allow a seller to hide inferior merchandise underneath better merchandise in a way that people are fooled into thinking it's all the same quality. In addition, giving a favorable judgment does not stop us from making efforts to protect ourselves from a past loss or a possible future loss. A buyer can go back to the store with any merchandise he feels is defective, or in any way questionable, and should watch out in the future.

While there are cases of dishonesty, nonetheless there are many situations of supposed dishonesty which, if we would take the time to reconsider and/or clarify, we would discover are in fact not so. It is unfair and in fact prohibited to transform an innocent occurrence into a malicious act unless it has been proven to be one. It is *limud zechus* which forces us to consider the distinction.

Are you sometimes less than energetic? Then be lazy about deciding! Are you sometimes slow? Be slow to condemn!

If we can slow down our judgment of people, if we can say to ourselves, "I'm going to keep on collecting more information before I come to any conclusions," we can save ourselves a lot of anguish. No one is forcing us to condemn that person right now, before the hour's up. It's not a timed test in school. We can take as much time as we need to come to a favorable decision.

Remember: In judging favorably, coming up with the "real" and the "right" answer is not the goal. The purpose is to come up with something meaningful which *may* be the explanation. No matter what we come up with, the exercise is an achievement and a goal in itself.

The important thing is to persevere, and the Chofetz Chaim guarantees our success: "The pathways of *zechus* will never be closed to one who wants to judge favorably.[1]

19
The Clouds Part...

✐ . . . And there's the sun!

Sometimes we're in a big huff, or, worse still, consumed by stormy indignation. Then all of a sudden, the clouds part and there's the sun!

We had a broken radio/cassette recorder which had been lying around the house unused for about a year. Finally we decided to get it repaired. My husband brought it in. When it was ready a week later, he was busy, so he explained to me where the store was and I went to pick it up.

The shopkeeper searched for the tape recorder but didn't find it. "Sorry, lady," he said. "The technician who does repair work for me is behind on all his work. Unfortunately, his daughter is ill in the hospital and he can't work his regular hours."

I told the shopkeeper that I wished the daughter a speedy recovery and returned home. A week later, my husband retrieved the tape recorder and I began using it. I noticed, however, that the speed was slightly slow; lively music seemed a bit subdued, and slow songs came out funereal. After my husband listened carefully to some music played on the machine, he agreed that the speed was faulty. We decided to bring the tape recorder back to the repair shop.

I lugged the large, bulky machine into the shop and told the shopkeeper about the problem.

"Maybe the cassette you're listening to is an old one," he suggested.

I felt slightly annoyed and answered defensively that the cassette I had used to test the tape recorder was fairly new, and that in any case, we had tried the machine out with several cassettes.

The man took down another tape recorder and a couple of music tapes. He quickly compared its speed with ours, and told me that there was nothing wrong with our tape recorder.

I began to lose my patience, since my husband and I had both already listened carefully to various tapes before we had decided the tape recorder wasn't working properly. The shopkeeper seemed to be trying to avoid taking responsibility for a shoddy repair job.

"Anyway," the shopkeeper continued, "where is your receipt for the repair job, with the guarantee?"

"I don't know about any receipt. I'll ask my husband about it. Maybe you didn't give him one."

"I always give a receipt to every customer who brings a repair," he insisted.

I know my husband to be very careful about matters such as receipts and records, and if the shopkeeper had ever given him one, my husband would surely have supplied me with it. Armed with this confidence, I decided to give the shopkeeper a little speech on the subject of saying 'always.'

"Isn't it possible that there may have been five customers in the shop and that just this once you didn't manage to give a receipt?" I asked him. "And don't you remember me? I came in once for the machine and you told me that your technician's daughter was in the hospital and the work would be delayed. Anyway, this label stuck on the machine with our name and telephone number in red ink must be from your shop!"

"It's not my handwriting!" he had the audacity to answer. I shrugged my shoulders and went home in frustration, leaving the tape recorder in the shop. I could see that this was a job for my husband.

At home, I asked my husband if there had ever been a receipt. "Never," he responded. He then asked me which man had helped me in the shop. "Was it the short guy with round glasses and a mustache?"

"Yes, that's him," I said.

"I guess he doesn't recognize you. But when he sees me, it'll click," my husband assured me.

He left purposefully and went to the repair shop, heading straight for the short man with the round glasses and mustache.

"It's about our tape recorder," my husband began firmly.

"Yes?" asked the shopkeeper politely.

"It's the speed — it's slightly slower than normal," my husband continued, in a tone no less determined.

The shopkeeper looked up at him in surprise. "So bring it in then!"

"But my wife just brought it in!" my husband answered, mystified.

The shopkeeper checked all the machines on his repair shelf but could not come up with our tape recorder.

Then he asked my husband slowly, "Are you sure she brought it in here . . . and not to the shop three doors down?"

The look on my husband's face said it all.

He left the shop and went down the street to the other shop. He found the shopkeeper there — who was also short, wore glasses and had a mustache! — hunched over our tape recorder, a pile of cassettes in front of him, testing its speed.

"I'm here about that machine," my husband mumbled, not sure how to extricate himself in a dignified way from this fix.

"Maybe it is just a tiny drop slow," the man admitted.

"It's okay — maybe it's playing at the right speed after all. You can't be sure," my husband said quickly and edged out of the store, tape recorder in hand. "But thank you very much for looking into it. All the best, then."

My husband came home holding the tape recorder and said to me, "Sit down. I have something to tell you." As the story unfolded, my jaw dropped lower and lower.

Who would have thought that there were two repair shops only three doors away from each other with repairmen who looked so much alike!

As my husband and I, both still incredulous, talked about it, I realized that the shopkeeper I had been dealing with was really not that short, and that his glasses were really not that round. I had just felt swept along with the current of certitude that we were in the right!

It didn't take us long to conclude that it was only proper to go back and explain to the shopkeeper about our mistake. We certainly didn't want him to wrongly suspect his own techni-cian, who was completely innocent, of having made an error. We also felt we should offer to reimburse him for the time he spent checking over a machine which he had never repaired in the first place.

In these stories we are watching people see their suspicions dissolve in thin air, looking on as they experience the shock of finding out that they were wrong and the other fellow wasn't.

Discovering a person's *zechus* is like being in a dark room and suddenly having a light turned on.

My friend Faigie was invited by close friends, Ruchama and Akiva Lerner, to the bris of their first-born son. It was a lovely spring day. Putting a lightweight blanket over her own newborn, Faigie strolled leisurely, enjoying the fifteen-

minute walk to the home of Ruchama's parents.

As she entered, a roomful of happy faces greeted her. After mazel tovs were exchanged, the Lerners graciously guided their guests to their places at the carefully arranged tables. Faigie was happy to find herself among old friends. She parked the carriage in a quiet corner near the table so she could keep her eye on the sleeping infant. It felt wonderful to relax and meet people she hadn't seen in ages. She was in the middle of listening to a fascinating story when a lady approached her. "Why don't you take your baby over there?" she said, pointing to another table.

"Over there," Faigie said as she told me this story, "was the other side of the crowded room, not near anyone I knew, and was difficult to get to. I thought to myself, The baby's sleeping, not bothering anybody. And the carriage isn't in anybody's way.

"But what bothered me more than anything else," she went on, "was the lady's attitude. She sounded like the type who just didn't like babies around. I smiled and hoped she'd leave it at that.

"But the woman was insistent. 'This is not a place for a baby.'

"I didn't want to make a commotion in front of everyone, so I decided just to move with the baby. I had to weave through tables and squeeze past a pole till I got to the other side of the room — 'over there.'

"Sitting in my new seat, not near anyone I knew, do I have to tell you how I felt?" She didn't have to tell me.

I thought it was the end of the story, but one look at Faigie and I sensed there was more to come.

"With no one to talk to and nothing to do, I glanced back to where I had been sitting. And blinked.

"For the first time, I noticed the very large fan that was blowing strongly exactly on the spot where the carriage had been parked."

That "light" that is turned on is the newfound clarity that we experience. Here, Faigie discovered that the lady who "just didn't like babies" was not the person she had "typed" her to be. In fact, the exact opposite was true — she only had the well-being of a young mother's baby in mind.

We were making a party for fifty people and decided to buy all the pastries and bread from Katz's Bakery. I called up Information to get the number so I could place the order.

Two hours before our guests were due to arrive we went to the bakery to pick up the order. When we got there we were shocked to find out that nothing had been prepared! It was the end of the day and the store was almost empty. With a sinking feeling, we realized that other bakeries would also be just as empty at this hour.

The proprietors understood our predicament and wanted to help. They said they would call their other branches around the city to see which had rolls and cakes left, and if not, they would see if there was something in their freezers. Somehow they would try to get together what we needed.

We stood there while they made the calls, and within a short time we had what we needed. It was hard for us to fathom how such nice people could have been so irresponsible.

Don't think the story ended there. Here's the P.S.:

When we finally got home, there was a message that Kass's Bakery had called and wanted us to call back immediately. Although we were pressed for time, I returned the call.

"Why haven't you come to pick up your order?" the voice asked. "We're closing in a few minutes."

"Pick up our order?" I repeated. "There must be some mistake." And a mistake there was.

The operator had given us the number of Kass's bakery instead of Katz's.

Between the hustle and bustle, the stress and pressure of being a working mother, I relish the peace and quiet of a fifty-minute commute to and from New York City on our suburban train line. I board at an early station, when most of the rows of seats are still empty. There are three seats abreast and

I always take the window seat. The middle seat is usually left empty, as any incoming passenger usually chooses an aisle seat to get a bit more stretching space. Then both of us put our bags and other belongings in the middle.

One morning I was settled and comfortable in my usual spot when a woman got on and approached my row. She moved in next to me and left the aisle seat empty. I begrudgingly picked up my briefcase, pocketbook and other belongings from the middle seat, piled them up on my lap, wondering why she had to sit right next to me, rather than at the end.

Naturally, I couldn't say anything, but I could give her a hint. I opened up my newspaper a little more fully so she could see that it would be more spacious for her to move over. Well, she just continued sitting there, and turned herself a little more diagonally away from me. She took out a mirror, tubes of lipstick, cases of powder, eye shadow, mascara and a whole bag of sundry cosmetics, and began to apply her makeup very carefully, trying not to jut her elbow into me and my newspaper. Occasionally my belongings slipped onto the floor. Feeling hot and cramped, I was getting more fed up by the minute. I turned the pages of the newspaper one after the other, letting them flutter in her face, too annoyed to read what was on the page. Couldn't she just move over and make us both happy?

About fifteen minutes later we arrived at a busy station, and passengers poured into the train. A man approached our row. As he was about to sit down on the end seat, I heard my neighbor say to him, "Watch it, that seat's wet."

Contritely, I closed the paper and moved over to give my seat partner more room.

20
Never Too Young or Too Old

When I learned about the idea of people being like "Chapter Three" of a continuous story it fascinated me — and made a lot of sense. If we don't know what went on in the previous chapter, which more often than not is the case, how can we feel sure about our condemnations?

I found that the image helped me rein in thoughts that could otherwise gallop off with more freedom than I would care to give them.

I shared my enthusiasm with my family. I was hoping it would be useful for them too. I wasn't disappointed.

One Shabbos, I was walking with my eight-year-old daughter on our quiet street when an ambulance pulled up. The back door opened and out jumped one of our neighbors.

My daughter looked at me quizzically. "Mommy, he's not a doctor, is he?"

"Not that I know of, Rochy."

We continued to walk, as we watched our neighbor go into his house.

"He doesn't look sick, does he, Mommy?"

"He certainly doesn't," I answered.

"Right, Mommy," Rochy said thoughtfully, "you can take a person to the hospital on Shabbos if he's sick? But," she went on, obviously in a dilemma, "you can't ride back!"*

Rochy thought for a moment, then looked up at me and announced brightly, "You know what? That man is 'Chapter Three!'"

The children are listening and learning. And sometimes teaching us.

We were driving down a four-lane highway with the younger children when a car bellowing clouds of black exhaust fumes suddenly pulled in front of us. The adults in the car made a few comments: "He should have that fixed immediately!" "The nerve of someone driving like that nowadays!" "What a smell!" "They ought to give him a ticket!" The children asked questions about pollution and the ozone layer, and they got answers they could understand. After a moment's silence the small voice of our nine-year-old piped up excitedly: "Maybe it just happened to him now. Maybe he left the house and everything was okay and all of a sudden he sees this black smoke coming out of his car. Just think how he must feel! He's probably rushing to get it fixed right now!" Addressing no one in particular, the voice continued, "How would we feel if it happened to us?"

As parents, we are hoping — and praying — that we are making an imprint. And that's why stories like the following are heartening.

---

* There are times when a person might be allowed, according to halachah, to return home.

I piled the children into the car and went to pick up my daughter Tzippy, age six, from her dance class. It was a difficult ride home. Tzippy kept poking her older brother Yehoshua, age eight. When we got into the house, I tried to get dinner on the table as soon as possible. I knew that would quiet the children down.

Yehoshua came into the kitchen to complain about his sister Tzippy, who, he claimed, was the instigator of the fighting that had taken place in the car earlier which had still not come to a peaceful conclusion. In the midst of his complaining, he surprisingly switched gears, changed his tone and said, "Mommy, maybe something happened to Tzippy at her class that upset her."

Sure enough, a few minutes later Tzippy described to me how she had fallen in dance class and how embarrassed she had been. After some words of reassurance and some hugs and kisses, she felt much better. The supper that was warming up burned a little bit, but I didn't care. What a pleasure to watch children who can tune in to other people's feelings.

We all know it is important to establish proper patterns in childhood. In classes through the years, stories have elicited comments like:

"If only I had known about this forty years ago. It would have made such a difference in my life."

"I wish I could have been fed this with my baby food."

It is true that once we establish patterns it is hard to change them. But let us be inspired by the following story.

I teach "Jewish Thought" at a nursing home. Having been introduced to the concept of judging favorably, I decided to present it to the people there, and I see it is changing the quality of their lives.

One day as I walked through the door, a familiar face greeted me. It was Sarah, who had come to tell me her woes. Someone had stolen her wheelchair. She was using a different one, but the original was the one she had gotten used to, and she was terribly upset. I realized this was the perfect example for a class. They would all be able to identify with it since most of them were in wheelchairs.

I started out by giving an example of a distressing incident and asked everyone how they would feel if it happened to them. They expressed feelings such as anger and frustration. Then I told them about judging favorably and tried to get them to think of zechuyos. But they had trouble finding one. Then I decided to ask Sarah to tell her story about the wheelchair:

". . . and when I came out of the shower, it was gone. It was such a good one, somebody probably took it to sell," she concluded. Once again, I tried to get everyone to think of a zechus, trying to keep them on the track of positive thinking. With some coaxing, I got them started. "Maybe a worker took it to repair," one lady suggested. From the back row, we heard a voice say, "Someone probably thought it was hers and took it by mistake." They were getting warmed up. It encouraged other people to make comments like, "I once saw someone's visiting grandchild playing with a chair."

The director of the nursing home was sitting in on the class. When the residents had taken turns, the director announced to all of us, "Would you like to hear what really happened?" and of course, we were all anxious to hear what she had to say.

"While Sarah was taking her shower, one of the nurses had an asthma attack and couldn't breathe. We immediately called an ambulance and grabbed the first available wheelchair to take her down the elevator. We're short on help, so there hasn't been a chance to bring it up yet, but it's downstairs waiting for her."

Everyone, especially Sarah, was thrilled to hear what really happened (although we were sorry about the nurse's illness).

As we practice this skill more and more, I see how much happier the lives of the nursing home residents have become now that they are able to put judging favorably to use in everyday life.

Judging favorably can be used beneficially at every age and in all circumstances, by scholars and lay men,

by the poor and the rich,

when healthy or ailing,

with family and neighbors,

by both men and women, singles or marrieds, spouses or roommates;

with friends and adversaries, associates and competitors;

for landlords and tenants, hosts and guests, professionals and the unskilled;

by those in authority as well as those taking orders,

by they who give and those who get,

at reunions, receptions, dinners, weddings, luncheons;

when visiting or entertaining,

for those near and those far,

on the job, on vacation, on the road, or at home;

by experts in this art or those just beginning;

in every weather and in all seasons or at any time of the day . . .

21
The Other Side of The Story

🖎 This is the way it seemed:

My wife is a 'last-minute' person. It's especially trying on erev Shabbos because of the last-minute commotion. One week we sat down together and discussed how we could improve the situation. We went over the menu and decided what could be eliminated. Two salads were enough; we didn't need a third. Fresh fruit for dessert instead of cake. And this week, no potato kugel, because we already had enough side dishes. My wife seemed happy about our decisions. She also wanted a more relaxed Friday.

I came home Friday afternoon. The house looked clean. Everyone seemed relaxed. I walked into the kitchen, all ready to compliment my wife. She was standing near the stove and I see . . . she's frying the potato kugel we agreed she wasn't going to make.

❧ And this is the other side:

I'm a 'last-minute' person, so I was really happy when my husband told me he'd sit down with me and plan out a strategy for Fridays. Cleaning the house, setting the table — all the details. We'd get it all organized, particularly the cooking. I tend to overdo it and I need his input on what to eliminate. And you know what! It really helped — getting organized and eliminating the non-essentials.

By noon on Friday I was almost done when my neighbor's teenage daughter Shira came over. She said that her mother wasn't home and she wanted to help out by making a potato kugel. Could she have my recipe for that scrumptious kugel we fry on top of the stove every week? Shira wrote it out and went home eagerly. A half hour later, Shira knocked at the door, holding a bowl with the kugel batter. She wanted to know if it was the right consistency. It looked fine to me. She hesitated and I saw she wanted to say something. "Mrs. Stein," she said to me, "I really don't want to bother you, but I'm afraid that I won't be able to turn the kugel over without it flopping. Would you be able to come next door just to turn it over for me?"

"Sure," I answered. And then I thought, Her mother's not home; why should she have to fool around with hot oil? So I said, "Listen, Shira, you've never done this before. You know what, just give me the batter and I'll do it on my stove. Come back in about an hour and it'll be done." She thanked me and left and I poured her batter into my frying pan. As it sizzled, I went about my work. Then my husband walked in . . .

_T_hursday evening Shani heard a knock at her door. Her downstairs neighbor, Toby Goodman, was having guests, Shaya and Rena Shapiro. Could she borrow a playpen? Shani was happy to do the favor.

Then it was Shabbos afternoon, a warm and sunny day. The Goodmans and the Shapiros were resting. Baby Gila was on the porch in the playpen cooing peacefully. But soon the cooing became a whimper. A few minutes passed, and the whimper escalated to a wail. And after a while that wail turned into a howl which eventually awakened Rena. Oh, you poor dear, I just lay down for a minute, she mumbled as she jumped from her bed. I must have been more tired than I realized. How long was I sleeping? she wondered, as she rushed to the door. As she opened the door, her hand flew to her mouth to stifle a scream. To her horror, someone was throwing things down on her baby from the porch above. She bolted to the railing, leaned over, and in an angry voice called up: "Stop that right away!" She watched as the upstairs children scampered off. Rena calmed little Gila and then tried to calm herself. "Beyond belief," she shuddered, as she finished telling the story to the others later that day.

And this is the other side:

_S_unday morning, Toby Goodman returned the playpen to Shani. She thanked her neighbor and then added a bit caustically that she felt obligated to mention to Shani something about her children's behavior on Shabbos afternoon. She asked her, with obvious restraint, to explain to them that it is both unkind and unsafe (to say the least!) to throw things on a baby.

Shani thought back to Shabbos afternoon, replaying the scene. "You know, the baby was crying for a long time. We all felt so sorry for her but we didn't know what to do. We looked *down, and we saw the poor thing was sitting in the playpen, all alone, with no toys and nothing to do, screaming her head off. We waited. We saw no one was coming and assumed you were all resting. I sent down one of the kids to knock, but no one answered. So I told the children to take out our soft, cloth toys, and drop them down to the other side of the playpen so that they wouldn't hit the baby. We thought that if she were occupied, she might stop crying."*

Perhaps you're thinking, I would never do that! I would never throw down toys near a baby — I don't care if they *are* cloth.

You don't have to agree. But admit it: Could you ever have imagined that there was another side to such a story?

✍ This is the way it seemed:

*W*e *were in a pinch. Our school was running a bazaar that evening, and we were short of help. I called up Ilana, one of the mothers, and asked if she would have time to help. She said that she had hurt her foot that morning and the doctor said she would need three to four days off her feet.*

The next day I saw her in the bank. I felt like saying, "Ilana, you don't have to lie. You could have just said you can't help."

✍ And this is the other side:

I twisted *my foot again. This time it was a hard turn. The last time it happened, I just took it easy, and in a day or two I was back to myself. But this time I was worried that it was more serious. I hobbled over to my doctor and he gave me an encouraging report. Nothing serious, but it would take three to four days to heal.*

I got into bed, trying to look at the bright side. At least I'd have a chance to catch up on some reading and maybe even get some letters written. The phone was beside my bed and I let whoever called know that the doctor said I'd be out of commission for a few days.

I woke up the next morning and cautiously put my foot down. What a pleasant surprise! It hardly hurt. I had important errands to take care of that I had thought I would have to postpone. I was glad that the slight pain and almost indiscernible limp wouldn't deter me.

✍ Here's one side of the story:

*I*t was a special day for Zev and Penina Miller. Tonight their daughter Ahuva was getting married.

Ruthie Fried was on her way to the wedding. She and Penina had been high school friends and the friendship stuck.

It was a long ride and Ruthie had plenty of time to reminisce. Scenes from the past . . . Penina's first marriage, the accident, the shivah, the rivers of tears they shed together. And then Penina met Zev Miller. It was a happy marriage from the start. And the best part was the wonderful relationship Penina had developed with Zev's children — their children. The Millers had become a close loving family.

That's why Ruthie was so surprised as the wedding festivities began and she watched her friend Penina standing quietly off to the side, not really participating in this joyous occasion the way Ruthie had expected she would.

Well, there's a long night ahead of us and plenty of time to join in, thought Ruthie, trying to be positive.

But as the evening progressed, Ruthie was both shocked and disappointed to see Penina remain off to the side. Aren't you happy for Ahuva? Don't you want to share in this simchah? she mumbled under her breath. If there's friction in the house, this is not the time to show it. Swallow your differences at least for tonight!

Of course, it wasn't appropriate for Ruthie to say anything, even though they were good friends.

Months passed. Ruthie and Penina were spending the afternoon together. Penina took out Ahuva's wedding album.

As they looked through the pictures, Ruthie found the opening to ask what had been bothering her for a long time.

"Penina, I hope you don't mind my asking, but look at the album. You're not in most of the pictures. Why didn't you get into the middle and dance?"

Penina leaned forward in her chair. Her hand rested on Ruthie's arm as she explained gently, "Ruthie! Did you think of Ahuva's grandmother, how she must have felt at this simchah? With the real mother of the kallah, her daughter, not there? Don't you think that making my presence obvious would only add pain to a situation that was already painful?"

✃ And this is another side:

Tears of joy mingled with sadness filled my eyes as I watched my best friend's daughter Shevi being escorted down the aisle. It was hard to believe that only two years had gone by since Devorah had passed away . . . and now here was Shevi, suddenly grown up and looking just like her. If only Devorah could be here now, I wished unreasonably. As I looked around, I knew I was not alone. Although the crowd was smiling, there were quite a few of us on the bride's side with teary, red-rimmed eyes.

One person, though, seemed to be unaffected by any memories. With an easy smile and a hug for everyone, Shevi's stepmother Leah (Devorah's replacement, I couldn't help thinking) was the center of the festivities and seemed to be enjoying every minute. She was busy welcoming guests, directing the photographer — making sure she was in plenty of pictures, too — and acting the perfect mother of the bride.

Couldn't she have a little more sensitivity? I wondered bitterly. Doesn't she realize how much we all miss Devorah? Why doesn't she let Devorah's family take over? That would certainly be more appropriate. Although I never said a word to anyone, I was left with a hurt that my friend's memory had been dishonored.

The family friendship was too precious to forgo, and over a period of time I stopped seeing Leah as "Devorah's replacement" and instead grew to appreciate her for herself. Gradually, our relationship developed to the point where I felt she was a real friend.

One day we were talking and out of the blue she told me how hard she had worked to make Shevi's wedding a happy occasion. "I knew the memory of the tragedy would loom large that evening and I decided that come what may, Shevi deserved to have the happiest moment in her life as unspoiled and as joyous as it should be for every bride. My husband and I talked it over and we made up our minds that we would do everything we could to give her a wedding every girl dreams of. It wasn't easy for me — but I wanted her to have those precious moments."

A Final Thought

When a Jew is in need, he knows there is one address, one door to knock at. We turn to our Creator not only for our many physical and material requests, but we are also taught to beseech Him for spiritual success.

The ability to see people and situations in a positive light is a blessing and should be a spiritual goal for all of us. Our desire to be counted amongst those who resist the temptation to be faultfinders, is expressed in this excerpt from an inspiring supplication found on the walls of Kever Rachel (Rachel's Tomb):

ד׳ אֱלֹקַי וֵאלֹקֵי אֲבוֹתַי שֶׁתַּעַזְרֵנִי בְּרַחֲמֶיךָ וְתַדְרִיכֵנִי וְתוֹרֵנִי דֶּרֶךְ יְשָׁרָה בְּאוֹפֶן שֶׁאֶזְכֶּה לִשְׁמֹר עַצְמִי בְּרַחֲמֶיךָ שֶׁלֹּא אֶכָּשֵׁל בְּשׁוּם דָּבָר שֶׁאֵינוֹ טוֹב וְלֹא אוֹמַר דָּבָר שֶׁלֹּא כִּרְצוֹנֶךָ וּתְזַכֵּנִי לִהְיוֹת טוֹב לַכֹּל תָּמִיד וְלֹא אַחֲקֹר לְעוֹלָם אַחַר חוֹבוֹת בְּנֵי אָדָם חַס וְשָׁלוֹם.

רַק אַדְּרַבָּה, אֶזְכֶּה לְהִשְׁתַּדֵּל תָּמִיד בְּכָל כֹּחַ וָעֹז וּגְבוּרָה לִמְצֹא תָּמִיד זְכוּת וְטוֹב בְּכָל אֶחָד וְאֶחָד מִבְּנֵי יִשְׂרָאֵל עַמְּךָ הַקָּדוֹשׁ אֲפִילוּ בַּפְּחוּתִים שֶׁבַּפְּחוּתִים וַאֲפִילוּ בַּקַּל שֶׁבַּקַּלִּים, אֲפִילוּ בַּלּוֹחֲמִים וְהָרוֹדְפִים אוֹתִי כּוּלָם אֶזְכֶּה בְּרַחֲמֶיךָ לְדוּנָם לְכַף זְכוּת תָּמִיד. וְתִתֶּן לִי שֵׂכֶל לָדַעַת מֵאִתְּךָ אֵיךְ לְחַפֵּשׂ וְלִמְצֹא בָּהֶם זְכוּת וּנְקוּדוֹת טוֹבוֹת תָּמִיד.

Hashem, please help me, guide me and show me the straight path so that I avoid stumbling in unworthy pursuits and refrain from speaking in a way that is not in accordance with Your will. May I merit to be good to everyone and may I not seek out people's failings.

Rather, may I always be worthy to do my utmost, using all my capabilities to find zechus and worth in each and every person in *Klal Yisrael*, Your holy nation, even the smallest of the small and even those who stand up against me. Through Your mercy, may I always merit to judge others favorably; may You bestow upon me the intelligence to understand how to search for and find redeeming factors, strengths and virtues in my fellow man at all times.

Notes

Introduction

1. Rambam, *Hilchos Chanukah* and *Megillah*, chap. 4, *halachah* 14:
גדול השלום שכל התורה ניתנה לעשות שלום בעולם שנאמר דרכי נעם וכל נתיבותיה שלום

Chapter Three

1. Based on R' Zalman Sorotzkin, *Oznaim LaTorah, Vayikra* 19:3
2. *Sefer HaMitzvos*: 273
3. Rashi on *Vayikra* 19:15
4. Ibid.
5. Rambam, *Hilchos Sanhedrin* 21:1
6. *Sefer HaMitzvos*: 275
7. *Sefer HaChinuch* 235
8. Ibid.: ועוד יש בכלל מצוה זו שראוי לכל אדם לדון את חבירו לכף זכות ולא יפרש מעשיו ודבריו אלא לטוב
9. *Rosh, Berachos* Chapter 9-23
10. *Vayikra* 19:15, לדון את חבירך לכף זכות
11. Rabbeinu Yonah, *Shaarei Teshuvah*, 3:218: אם האיש ההוא ירא אלקים . . . נתחיבת לדון אותו לכף זכות גם כי יהיה הדבר קרוב אצל הדעת לכף חובה
12. אם ראית ת״ח שעבר עבירה בלילה אל תהרהר אחריו ביום ודאי עשה תשובה (ברכות יט)
13. בינוני ספק השקול.
14. בינוני נוטה לחוב
15. *Pirkei Avos* 1:6

Chapter Four

1. *Mitzvos HaLevavos*, p. 41: מ״ע זאת גורם לקיום של כל התורה של בין אדם לחבירו שכיון שמטה משפט חבירו לכף זכות גורם זאת שיאהבהו. ולא יעבור על לא תשנא ולא תקום ולא תטור ושאר כל המצוות
2. *Sefer HaChinuch* 235: שכל אדם חיב לדון חבירו לכף זכות שהוא בכלל . . . יהיה סבה להיות בין אנשים שלום ורעות; ונמצא שעיקר כל כונת המצוה להועיל ליישוב בני אדם עם יושר הדין ולתת ביניהם שלום עם סלוק החשד איש באיש
3. *Shabbos* 127a
4. Rashi, *Shabbos* 127b: דן את חבירו לכף זכות בכלל לכף הבאת שלום. מדתוך שהוא מכריעו לזכות ואמר לא חטא לי בזאת, אנוס היה, או לטובה נתכוון, יש שלום ביניהם
5. The Vilna Gaon, *Siddur HaGra, Kesser Rosh*: אמר רבינו: דבר מנוסה: אם יהיה לאדם שונאים או אם יפעול אצלו שהם צדיקים גמורים,

וידון אותם לכף זכות, תיכף יתהפך לבבם לאוהבים לו
6. The Vilna Gaon on *Mishlei* 27:19: ״כמים הפנים לפנים כן לב האדם לאדם״ כמו המים שמראין פני האדם כפי מראהו להמים אם יעקב פניו גם המים יתראו, כן לב האדם לאדם. אם לבו טוב לאותו אדם הוא גם כן טוב עמו אף שאינו יודע לבו של אדם
7. *Midrash Tanchuma, Vayeira* 68: בזמן שהבריאות חוטאין ומכעיסין לפניו והוא כועס עליהן, מה הקדוש ברוך הוא עושה, חוזר ומבקש להן סניגור שילמד עליהן זכות, ונותן שביל לפני הסניגור
8. *Midrash Bereishis* 49
9. *Ruach Chayim* on *Pirkei Avos* 5:3
10. אולים יליץ אשם ובין ישרים רצון
11. *Shaarei Teshuvah* 3:217
12. *Sefer Chofetz Chaim, Mitzvas Asei* 2: להראות לנו את גדולת המדה הזאת שצריך האדם לחפות על גנות חבירו בכל כוחו כמו על של עצמו
13. *Chovos HaLevavos, Shaar Hacniya,* chap. 6: ונאמר על אחד מן החסידים שעבר על נבלת כלב מסרחת מאד ואמרו לו תלמידיו כמה מסרחת נבלה זאת אמר להם כמה לבנים שניה
14. *Shemiras HaLashon, Shaar HaTevunah* 17
15. Reprinted with permission from *Tehillim Treasury* by Rabbi Avrohom Chaim Feuer (Mesorah Publications)
16. *Vayikra* 19:15, 16
17. *Shemiras HaLashon, Shaar HaTevunah* 4: והנה לפי רב הרגלו של אדם במדה זו כן נגד זה יתמעט ממנו עון לשון הרע
18. *Sichos Mussar, תשל״א*
19. *Sefer Chofetz Chaim, Hilchos Lashon Hara,* chap. 3. See *Beer Mayim Chaim* 11, דעל ידי שלא דנתה [מרים] למרע״ה לכ״ז לומר דמסתמא כדין עשה מה שפירש ממנה אשתו חשבה הכתוב למדברת לשה״ר ממש ונענשה על זה בצרעת . . . וכאשר תדייק תמצא כמעט כל הסיפורים שנאמרו בתורה . . . הוא הכל מענין זה [שלא דנו לכ״ז]
20. *Sefer Chofetz Chaim, Hilchos Lashon Hara* 8:1 *Beer Mayim Chaim* 1
21. Adapted from a story by R' Eli Teitelbaum
22. *Erech Apayim, siman* 1:53: אם היה . . . אם אדם דן את חבירו לכ״ז . . . ודאי שהיה ניצול ברוב פעמים מלכעוס עליו. שאם חבירו חרף על איזה דבר שעשה לו ידינהו לכ״ז. אפשר שהוא שכאי בזה ואם היה להיפך אפשר שהייתי מחרפו יותר. וכן על כל ענין רע שסובל מחבירו ידינהו לכ״ז. אפשר

שלא כיוון להרע לי או אפשר שזכאי בזה או אולי
טועה הוא וכי"ב. ואם היה חושב כן ודאי היה
ניצול רוב פעמים מכעס

Chapter Five

1. *Mitzvos HaLevavos*, page 41: במסכת ב"מ:
לא חרבה ירושלים אלא בשביל שהעמידו דבריהם
על דין תורה. הורו לנו חז"ל אשר במדות האדם יש
כמה דברים אשר אם יעמיד על דין תורה הוא
חורבן לעולם. והוכרח לנהוג במדת החסידות
במדה שאדם מודד בה מודדין לו 2.
3. *Shemiras HaLashon*, *Shaar HaZechira*h:
כי ידוע הוא, כי לפי מה שהאדם מנהיג את עצמו
במדותיו בעולם הזה, הוא מעורר כנגדו למעלה
בעולם העליון, כל מדה לפי עניינה. אם דרכו
להעביר על מדותיו ומתנהג עם אנשים במדת
החסד והרחמים, הוא מעורר כנגדו למעלה את
מדת הרחמים ומרמים הקב"ה על העולם בשבילו...
ואם מדתו להתנהג עם אנשים שלא לוותר להם
כלום משלו ולא לרחם עליהם, הוא מגביר בזה
למעלה את מדת הדין על העולם וגם לעצמו...
ואין מוותרין לו כלום ממעשיו
4. *Shabbos* (127b): הדן את חבירו לכף זכות דנין
אותו לזכות
5. The *Tiferes Yehoshua* (p. 102) tells us an
insight from *Pirkei Avos* (2:6) which
strengthens this point: *havei dan es kol ha
adam l'kaf zechus*. Why insert the word *kol*
(כל) *ha'adam*? Wouldn't it be enough to
state *havei dan es ha'adam*? The two letters
can be reversed to read *lecha* (לך), to hint to
us that if we judge others favorably, then
lecha, the same judgment will come back
to us
6. The RiMiGash as quoted by HaRav
Zeitchik, *Ani Tefillah*: שע"י שאדם דן לזכות את
חבירו ומדבר במעלותיו אז הוא מעורר רחמים
וזכותים בשמים, שגם בשמים מזכירים את חבירו
לשבח ולזכות...האדם מלמטה הוא גורם על ידי
ברכתו והזכרת שבח חבירו לעורר רחמים וזכותים
על חבירו

תפארת שלמה: (חלק ב' אבות) אכן הורו לנו בזה,
גודל כח האיש הישראלי ורב-פעלו בדבורו בעולם
הזה. אשר לו הכח והיכולת להתעורר כן בעליונים
למעלה כמוהו, הן אשר יצא מפיו הן לחוב, הן
לזכות. כי כאשר האדם מלמטה מליץ יושר ומדבר
זכות על חבירו, מעורר על ידו גם למעלה מליץ
טוב ומזכיר זכות על רעהו להגיד עליו יושר
מלמעלה... כי דיבורו עושה רושם למעלה.
7. *Chidushei HaMeiri al Maseches Shabbos*
8. *Pele Yoetz: Os Samech* (סניגורא):
...וביותר צריך ליזהר כשאדם נתון בצרה ללמד
עליו סניגוריא, ושלא להזכיר עוונותיו כמנהג קלי-
הדעת שאומרים זה וזה גורם ועל-כן באה עליו
הצרה הזאת כי ידוע שאין השטן מקטרג אלא

בשעת הסכנה... וביותר צריך ליזהר שלא להזכיר
חובת שוכני-עפר שהם עומדים בדין... ואיש טוב
מדבר טוב על ישראל ומביא גאולה לעולם
9. *Shmiras HaLashon*, *Shaar HaZechirah* 2:
...מרחם הקב"ה על העולם בשבילו
10. Ibid.: מעורר – אם נוהג אדם ברחמים למטה
רחמים על אותו יום ומתעטר ברחמים בשבילו...
11. *Sefer Shemiras HaLashon*, *Shaar HaTev-unah* 4: והנה מה מאד צריך האדם להחזיק את עצמו
במדה זו לדון את כל האדם לכף זכות, כי על ידי
מדה זו דרך זכות וכן להפך חס ושלום, נקל לאדם
לעלות על עצמו שם צדיק או רשע לעולם
12. *Likutei Halachos* of the Chofetz Chaim,
Second Preface, ...ואין לי אפילו מצוה אחת
בשלימותה כפי מה שנצטוינו מפי אדון העולם
ית"ש...
13. *Sefer Shemiras HaLashon*, *Shaar Ha-
Tevunah*, chap. 4: והנה כל זה תלוי לפי ההנהגה
שהנהיג את עצמו בימי חייו עם הבריות. אם דרכו
היתה לדון אותם לכף זכות, דנין אותו גם כן לזכות
כדאיתא בשבת קכו. ואם דרכו היתה ללמד חובה
על הבריות ולדבר עליהם רע, גם מלאכי השרת
מדברים עליו רע למעלה כדאיתא במדרש משלי.
על כן צריך שידע האדם בנפשו בין לטב בין למוטב, אז
בעת שהוא דן את חבירו בין לטב בין למוטב, אז
בדבוריו ממש הוא מסדר דין לעצמו
14. Ibid.

Chapter Six

1. *Tanna D'Vei Eliyahu Zuta* 16: מפני הורקנוס
בני כדי שיעסוק בתורה
2. *Rif*, *Ein Yaakov*, Shabbos 127b
3. Ibid.
4. *Maharsha*, on Shabbos 127b
5. Ibid.
6. There are two approaches to the story in
the commentaries. One is that the last
zechus was the real *zechus* — everything
was pledged. The boss was able to pay because his colleagues were able to find a way
to annul his vow. But our discussion is
based on a second interpretation which
states that all the *zechuyos* were true and
only part of his possessions (the pillows and
blankets) were pledged.
7. *Maharsha*
8. *Yesod V'Shoresh HaAvodah*, Gate I, chap.
7: אפילו שהזכות יהיה רחוק מן השכל צוה הבורא
ית" לקרב אל לבו דוקא זכות. Even if the *zechus*
is far-fetched, the Creator commanded us
to consider [even an unlikely] *zechus*, to
open up our minds to find *zechus*.

Chapter Seven

1. *Yesod V'Shoresh HaAvodah*, Gate I, chap

... ויחשוב במחשבתו בזה "הריני מוכן ומזומן :8
לקיים מצות עשה של בצדך תשפוט עמיתך...".
2. Ibid. ...ויתאמץ בהתאמצות גדול במחשבתו
למצא לו איזה זכות במעשה בדבור ההוא
3. Ibid.
4. *Anaf Yosef* in *Ein Yaakov* on *Yoma* 29a:
קשה הרהורי עבירה מעבירה
5. *Sefer Chofetz Chaim, Hilchos Lashon Hara,* 10-14
6. *Yesod V'Shoresh HaAvodah, Shaar Ha-Gadol:* אף שהיה טועה בדבר זה במה שדן אותו
לכף זכות, עכ"ז עשה רצון הבורא ית' שצוה ע"ז
במ"ע בצדק תשפט עמיתך

Chapter Eight

1. *Yesod V'Shoresh HaAvodah; Shaar Ha-Rishon,* 3:7
2. *Yad HaKetanah, Hilchos Dei'os,* chap 5, *asei* 3: ואף אין החיוב שיאהבהו כאהבתו את נפשו
ולעסוק ולטרוח עבורו כמו שהוא עוסק וטורח בכל
בשביל עצמו ... כי אם לאהוב שיזכה חבירו בכל
הטוב כאשר אוהב עצמו לזכות בכל טוב
3. *Pirkei Avos* 4:28
4. *Mesillas Yesharim* 11: הכבוד הוא הדוחק את
לב האדם יותר מכל התשוקות והחמדות שבעולם
5. Ibid.: כלל הדברים הכבוד הוא מן המכשולות
היותר גדולים אשר לאדם
6. Even when we do things for the wrong motivation, we are still habituating ourselves in proper behavior, and hopefully, this habituation will become internalized, as it says in *Pesachim* 50: לעולם יעסוק
אדם בתורה ובמצוות אע"פ שלא לשמה שמתוך
שלא לשמה, בא לשמה
7. *Mishnah Sanhedrin,* chap. 4; *mishnah heh:* כל אחד ואחד חייב לומר בשבילי נברא
העולם — "The world was created for me."
8. *Alei Shur,* R' Wolbe
9. Rambam, *Hilchos Dei'os,* chap. 6. hal. 3: מצוה על כל אדם לאהוב את כל אחד ואחד
בישראל כגופו, שנאמר, ואהבת לרעך כמוך,
לפיכך צריך לספר בשבחו ולחוס על ממונו כאשר
הוא חס על ממון עצמו ורוצה בכבוד עצמו
10. *Sefer HaChinuch* 338

Chapter Nine

1. Reprinted with permission from Chanie Friedman from *Coalition Magazine* (Sept. 1992/Elul 5752)
2. *Sefer Chofetz Chaim, Hilchos Lashon Hara,* 10, Be'er Mayim Chaim §30
3. *Mishlei* 10:12: ועל כל פשעים תכסה אהבה
4. לא תעשה עול במשפט (*Vayikra* 19:15); *Kli Yakar* on this verse: יש בו אזהרה שלא יתיר...
לעצמו מה שאוסר לאחרים ...

Chapter Ten

1. Rashi on this Mishnah
2. Baal Shem Tov on *Pirkei Avos*: לפיכך
אמרו חכמים הוי דן את כל האדם לכף זכות לא
תהא בהול לחרוץ את משפטו של הזולת, כי אל
תדין את חברך עד שתגיע למקומו להיות ידוע לך
שמראים לך זאת אצל חברך על מנת שתדון אותו,
כיון שאתה כבר הגעת למקומו וכבר עשית כעין
מעשה זה, כך או אחרת. והמשפט אשר תחרוץ
עליו יהיה משפטך אתה. אם תדין את חברך לכף
זכות הרי אתה מיטיב לעצמך
3. Rabbeinu Yonah, *Shaarei Teshuvah* 217:
כל הפסול פוסל ... ודרכו לפסול בני אדם במומו
4. Based on Rav Wolbe, *Alei Shur* chap. 11, pp. 162-164
5. *Sfas Emes* on *Pirkei Avos* 2:5
6. *Sanhedrin* 102b
7. *The Jewish Observer,* September 1982

Chapter Eleven

1. *Tiferes Yehoshua* p. 103
2. *Sfas Emes* on *Pirkei Avos* 1:6
3. Chazon Ish, *Emunah u'Bitachon* 1:11
4. *Vayikra* 19-18
5. *Sfas Emes* on *Pirkei Avos* 1:6. את כל האדם
הול"ל כל אדם ונראה דהפ' דוודאי הגם שבדבר
פרטי אינו עושה טוב מ"מ את כל האדם בכלל יש
בו דברים ומדות אחרים של זכות המכריע זה הדבר
ופי' האדם לפי המצב בכלל

Chapter Twelve

1. כנגד עין הרע

Chapter Thirteen

1. *Shemiras HaLashon, Shaar HaTevunah* 4:
... אולי חסר המספר פרט אחד
1a. *Sefer Chofetz Chaim Mitzvasa Asei* 3, *Beer Mayim Chaim* 3
2. *Sefer Chofetz Chaim, Mitzvas Asei* 3: ופעמים הרבה מחמת שהיה לו בשעת מעשה כעס
על ענין אחר ונזדמן לו ענין זה בשעת מעשה ומרוב
צערו נתהוה זה מה שדבר או שעשה כי אין אדם
נתפס על צערו כמו שאמרו חז"ל
3. *Shemiras HaLashon, Shaar HaTevunah* 4: והענין של כף זכות הוא בין אם יש לצדד בעצם
הענין שנשמע עליו שעשה או שדבר לומר שהדין
עמו
4. Based on the laws of reproof, *tochachah*
5. *Sefer Chofetz Chaim, Hilchos Lashon Hara* 4:3: יש לתלות שעשה דבר זה שלא במתכון
6. Ibid.: שלא היה יודע שדבר זה ... יש לתלות
אסור
7. *Shaar HaTevunah* 4: ... או שלא ידע את
חומר אסרו ...
8. *Hilchos Lashon Hara* 4:9: ואפילו אם הוא

רואה עליו שהורגל באותן המדות הרעות ואין לבו
מר עליהם כלל, אעפ"כ אסור לילך ולהלעיג עליו
דאולי אינו יודע את חומר איסורן. כי באמת זה אנו
רואין בחוש לכמה אנשים . . . שאין מחזיקין
המדות הרעות האלו לאיסור כל כך כמו שהם
על פי אמת למתבונן בהם בכתובים ומאמרי חז"ל.
רק לדבר שאינו הגון סתם. ואולי גם החוטא הזה
דעתו כן, ואם היה יודע את חומר איסורן כמו שהם
אפשר שהיה מתחזק בכל כחותיו שלא לעבור
עליהם

9. Ibid. 4:3: או שהיה סבור שהוא חומרא ומדה
טובה בעלמא שהכשרים נזהרים בזה

10. הנהגה ישרה ומדה טובה

11. *Ahavas Chessed*, chap. 9: ויש אנשים
שרפוי המצוה של גמ"ח [הלואה] בידם מחמת
העלם ידיעה. היינו שנעלם מאתם גודל חיוב של
המצוה וגודל שכרה שהם סוברים שהיא רק הנהגה
ישרה ומדה טובה בעלמא ואינם יודעים שהיא
מצות עשה דאורייתא כמו סוכה ולולב ותפילין

12. *Sefer Chofetz Chaim, Mitzvas Asei 3*:
ופעמים הרבה יוצא הדיבור מפי אדם שלא
במתכוין והוא עצמו מתחרט אחר כך על זה

13. *Midrash Shmuel*, quoted in *Dover
Shalom*, page 299, compiled by Rav S.D.
Eisenblatt: השי"ת מעריך מעשה בני אדם לפי
טבע שנולדו. ולפעמים יתן הדין ליתן לרשע שכר
לפי שנולד במזג רע מאוד רק שמתגבר על יצרו
ואינו חוטא כ"כ לפי ערך הטבע שנולד ולפעמים
יתן הדין להעניש לצדיק לפי שנולד בטבע טוב
מאד, ואלו היה מתחזק את עצמו בעבודת השם,

אזי היה צדיק גדול יותר ממה שהוא . . . לכן צריך
לדון אדם לכף זכות כי אולי נולד בטבע רע מאוד
רק שמתגבר על יצרו והוא יותר צדיק ממך

Chapter Fourteen

1. *Bamidbar* 32:22: והייתם נקים מד' ומישראל
2. *Mishnah Shekalim*, chap. 3, *Mishnah* 2.
3. Ibid. The Mishnah states: "A person must
be concerned to please people in the same
way he must be concerned to please the
Omnipresent." ומצא חן ושכל טוב בעיני אלקים
ואדם
4. *Sefer Chofetz Chaim, Hilchos Lashon
Hara*, 7:2

Chapter Fifteen

1. *Berachos* 31b: אמר רבי אלעזר מכאן לחושד
את חברו בדבר שאין בו שצריך לפייסו ולא עוד
אלא שצריך לברכו
2. *Sefer Nishmas Chaim*, *be'ur al HaMa-
haral*, *Pirkei Avos*: מי שיש לו עין טובה מביט רק
על הטוב היינו בכל ענין צד הטוב שבו וצד הרע
אינו מתבונן ודנו לכף זכות
3. *Vayikra* 26:6, Rashi: הרי מאכל והרי משתה,
אם אין שלום אין כלום

Chapter Eighteen

1. *Sefer Chofetz Chaim, Mitzvas Asei 3, Beer
Mayim Chaim* §3: והכלל מי שירצה לדון לכף
זכות לא יסגרו לפניו דרכי הזכות.

Glossary

The following glossary provides a partial explanation of some of the foreign words and phrases used in this book; not included are words appearing in the dictionary. Foreign words and phrases which are immediately followed by a translation in the text are also not included. The explanations reflect the way the specific word is used in context.

ahavah : love
ahavas Hashem: love of G-d
aidelkeit (Yid.): refinement
beis din: rabbinical court
bentching (Yid.): blessings after the meal
berachah: blessing
bris: circumcision
chassan: groom
cholent: food prepared before the Sabbath to be eaten hot at the Sabbath day meal
chuppah: wedding canopy
derashah: learned discourse
erev: eve
gemilas chesed: act of kindness
ganev: thief
Gemorah: Talmud
gut Shabbos (Yid.): a salutation for a good Sabbath
HaKadosh Baruch Hu: the Holy One, blessed be He
Hashem: G-d, lit. "the Name"
Hashem (Yisbarach): G-d

Hatzoloh: paramedic emergency service

hishtadlus: effort

kallah: bride

Kedushah: part of the prayer service

Klal Yisrael: the Jewish People

krias HaTorah: reading of the weekly Torah portion

lulav: palm branch

Ma'ariv: evening prayer service

machateineste (Yid.): married child's mother-in-law

maftir: final honor in the Torah-reading service

mechutan (Yid.): married child's father-in-law

mechutanim (Yid.): married child's in-laws

mein kind (Yid.): my child

motzaei Shabbos: the night following the sabbath day

morah d'asrah: Torah authority of that neighborhood

Mussaf: additional prayer service

nachas: joy

Pirkei Avos: the Ethics of the Fathers

rav: rabbi

Rosh Yeshivah: dean of a Torah institution

sefer: book

sefiras haOmer: counting the 49 days between Pesach and Shavuos

shemiras halashon: guarding the tongue

shmoozing (Yid.): chatting

sifrei kodesh: holy books

simchah (simchos): a happy occasion

shiur: class

shmattah: rag

succah: temporary dwelling essential to the holiday of Succos

talmidim: students

talmidei chachamim: Torah scholars

tante: aunt

tzitzis: the fringes worn on a four-cornered garment

Yerushalayim: Jerusalem

yiras Shamayim: Fear of Heaven

Yom Tov: holiday

This volume is part of
THE ARTSCROLL SERIES®
an ongoing project of
translations, commentaries and expositions
on Scripture, Mishnah, Talmud, Halachah,
liturgy, history and the classic Rabbinic writings;
and biographies, and thought.

For a brochure of current publications
visit your local Hebrew bookseller
or contact the publisher:

Mesorah Publications, ltd

4401 Second Avenue
Brooklyn, New York 11232
(718) 921-9000